Hands-On Embedded Programming with Qt

Develop high performance applications for embedded systems with C++ and Qt 5

John Werner

BIRMINGHAM - MUMBAI

Hands-On Embedded Programming with Qt

Commissioning Editor: Richa Tripathi
Acquisition Editor: Shriram Shekhar
Content Development Editor: Tiksha Sarang
Senior Editor: Afshaan Khan
Technical Editor: Gaurav Gala
Copy Editor: Safis Editing
Project Coordinator: Prajakta Naik
Proofreader: Safis Editing
Indexer: Manju Arasan
Production Designer: Arvindkumar Gupta

First published: July 2019

Production reference: 1120719

Published by Packt Publishing Ltd.
Livery Place
35 Livery Street
Birmingham
B3 2PB, UK.

ISBN 978-1-78995-206-3

www.packtpub.com

Subscribe to our online digital library for full access to over 7,000 books and videos, as well as industry leading tools to help you plan your personal development and advance your career. For more information, please visit our website.

Why subscribe?

- Spend less time learning and more time coding with practical eBooks and Videos from over 4,000 industry professionals

- Improve your learning with Skill Plans built especially for you

- Get a free eBook or video every month

- Fully searchable for easy access to vital information

- Copy and paste, print, and bookmark content

Did you know that Packt offers eBook versions of every book published, with PDF and ePub files available? You can upgrade to the eBook version at www.packt.com and as a print book customer, you are entitled to a discount on the eBook copy. Get in touch with us at customercare@packtpub.com for more details.

At www.packt.com, you can also read a collection of free technical articles, sign up for a range of free newsletters, and receive exclusive discounts and offers on Packt books and eBooks.

Contributors

About the author

John Werner is an internationally published author, engineer, consultant, and conference speaker with more than 15 years' experience. He has earned patents for inventions ranging from Inkjet printers to automotive ignition systems. John was one of the early users of Qt on QNX and contributed to the early knowledge of how to make it work. He is a contributor to the Qt-related information on Stack Exchange. He is currently a senior software engineer, specializing in Qt development, for Caliber Imaging & Diagnostics.

I would like to acknowledge the following people and companies:

- *Qt, for providing trial licenses of their embedded products*
- *My GoG family for their support and their endless humor*
- *The team at Caliber Imaging & Diagnostics, my employer, for their support and encouragement*
- *Nick at La Salon Bianca, for making me look good*
- *The editorial staff at Packt, for helping me walk through this process of writing my first book*
- *Most of all, my wife and children for their infinite understanding, patience, and support*

About the reviewer

Pablo Rogina was born and lives in Buenos Aires, Argentina. He earned his bachelor's degree in computer science at Universidad de Buenos Aires (UBA) and holds a postgraduate degree in information security, also from UBA. He has more than 25 years' extensive experience and exposure to several different positions and responsibilities in IT environments, ranging from programming to network administration, and including system analysis and design, end user support, and database design and management. Over the last few years, he has been focusing on embedded system development, with specific exposure to IoT and computer vision solutions.

Packt is searching for authors like you

If you're interested in becoming an author for Packt, please visit `authors.packtpub.com` and apply today. We have worked with thousands of developers and tech professionals, just like you, to help them share their insight with the global tech community. You can make a general application, apply for a specific hot topic that we are recruiting an author for, or submit your own idea.

Table of Contents

Preface

Welcome to *Hands-On Embedded Programming with Qt*!

By means of the pages, examples, and projects in this book, you will get hands-on experience of developing a Qt application on an embedded target. Through the development of an overarching project, `BigProject`, you will learn about and gain experience with the many technologies that the Qt framework has to offer the embedded developer.

You will also be exposed to safe programming practices that will help you save time and prevent bugs in the field.

Who this book is for

This book is intended for software and hardware professionals with experience in a variety of different fields who are seeking to learn about embedded and IoT programming using the Qt framework. Whether you are new to embedded programming, a less experienced embedded programmer, or quite familiar with embedded development and are looking to add Qt to your toolbox, you will find something for you.

What this book covers

Chapter 1, *Setting Up the Environment*, covers the setup of the host and target environments we will be using for the rest of the book. It starts by specifying the host hardware we will be using for learning purposes. From there, it moves on to covering how to set up the host development environment with Qt and other tools. Cross-compiling Qt for the target environment and preparing the target operating system are also covered. Parts of this chapter can be completed without the need for the host.

Chapter 2, *Writing Your First Qt Application*, has been written so that you can continue learning without the target system. In this chapter, we'll write our first Qt program and execute it on the host. In the process, you will learn how to start Qt Creator; build a widgets-based Qt application; compile it for the host, run it, and even debug it; all from within the Qt Creator IDE.

Chapter 3, *Running Your First Application on the Target*, takes the application we wrote and ran on the host in Chapter 2, *Writing Your First Qt Application*, and focuses on running that application on the target. You will learn how to set up a Qt Creator kit that will allow you to simply select all the proper tools and settings to cross-compile, deploy, run, and debug on an embedded target. You will also be introduced to the problem of differing screen resolutions and sizes and how to easily solve it in Qt.

Chapter 4, *Important Qt Concepts*, starts laying the groundwork for the remainder of the book by exploring some of the basic, underlying concepts that are found throughout Qt. We will look at signals and slots, Qt's introspection system, the model/view architecture, and how Qt abstracts hardware and software platforms so that we can easily write code once and run it on many different systems.

Chapter 5, *Managing the Overall Workflow*, starts by looking at how we develop safe software systems with the highest possibility of success, both in terms of quality and time to market. From there, we start BigProject. We will work on this as we learn how to develop embedded software with Qt. As we move through the book, the mythical marketing and management teams reveal the new requirements of BigProject, just like they have done in real-world projects I have worked on. To overcome one of the first changes they make, we will learn about mocking.

Chapter 6, *Exploring GUI Technologies*, starts by examining the two different GUI technologies, widgets and Qt Quick/QML, which are available in Qt. As we finish up exploring the differences between them and the different ways in which they are developed, there are new requirements given to us for BigProject , leading us to learn how we can combine the two GUI technologies in a single application.

Chapter 7, *Adding More Features*, introduces a number of new requirements. In order to satisfy these requirements, we will learn how to interact with SQL databases using Qt, design state machines graphically in Qt Creator and have them automatically converted to C++ code, deploy a virtual keyboard, and use Qt's WebSocket support. Throughout this journey, we will be adding to BigProject. We will also look at the often overlooked world of IoT security, learning why it is important, and how we can find out more about it.

Chapter 8, *Qt in the Embedded World*, takes a step back and looks at Qt's place in the embedded world. We will learn how the computer and embedded markets have changed since Qt was first written. We will then examine how Qt is licensed and learn what we need to be careful of in terms of which license we develop and release our product under. We will then look at some of the commercial products Qt offers to make embedded development even easier, and even see some of the specific packages Qt has developed for targeted markets, such as medical, automotive, and safety-critical systems.

Chapter 9, *Exploring the IoT with Qt*, brings us to IoT. Here, we will learn how IoT and Qt fit together. After receiving yet more requirements from our mythical marketing and management teams, we will learn about accessing Web APIs from within BigProject, and how to interact using the MQTT IoT protocol. In between, we will learn about Qt's sensor support, and configure and build tools to allow the user to read the target's temperature, humidity, and pressure sensors within Qt.

Chapter 10, *Using More Qt-Related Technologies*, continues the theme of new requirements for BigProject and explains how we can fulfill them using Qt. In this case, we will learn how to save settings, perform inter-process communications using D-Bus, write a GUI that can be accessed from a web browser, and how to print to PDF files.

Chapter 11, *Debugging, Logging, and Monitoring Qt Applications*, teaches us various ways to test, debug, and monitor Qt applications. We will learn about different methods for verifying software, ranging from analysis to testing, and the tools that come with Qt Creator to help us do both of these. We will also look at using Google and the Qt Test frameworks and uncover and fix a couple of latent bugs in BigProject. We will then take a quick look at some old and new debugging tricks, and finish off learning about how we can use Qt's built-in logging system.

Chapter 12, *Responsive Application Programming – Threads*, dives into a fun topic—threading. In this chapter, we will learn about the different threading models that Qt supports and actually compare how they work on some sample problems. Speaking of problems, we will also look at the types of problems with which the threading models work. Finally, we learn how we can communicate between threads and safely synchronize multiple threads.

Chapter 13, *Qt Best Practices*, wraps up our learning. Over the course of the book, we have learned the *Qt Way* of doing things, and that has probably gotten you wondering, *Why did they do that?* To answer this question, we will look at just that question. We will then try to come up with some guidelines as to when we should be using modern C++11 (or later) features, and when we should be using the Qt approach. Finally, we will look at how to write efficient Qt code and learn about some of the powerful tools Qt Creator has incorporated into it to give you advice on how to improve the efficiency of your code.

Appendix A, *BigProject Requirements*, contains the requirement list for BigProject.

Appendix B, *Bonus Code - Simplifying Q_PROPERTY*, contains macros that will make the Q_PROPERTY coding simpler.

To get the most out of this book

The reader is expected to have basic knowledge of C++. While some knowledge of C++11 is helpful, new features are explained when we come to them. You should also have experience with using Linux shell commands. You will also want to get an embedded target. For this book, we will be using a Raspberry Pi 3B+ with a couple of extra pieces of hardware. The details can be found in Chapter 1, *Setting Up the Environment*. However, you can work through most of the first two chapters without having the hardware!

Download the example code files

You can download the example code files for this book from your account at www.packt.com. If you purchased this book elsewhere, you can visit www.packt.com/support and register to have the files emailed directly to you.

You can download the code files by following these steps:

1. Log in or register at www.packt.com.
2. Select the **SUPPORT** tab.
3. Click on **Code Downloads & Errata**.
4. Enter the name of the book in the **Search** box and follow the onscreen instructions.

Once the file is downloaded, please make sure that you unzip or extract the folder using the latest version of:

- WinRAR/7-Zip for Windows
- Zipeg/iZip/UnRarX for Mac
- 7-Zip/PeaZip for Linux

The code bundle for the book is also hosted on GitHub at https://github.com/PacktPublishing/Hands-On-Embedded-Programming-with-Qt. In case there's an update to the code, it will be updated on the existing GitHub repository.

We also have other code bundles from our rich catalog of books and videos available at https://github.com/PacktPublishing/. Check them out!

Download the color images

We also provide a PDF file that has color images of the screenshots/diagrams used in this book. You can download it here: `https://static.packt-cdn.com/downloads/9781789952063_ColorImages.pdf`.

Code in Action

To see the code being executed, please visit the following link:

`http://bit.ly/2Jb2Yzv`.

Conventions used

There are a number of text conventions used throughout this book.

`CodeInText`: Indicates code words in text, database table names, folder names, filenames, file extensions, pathnames, dummy URLs, user input, and Twitter handles. Here is an example: "Because we are using a Raspberry Pi 3B+, you will want to use the `qt-raspberrypi3-2gb.img.xz` file."

A block of code is set as follows:

```
void MainWindow::on_pushButton_clicked()
{
    QString name = ui->lineEdit->selectedText();
    ui->label->setText(QString("Nice to meet you %1!").arg(name));
}
```

When we wish to draw your attention to a particular part of a code block, the relevant lines or items are set in bold:

```
// find the sensor and start it
m_sensor = new QAmbientTemperatureSensor(this);
m_connected = m_sensor->connectToBackend();
m_sensor->start();
```

Any command-line input or output is written as follows:

```
[On Host]$ # fetch the code
[On Host]$ cd ~/raspi
[On Host]$ git clone https://code.qt.io/qt/qtknx.git
[On Host]$ cd qtknx/
```

Bold: Indicates a new term, an important word, or words that you see on screen. For example, words in menus or dialog boxes appear in the text like this. Here is an example: "You can always jump back to the **Welcome** screen by hitting the **Welcome** icon at the top of the left-hand icon menu."

 Warnings or important notes appear like this.

 Tips and tricks appear like this.

Get in touch

Feedback from our readers is always welcome.

General feedback: If you have questions about any aspect of this book, mention the book title in the subject of your message and email us at customercare@packtpub.com.

Errata: Although we have taken every care to ensure the accuracy of our content, mistakes do happen. If you have found a mistake in this book, we would be grateful if you would report this to us. Please visit www.packt.com/submit-errata, selecting your book, clicking on the Errata Submission Form link, and entering the details.

Piracy: If you come across any illegal copies of our works in any form on the internet, we would be grateful if you would provide us with the location address or website name. Please contact us at copyright@packt.com with a link to the material.

If you are interested in becoming an author: If there is a topic that you have expertise in, and you are interested in either writing or contributing to a book, please visit authors.packtpub.com.

Reviews

Please leave a review. Once you have read and used this book, why not leave a review on the site that you purchased it from? Potential readers can then see and use your unbiased opinion to make purchase decisions, we at Packt can understand what you think about our products, and our authors can see your feedback on their book. Thank you!

For more information about Packt, please visit packt.com.

Section 1: Getting Started with Embedded Qt

In this section, we will be learning how to set up an embedded development environment. In Chapter 1, *Setting Up the Environment*, we will go over the software setup for our host and target machines and learn what hardware you will need as we move forward. In Chapter 2, *Writing Your First Qt Application*, we will focus on setting up and running our first Qt application on the host system. We won't be using the target system yet, so the host system can be completed while you are waiting for the target to arrive. In Chapter 3, *Running Your First Application on the Target*, we will take the application we wrote in Chapter 2, *Writing Your First Qt Application*, and run it on the target.

The following chapters will be covered in this section:

- Chapter 1, *Setting Up the Environment*
- Chapter 2, *Writing Your First Qt Application*
- Chapter 3, *Running Your First Application on the Target*

Setting Up the Environment

Did you ever buy something marked *Some Assembly Required* only to get it home and find out *Some* actually means several hours of work and that the tools you need aren't included? I feel guilty, because this chapter should be labeled *Some Assembly Required*, but at least I will help you to find all of the free tools you need.

In this chapter, we will look not only at getting the software tools, but also getting the hardware set up and working toward getting the best experience with the rest of this book. We will walk through the basic setup of the Qt toolchain, embedded compilers, and reference hardware.

The following topics will be covered in this chapter:

- Creating our embedded environment
- Preparing the host machine compiler
- Building Qt for the target

Technical requirements

The following hardware will be needed in order to derive the most from this chapter and the rest of this book:

- A target device (Raspberry Pi 3B+) with supporting hardware. See the *Embedded Hardware and Firmware Setup* section for more information.
- A host development PC running Ubuntu 16.04 or higher. This can be running directly on a PC or in a VM with network access. Other Linux distributions may work, but this book is written for Ubuntu. (I am running Ubuntu 18.10 on dedicated hardware.) You will need the following access rights for your account on the host:
    - Administrative (or root) privileges for installing software on your development PC are needed.

- A web browser (Chrome is recommended) is required.
- Internet access is necessary.
- The following tools should be configured and working on the host:
  - `ssh`
  - `rsync`
  - `scp`
  - `tar`
  - `xz`
  - `bzip2`
  - `g++`
  - `patch`
- The Host PC must be connected to a network that can also connect to the target device.
- The Host PC must be able to read/write micro SD cards. You will want a fast SD card reader.

Additionally, this book assumes that you have at least a basic grasp of the following technologies:

- Installation of distribution provided software packages on your development PC
- A basic understanding of how to use Linux, including how to make files executable, run a program, edit a text file without a GUI, and safely reboot it
- C++11 programming and debugging

The code samples for this chapter can be found at `https://github.com/PacktPublishing/Hands-On-Embedded-Programming-with-Qt/tree/master/Chapter01`.

Creating our embedded environment

As much as I would like to get right down to writing software, there are some hardware issues that need to be taken care of first. I chose to cover this first so that you have time to get everything together before you need to use it.

The Raspberry Pi 3B+ was chosen because of its low cost, high availability, and good community support. We will also be using the Raspberry Pi 7" touchscreen display and a Raspberry Pi Sense HAT. Additionally, you will want a USB keyboard, USB mouse (optional), power supply for the Raspberry Pi, and a 16 or 32 GB micro SD card.

You will also want a network connection between your Raspberry Pi and your development host. If possible, you will want the Raspberry Pi on the same network that your host uses for its network access; however, you may also choose to add an additional network interface to your host and set up a separate network.

 Details on how to configure multiple network cards will depend on your exact version of Linux. A good place to start looking is the Ubuntu Stack Exchange forum (`http://askubuntu.com`) or the Server Fault Stack Exchange (`http://serverfault.com`). You may want to try searches like *multiple NICs* or *two network cards*.

Obtaining the hardware

While you can purchase all of these individually, there are several starter kits available that include everything you need but the Sense HAT. I chose to go with the NeeGo Raspberry Pi 3B+ Starter Kit and ordered the Sense HAT separately.

 To get the most out of this book, you will want to get the hardware as soon as possible, but don't let that stop you! If you are waiting for pieces to arrive, you can skip ahead to the section, *Installing Qt*, and get that going. One of the great things about using Qt is that you can do most of your early development and testing on the host computer, and then simply rebuild it for your target!

Once you have the hardware, assemble the main Raspberry Pi board and the touch screen display and its driver card, but don't put anything in a case. You will need access to the SD card slot on the main Raspberry Pi board, and most cases will not allow this. We won't need the Sense HAT for a bit, so don't try adding it yet.

Loading the firmware

After experimenting with setting up the stock Raspbian build to work well with Qt, I found it much easier to get a *Qt Ready* firmware image based on the Yocto Project.

Yocto is a project that simplifies creating embedded Linux images. Jumpnow Technologies has contributed a custom meta-layer for Raspberry Pi boards and generated prebuilt images. The images can be found on the Jumpnow Technologies website at `https://jumpnowtek.com/downloads/rpi/`. At the time of writing, the `thud` directory contains the latest images for the Raspberry Pi. The qt images support Qt OpenGL and QML out of the box, which is something I found a bit tricky to get running with Raspbian. Because we are using a Raspberry Pi 3B+, you will want to use the `qt-raspberrypi3-2gb.img.xz` file. This image does not have built-in support for Wi-Fi, so we will connect through the Ethernet port.

Take a second here to note the default root password for the image. It should be found in the `README.txt` file in `downloads/pi`. The first time you log in, you will be prompted to change the password.

More information on the Yocto Project can be found at `https://www.yoctoproject.org/`, and details on the Raspberry Pi layer for Yocto can be found at `https://jumpnowtek.com/rpi/Raspberry-Pi-Systems-with-Yocto.html`.

Backing up the SD card

If your Raspberry Pi came with an image pre-installed on a micro SD card, you should make a backup of that image before putting a new image on the card. Since you will be extracting an uncompressed image, you will need to have at least as much free space on your host PC as the size of the micro SD card.

Identifying the SD card device

First, you need to identify the Linux device ID of the micro SD card. The simplest way to do this is to use `dmesg` and a little logic.

If the SD card is already in the host PC, safely eject it.

In Command Prompt, enter the `dmesg` command. This will produce a list of kernel-level messages. Identify the last line of the output so that you can recognize new lines when they are added, as shown in the following code:

```
[On Host] $ dmesg
...
[175534.610523] Key type id_legacy registered
[183431.189380] usb 2-5: new high-speed USB device number 7 using ehci-pci
[183433.051881] usb 2-5: New USB device found, idVendor=0bda,
```

```
idProduct=0138
[183433.051889] usb 2-5: New USB device strings: Mfr=1, Product=2,
SerialNumber=3
[183433.051893] usb 2-5: Product: USB2.0-CRW
[183433.051896] usb 2-5: Manufacturer: Generic
[183433.051899] usb 2-5: SerialNumber: 20090516388200000
[183433.363950] ums-realtek 2-5:1.0: USB Mass Storage device detected
[183437.118622] scsi host5: usb-storage 2-5:1.0
[183437.119522] usb 2-5: USB disconnect, device number 7

[On Host] $
```

Now, insert the SD card, and immediately issue the `dmesg` command again. When the card is inserted, Linux will generate log messages noting what device it is assigned to:

```
[On Host] $ dmesg
...
[183433.363950] ums-realtek 2-5:1.0: USB Mass Storage device detected
[183437.118622] scsi host5: usb-storage 2-5:1.0
[183437.119522] usb 2-5: USB disconnect, device number 7
[183527.597445] usb 2-5: new high-speed USB device number 8 using ehci-pci
[183528.626641] usb 2-5: New USB device found, idVendor=0bda,
idProduct=0138
[183528.626645] usb 2-5: New USB device strings: Mfr=1, Product=2,
SerialNumber=3
[183528.626647] usb 2-5: Product: USB2.0-CRW
[183528.626649] usb 2-5: Manufacturer: Generic
[183528.626650] usb 2-5: SerialNumber: 20090516388200000
[183528.938856] ums-realtek 2-5:1.0: USB Mass Storage device detected
[183531.850735] scsi host5: usb-storage 2-5:1.0
[183533.307556] scsi 5:0:0:0: Direct-Access     Generic- Multi-Card
1.00 PQ: 0 ANSI: 0 CCS
[183533.309572] sd 5:0:0:0: Attached scsi generic sg2 type 0
[183534.866611] sd 5:0:0:0: [sdb] 62333952 512-byte logical blocks: (31.9
GB/29.7 GiB)
[183535.386748] sd 5:0:0:0: [sdb] Write Protect is off
[183535.386757] sd 5:0:0:0: [sdb] Mode Sense: 03 00 00 00
[183535.965682] sd 5:0:0:0: [sdb] No Caching mode page found
[183535.965693] sd 5:0:0:0: [sdb] Assuming drive cache: write through
[183538.506518] sdb: sdb1
[183540.690613] sd 5:0:0:0: [sdb] Attached SCSI removable disk
[On Host] $
```

The new lines referring to `sdb` (italicized) are shown in the preceding code. From looking at them, we see that the SD card is `/dev/sdb`.

Grabbing the image

Now that we know the device, we can grab a backup image of the pre-installed image. If you are using a new SD card, you can skip this section and refer to it when needed in the future.

You will want to use as fast an SD card and reader as you can. Making a backup will require reading the entire card—that's 32 GB of data on a 32 GB card.

We will be using the dd command to pull the image off of the card and bzip2 to compress it as it is stored. On Ubuntu systems, reading from the raw SD requires root privileges, for which we will use sudo. The following example also includes status=progress in the dd command so that it prints out progress as it's extracting:

```
[On Host] $ sudo dd if=/dev/sdb status=progress bs=1M | bzip2 -c >
BackupImage.img.bz2
```

Burning a new image

There are many ways to load the firmware on the micro SD card. One of the most basic ways is to use the Linux dd command, but that requires that the image is uncompressed. That's why I prefer to use the graphical balenaEtcher (https://balena.io/etcher). It can handle several different compression formats, including ZIP. Simply insert the SD card into your host machine, start balenaEtcher, choose the image, choose the micro SD card, and start flashing the image to the SD card.

When the flashing is done, ensure that the Raspberry Pi is powered off and insert the micro SD card into the micro SD card slot on the main Raspberry Pi board.

Connections and first boot

Now that your Raspberry Pi is assembled and the micro SD card has been inserted, it's time to connect it up and boot it, as follows:

1. Connect your keyboard and mouse to the USB ports on the Raspberry Pi. If you went with the NeeGo kit we mentioned previously, you will have received a combined wireless keyboard/mouse that uses a single USB dongle. Plug that in.
2. Next, connect an Ethernet cable to the Raspberry Pi.

3. There is no on/off switch on the Raspberry Pi, so I find it easiest to plug the power supply into a power strip with a switch. When powered, the Raspberry Pi automatically starts booting.

4. Now that the power supply is plugged into mains power, it's time to plug the other end into the USB OTG port on the Raspberry Pi or the video card (either will work). If you don't have a switch on the power supply, the Raspberry Pi will immediately start booting. If you do have a switch, now is the time to turn it on.

5. The screen will briefly display the Yocto logo as it boots then come up with a login prompt.

6. Log in as root using the password provided, then choose a new secure password for root. You will be using this password to log in later.

Network configuration

Now that you have logged in and set the root password, use `hostname` to find the hostname of the system. If needed, edit `/etc/hostname` and manually set your desired hostname. If you changed `/etc/hostname`, you must reboot the Raspberry Pi to make it take effect. This can be done by simply typing `reboot` at Command Prompt.

If your network is set up for DHCP connections, an IP address will have already been set for the board, and the Raspberry Pi will already be accessible through the hostname. If you don't have DHCP set up on your network, you will want to configure a static IP address for the Raspberry Pi and add the hostname and IP address to `/etc/hosts` on your host PC.

You can test the connection between your Host PC and the Raspberry Pi by issuing the following command on the host: `$ ssh root@raspberrypi`
Here, `raspberrypi` is the name of the device you found or configured previously.
If everything is correctly configured, you should be able to enter the root password and get Command Prompt on the Raspberry Pi.

The Yocto image we are using comes complete with a firewall. It is designed to help to make your Target more resistant to network-based attacks. But like many safety features (especially child-proof medicine bottles), the Target's firewall can get in the way. For the purposes of training, I suggest that you disable it and reboot your Target:

```
[On Target]$ update-rc.d firewall remove
[On Target]$ rm ./rcS.d/S60firewall
[On Target]$ reboot
```

If you want to avoid having to enter the root password with every connection to the Target, you can use ssh-copy-id to copy a unique key from your host PC to the Target. After doing this, ssh will try the key before asking for a password.

The format of the command is as follows:

```
[On Host] $ ssh-copy-id -f root@raspberrypi
```

If you don't have the ssh credentials on the host machine, the command will prompt you on how to create them. -f tells ssh-copy-id not to test whether the credentials already exist.

 The Yocto image comes with a custom firewall rule that will lock login for 30 seconds after three failed login attempts. ssh-copy-id can trigger this.

Installing RSync

RSync is a very powerful tool for synchronizing directories across machines. We will be using it fairly heavily during our setup. Unfortunately, rsync is not part of the Yocto image we are using, so we need to download, build, and install it ourselves on the Target. Let's get started:

1. From Command Prompt, you can download the sources for rsync using wget:

```
[On Target] $ wget
https://download.samba.org/pub/rsync/src/rsync-3.1.3.tar.gz
```

2. Once the tarball has been downloaded, untar and configure it to install in /usr/bin:

```
[On Target] $ ./configure --prefix=/usr
```

3. You can now build and install it, as follows:

```
[On Target] $ make && make install
```

Preparing the host machine

In this section, we will look at setting up the Linux host PC so that we can easily develop Qt applications.

Installing Qt

Qt comes in two basic licenses—Commercial and Open Source. We will be using the Open Source version.

 Projects developed with the Open Source version of Qt must comply with the applicable GPL and LGPL licenses.

Qt can be download from `https://qt.io/dowownload`. Make sure to download the Linux version of the online installer for the Open Source version.

 You might be wondering why we don't use the version of Qt already installed or installable from your Linux distribution. The answer is quite simple—to avoid confusion caused by different versions of Qt and its tools. Each version of each Linux distributions tends to come with a different Qt version. By downloading Qt for ourselves, we ensure that we are working with the same version and tools.

Once downloaded, make the installer executable (`chmod +x <file>`) and then launch it.

This book is written for Qt 5.12.0 that's been installed in `~/Qt`, along with Qt Creator. You can change the installation directory, but you will have to also adjust some of the steps that are provided.

We only need some of the Qt components, but you can install more if you like. From the Qt 5.12.0 section, select at least the following components from the Qt sub-menu:

- **Desktop gcc 64-bit**
- **Sources**
- **Qt Charts**
- **Qt Virtual Keyboard**
- **Qt WebGL Streaming Plugin**
- **Qt Debug Information Files**

Consider the following diagram for the preceding components:

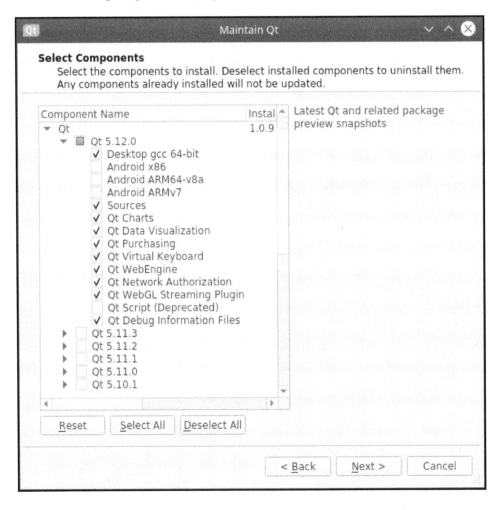

Also, be sure to install the latest version of Qt Creator (4.8.0 at the time of writing).

Just these few items pose a fairly large download. If you have a slow internet connection, you may want to find something else to do while it completes.

Setting up the cross compilation environment

There are several steps to setting up the cross compilation environment. We will put everything into the ~/raspi directory on the host so that you can create it.

Installing the cross compilation tools

Since the Raspberry Pi uses an ARM processor, we will need to install a cross compilation tool chain. A cross compile toolchain allows the host to build code that will run on a Target, even if the processor and possibly the OS do not match. A typical toolchain contains a compiler, linker, debugger, and other tools that run on the host, but generate code for the Target. You could think of it almost like a really cool translator that allows you to write a book in English and have it magically appear in Mandarin when it's done.

While we could build the cross compilation tools from sources, it is a lot easier to download pre-built binaries from https://github.com/raspberrypi/tools. We will want to put the tools in ~/raspi/tools. You can either use Git to pull them down or download the ZIP file.

To use Git, simply clone the directory, as follows:

```
[On Host] $ cd ~/raspi
[On Host] $ git clone https://github.com/raspberrypi/tools
```

You can grab the ZIP file from https://codeload.github.com/raspberrypi/tools/zip/master. Once you've download the ZIP file, extract the tools-master directory to ~/raspi/, then rename tools-master to tools:

```
[On Host] $ cd ~/raspi
[On Host] $ unzip tools-master.zip
[On Host] $ mv tools-master tools
```

Preparing for debugging

In order to successfully debug applications on the Target, we need to have a multi-architecture version of gdb (the debugger) installed. On Ubuntu, you can install it easily using apt:

```
[On Host] $ sudo apt install gdb-multiarch
```

Accessing the Target's root directory on the host

Cross compiling for the Linux target is best done when the host PC has access to parts of the root filesystem of the Target so that the proper includes and libraries can be accessed. There are a couple of different ways of doing this.

The first method is to share the filesystem between the host and target PC by remote mounting it from one system to the other. This is typically done using NFS.

The other method is by cloning the necessary parts of the target filesystem on the host. There are some definite advantages to cloning the filesystem, as follows:

1. The Target can be run independently of the host. This is perfect for demos or when the always available network is down.
2. The Target doesn't need to be present when compiling code for it. This seems to happen to me quite often when the software team grows and new Target hardware is limited. You will still need a Target at some point to transfer the code to it, just not while building.

For our purposes, we will clone the Target filesystem.

The required pieces of the root filesystem from the Target will be stored in ~/raspi/sysroot. RSync will be used to pull the copy:

```
[On Host] $ cd ~/raspi
[On Host] $ mkdir sysroot sysroot/usr
[On Host] $ rsync -avz root@raspberrypi:/lib sysroot
[On Host] $ rsync -avz root@raspberrypi:/usr/include sysroot/usr
[On Host] $ rsync -avz root@raspberrypi:/usr/lib sysroot/usr
```

3. The next step is to fix the symbolic links in `sysroot`. On the Target, they refer to absolute paths, but on the Host, they will need to refer to relative paths within `sysroot`. Once more, a script has been provided to take care of this for us, which can be found at `https://raw.githubusercontent.com/riscv/riscv-poky/priv-1.10/scripts/sysroot-relativelinks.py`. You can use `wget` to fetch it. Next, make it executable.

4. Run it by providing the location of the host copy of the Target's root filesystem:

```
[On Host] $ cd ~/raspi
[On Host] $ wget
https://raw.githubusercontent.com/PacktPublishing/Hands-On-Embedded
-Programming-with-Qt/master/Chapter01/sysroot-relativelinks.py
[On Host] $ chmod +x sysroot-relativelinks.py
[On Host] $ ./sysroot-relativelinks.py sysroot
```

Building Qt for the Target

While Qt can sometimes be obtained for a specific target, the version we are running isn't available for the Raspberry Pi. Instead, we will look at how to build Qt from the sources. At first, it may seem like a daunting task, but it really is straightforward. Let's get to it:

1. Before we start building Qt, we are going to make a backup copy of the source directory using `tar`. Open Command Prompt and `cd` to the installation directory for Qt 5.12.0. Next, tar up the `Src` directory, as follows:

```
[On Host] $ cd ~/Qt/5.12.0
[On Host] $ tar jcvf qt-5.12.0-src.tar.bz2 Src
```

Always keep the distribution sources untouched and don't build in the installed source directory. Use a copy of the directory instead. That way, should something happen, you won't have to re-download the sources.

2. Now, extract the tarball into `~/raspi/Src` and rename it `~/raspi/qt-5.12.0-src`:

```
[On Host] $ cd ~/raspi
[On Host] $ tar xvf ~/Qt/5.12.0/qt-5.12.0-src.tar.bz2
[On Host] $ mv Src qt-5.12.0-src
```

Experience is a great teacher. Over the years, I have found that the source code for Qt is so big that simply cleaning up from a build in order to make an adjustment and do another build can take a very long time. So, I discovered a trick—I build Qt in a separate directory from the source code! When I want a fresh build, I simply blow away the build directory and start again!

Fixing the sources

I would love to say that the sources are perfectly ready to build for our Raspberry Pi target, but I can't. There are a few source code issues with Qt 5.12.0 that are not supported by the cross compilers. To account for this, I have generated a patch set for the files. Download the patch file, that is, `qt-5.12.0-raspi.patch`, from the GitHub repository for this chapter and apply it using the following patch command:

```
[On Host] $ cd ~/raspi/qt-5.12.0-src
[On Host] $ patch -d qt-5.12.0-Src -p1 < qt-5.12.0-raspi.patch
```

This section only applies to Qt 5.12.0! If you download 5.12.3 (or later), all of this special setup isn't needed. You can use either version for this book.

Building a program

Now that the sources have been fixed, let's build it. There are two basic steps. The first is to configure the build, while the second is to actually build it.

Configuring the Qt build

Developers are so lucky these days. Back when I first started installing programs from the internet (which wasn't even called the internet back in those days), building a program for your machine meant editing configuration or making files by hand and tweaking various settings with the hope that you could figure out the right ones for your machine.

After what seemed like years, someone finally came up with a brilliant idea: *Let's build a program that will automatically test the system and set all of the proper values for building it automatically. We can call it* `configure`. Today, most packages have some sort of `configure` program that can be run to do all of the setup information.

Of course, Qt is one of these packages. If we were building for the host machine, it would be very straightforward to do, but since we are building for a target, we need to give `configure` some help.

So as not to pollute the source directory with built objects and to make it easier to "clean" the build should we need to rebuild, we will build in a separate directory.

The following three command lines (yes, the third line is really just one line!) will work for our purposes:

```
[On Host]$ mkdir build-raspi
[On Host]$ cd build-raspi
[On Host]$ ../qt-5.12.0-src/configure -release -opengl es2 -device linux-
rasp-pi3-g++ -device-option CROSS_COMPILE=~/raspi/tools/arm-bcm2708/gcc-
linaro-arm-linux-gnueabihf-raspbian-x64/bin/arm-linux-gnueabihf- -sysroot
~/raspi/sysroot -opensource -confirm-license -make libs -prefix /usr -
extprefix ~/raspi/sysroot/usr -hostprefix ~/raspi/qt5 -v -no-use-gold-
linker -webengine-embedded-build -webengine-pepper-plugins -webengine-
printing-and-pdf -webengine-proprietary-codecs -webengine-spellchecker -qt-
sqlite -feature-webengine-embedded-build -feature-webengine-printing-and-
pdf -skip qtscript -webengine-webrtc
```

There are no spaces after any dashes, even though the line may be wrapped at them. These commands should be issued in the `~/raspi` directory. Why don't you make the line run and, while it does its work, take a look at the *Decoding the configure command* section to understand what you told it to do.

Decoding the configure command

As the `configure` command has developed, cross compiling has actually become fairly easy to configure, even if it looks complex at first. The following table breaks down the parts of the command line so that you can understand what's happening a bit better:

Command	Function
`../qt-5.12.0/configure`	The command to run
`-release`	Build a release version
`-opengl es2`	Enable OpenGL ES2
`-device linux-rasp-pi3-g++`	Build for the Raspberry Pi 3 target
`-device-option CROSS_COMPILE=~/raspi/tools/arm-bcm2708/gcc-linaro-arm-linux-gnueabihf-raspbian-x64/bin/arm-linux-gnueabihf-`	What cross compiler to use

`-sysroot ~/raspi/sysroot`	The location of the Target's root filesystem on the host
`-opensource`	Build the Open Source version
`-confirm-license`	Accept the license without a prompt
`-make libs`	Make the libraries
`-prefix /usr`	Where to install on the Target's root filesystem
`-extprefix ~/raspi/sysroot/usr`	The installation location on the host copy of the root filesystem
`-hostprefix ~/raspi/qt5`	Where to put host files for cross compilation for the Target
`-v`	Be verbose about what is happening
`-no-use-gold-linker`	Don't use the Gold Linker
`-webengine-embedded-build`	Build WebEngine for an embedded environment
`-webengine-pepper-plugins`	Build the Pepper Plugin for WebEngine
`-webengine-printing-and-pdf`	Build support for PDF and printing in WebEngine
`-webengine-proprietary-codecs`	Build proprietary codecs for WebEngine
`-webengine-spellchecker`	Build the WebEngine Spell Checker
`-qt-sqlite`	Build support for the SQLite Database
`-skip qtscript`	Don't build the Qt Script component

 Most incarnations of `configure` can tell you more about what options they support. Try running `./configure --help` to see what else can be controlled, or refer to `http://doc.qt.io/qt-5/configure-options.html`.

Building the code

If the configuration step was successful, then it's time to build the code using the `make` command. If not, examine the output of `configure` and try to identify what is missing.

To speed things up, we will run a parallel build job. For most systems, you want to split the build into twice the number of threads as the number of processors. For a quad core processor, that means eight threads:

```
[On Host] $ make -j 8
```

If the build worked without error, install the build using the following command:

```
[On Host] $ make install
```

If there were errors during the build, try building without multiple jobs and look at where the build stopped for clues as to what needs to be fixed.

 More information on how to build Qt from sources can be found on the Qt website at `http://doc.qt.io/qt-5/build-sources.html`.

Synchronizing the new components with the target

When we built Qt, we built it into the local copy of the Target's root filesystem. Now, we need to push the changes back to the Target. Once again, we will use `rsync` to make that happen, as follows:

```
[On Host] $ cd ~/raspi/sysroot
[On Host] $ rsync -avz . root@raspberrypi:/
```

Running a quick test to ensure how the program works

If you've made it this far, your Qt for IoT Development environment and hardware should all be ready to go. Let's run a quick test to make sure this is the case. I've written a short test program to verify the basic setup of the Raspberry Pi itself. It can be found in the Git repository for this book. Download the single executable, `C01_01-ItWorks`, to `~/raspi`. Transfer it to the device and then execute it. Then, follow these steps:

1. On the host PC, enter the following command:

    ```
    [On Host] $ scp ~/raspi/C01_01-ItWorks root@raspberrypi:/home/root
    ```

2. Then, `ssh` into the Raspberry Pi and start it:

    ```
    [On Target] $ /root/C01_01-ItWorks
    ```

3. You should now see a picture with the words **It Works!** on the display. If not, verify your installation steps:

You can hit *Ctrl+C* in the `ssh` connection to terminate the program.

Summary

In this chapter, we learned how to set up a Raspberry Pi 3B+ for embedded Qt development. We also learned how to prepare a Linux host PC for cross compilation for the Raspberry Pi Target. We explored how to pull the parts of the root filesystem that are needed for development from the Target. Together, we also learned how to configure and build Qt from its source code and then push the updated root filesystem to the Target.

While we have only dealt with one particular Target, working with applications for other target systems is fairly straightforward. The differences will be in what initial target image you select, the cross compiling tool chain, and the way Qt is configured. Hopefully, by working through this chapter, you will be confident enough to be able to do it for any system you find.

In Chapter 2, *Writing Your First Qt Application*, we will write our first Qt program using Qt Widgets, test it on the host, and find out just how easy it is to find and fix a bug using Qt Creator.

Questions

1. Qt is available under what types of licenses? How are they different?
2. What project allows you to custom build a Linux distribution for embedded use?
3. How do you prepare to build Qt from its source code?
4. What command can be used to synchronize directories across remote machines?
5. What are two methods for sharing filesystems between remote machines?
6. Is it okay to use the Qt version that's installed through Ubuntu? Why?
7. What are the major steps that are needed to prepare Qt for working on a new device?
8. How can you identify the device that's assigned to an SD card?

Further reading

You may also find the following Packt books to be useful regarding your learning experience:

- *Embedded Linux Development using Yocto Projects – Second Edition*, by Otavio Salvador and Daiane Angolini
- *Embedded Linux Development Using Yocto Project Cookbook – Second Edition*, by Alex González

2
Writing Your First Qt Application

Now that we have built our target and set up our host development system, it is time to get down to actually writing a Qt application!

In this chapter, we will develop, test, and debug a Qt application using just the host computer. Qt is a cross-platform framework—we can write, test, and debug major portions of the code on the host.

 You can work through this chapter without target hardware and without having completed cross-compilation of Qt.

The following topics will be covered in this chapter:

- Qt Creator—the Qt IDE
- Greetings from Qt—your first Qt application
- Who are you?—adding features to the code
- Fixing a mistake—testing and debugging with Qt Creator
- Digging deeper—a closer look at some topics

By the time you have finished this chapter, you should have learned how to do the following:

- Start Qt Creator
- Navigate around Qt Creator
- Create a Qt widget project
- Create a widget form
- Test and debug an application with Qt Creator
- Use the Qt Creator help system

Technical requirements

This chapter assumes that you have successfully installed Qt 5.12.0 on the host PC in ~/Qt/5.12.0 as described in `Chapter 1`, *Setting Up the Environment*, and have a basic understanding of C++ and its techniques.

 You do not need to have completed the target setup or have built Qt 5.12.0 to achieve the objectives laid down in this chapter.

Completed code for the application in this chapter can be found in the GitHub repository at:
`https://github.com/PacktPublishing/Hands-On-Embedded-Programming-with-Qt/tree/master/Chapter02`.

Introducing Qt Creator

There is a lot to Qt Creator, but for now, I just want to give you an overview. We will devote a section later in this book to looking at some of Qt Creator's advanced capabilities.

Qt Creator is the cross-platform IDE for developing Qt applications. It supports code editing and development in C++, JavaScript, QML, XML, HTML, and other languages. It can create and edit QMake project (`.pro`) files for both simple and complex projects. You can use it to visually design user interfaces. It works directly with version control systems such as Mecurial, Git, and SVN. It executes compilation, and it even does source-level debugging. It also does static C++ code analysis with Clang!

It is a very complete, fast, IDE written in Qt for developing Qt GUI and console applications along with Qt plugins and libraries.

With such a powerful IDE, you would expect that there is a great deal to learn about it, and you would be right. For now, I am going to cover just the key points. We will start with how to start Qt Creator, and then we will learn about most of the different screens and areas of Qt Creator's interface.

Starting Qt Creator

In Chapter 1, *Setting Up the Environment*, we talked a little bit about why we installed our own version of Qt—to make sure we knew exactly what we are running regardless of what packages may already be installed on the host PC. Once more, we need to be careful to make sure we get the version we want, but this time for Qt Creator.

To make sure we start the version we installed, we will specify the path to the version we installed. It is located in ~/Qt/Tools/QtCreator/bin, so we will start Qt Creator by using the following command line:

```
[On Host]$ ~/Qt/Tools/QtCreator/bin/qtcreator
```

In a few seconds, Qt Creator will start up, so let's examine Qt Creator's screens.

Qt Creator welcomes you

Each time you start Qt Creator, you will be greeted with the **Welcome** screen. There are three basic pages to the **Welcome** screen—the **Example** screen allows us to look through the examples provided, the **Tutorials** screen gives fast access to a variety of Qt tutorials, and the **Projects** screen allows us to look at the projects we have opened.

 You can always jump back to the **Welcome** screen by hitting the **Welcome** icon at the top of the left-hand icon menu.

Let's look at each one of these. We will start with the **Examples** screen, move to the **Tutorials** and the **Projects** screens, and finally, examine the left-hand icon bar.

The Examples screen

When you start Qt Creator, you are presented with one of three **Welcome** screens. The following screenshot gives you an overview of the **Examples** screen. The content isn't as important as the ability to recognize the general layout of the screen:

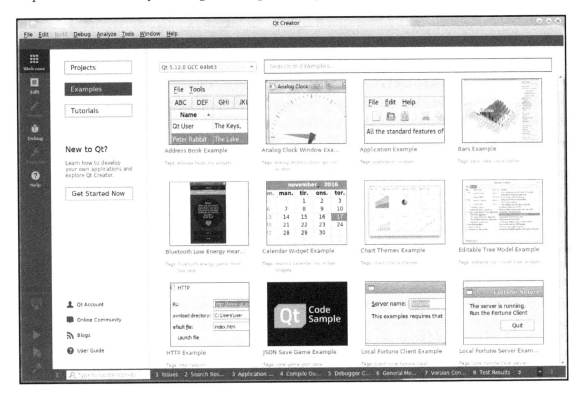

The left-most side is an icon bar. We will discuss that in a minute.

The section to the right of the icon bar allows you to switch between **Projects**, **Examples**, and **Tutorials**.

The **Examples** screen is the gateway to a plethora of Qt examples. It's a great place to look when you are trying to explore a new idea or just want to see what could be done. (I might even have referred to it while I was writing this book.)

The **Examples** screen even includes a search bar at the top that allows you to look for specific topics and ideas.

Almost all of the examples can be run on both the host and target. You will learn about how to run on the target in `Chapter 3`, *Running Your First Application on the Target.*

We won't be looking more at these, but feel free to explore them when you can. Make sure you have selected the **Qt 5.12.0 GCC 64bit** installation as it is the one we will be using.

Maybe you want more than simple examples. Perhaps the **Tutorials** screen will help you.

The Tutorials screen

Similar to the **Examples** screen, we see here the **Tutorials** screen in the following screenshot. Again, don't worry about the details. The goal for now is to identify which screen it is and learn what you can do from here:

The Qt Company has created many great tutorials on using Qt. These can be accessed from this screen. Even though I have been using Qt for years, I will often look at the tutorials when I am learning another part of Qt.

Qt is a huge framework that is continually being updated. Every time I think I know everything, I find another part worth exploring and applying. It is like finding that perfect gadget that makes it so much easier to do a mundane task.

If you are having to work hard to solve a problem in Qt, it probably means you are either not doing things *the Qt way*, or (more often) missing something that Qt has already solved for you. We will explore some of the more interesting ones later in this book.

Let's now have a look at the **Projects** screen!

The Projects screen

This is the **Projects** screen. Again, the content is not as important as the layout:

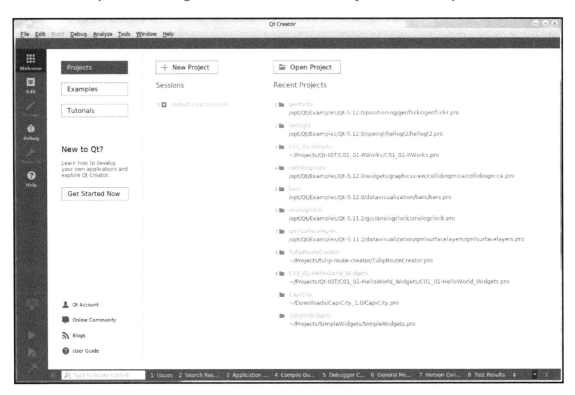

For me, the **Projects** screen is the most useful screen. From this screen, you can jump back to where you were last working, including the last files that were open using the "default (last session)" button. You can also choose from a list of recent projects (the right side), create a new project, or open another project.

The left icon bar

On the left-hand side of the Qt Creator window is an icon bar. It is always visible so that you have immediate access to a variety of items:

Icon	Description
Welcome	Open the **Welcome** screen. You can find **Projects**, **Tutorials**, and **Examples** here.
Edit	Switch to the **Edit** screen.
Design	Switch to the **Design** screen (only active when a GUI element is in the active edit window).
Debug	Open the **Debug** screen.
Projects	Open the **Projects** options screen for the currently active project.
Help	Open the **Help** Screen.
Debug	Select the active project configuration.
▶	Build and run the currently active project.

	Build and debug the currently active project.
	Build the currently active project.

Greetings from Qt

Now that we have looked at some of the basics of Qt Creator, let's use it to create our first program!

There is a long tradition in programming that the first program every programming class uses is *Hello World!* While I love traditions, I also love mixing things up a bit, so our first program will be *Greetings from Qt!* Obviously, our program will be an entirely different program from *Hello World!*

We will start by creating a project for Qt, and then we will learn about the text edit screen and how to design a simple UI. Of course, we will need to learn how to run our code. Finally, we will learn how to make sure our code stays safe as we develop and change it. The latter will become very important once we start working on our BigProject, something that will span most of this book.

Creating a project

Qt organizes code into projects. Projects can be defined by QMake files or CMake files. We will be using QMake files, and we will let Qt Creator create them for us.

We already know that we can start to create a new project from the **Projects** screen of the **Welcome** page. Let's try a different way this time.

From the **File** menu, select **New File or Project...** to launch the **New File or Project** wizard:

The **New File or Project** wizard will now open to guide you through creating a new file or project. Let's take a walk through the wizard and create a new project.

Walking through the New File or Project wizard

The **New File or Project** wizard is used for creating everything from Qt projects to C++ classes, to Python files, and even state machines. (We will see how to add a state machine in Chapter 7, *Adding More Features*.)

This walk-through will show you how to create a Qt widget application project using the wizard. The basic steps are as follows:

- Choosing the template
- Picking a name and location for the project

- Selecting the kit to use
- Defining the name of the main window
- Selecting the source control for your project

Choosing a template

There are many different templates for things that Qt Creator can create. We are creating our first application, Greetings from Qt, so we will select **Application** in the left selection box. This will be a Qt Widgets application (more on the other types later), so we then select **Qt Widgets Application** from the middle selection box.

 Did you notice that you can also create non-GUI (console) applications, libraries, and source files here? You can even import projects from version control systems!

Once you have selected these, click on **Choose...**:

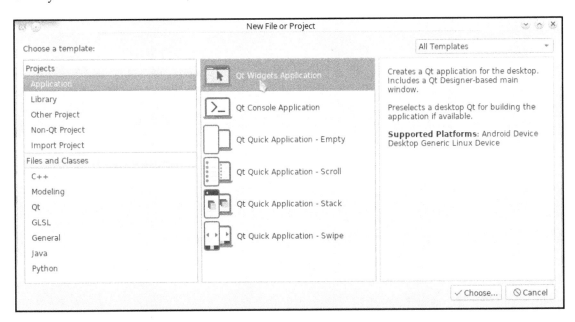

When you click on **Choose...**, you will be given a chance to pick a project name and location.

Picking a name and location

The next step in creating our application is picking a name for the project and a location to store it. The name is used both for the name of the executable and for the sub-directory for the project files. For the name, let's use `HelloFromQt`.

The project sub-directory will be created in the directory specified by the **Create in:** field. For our purposes, we will create all of our projects in `~/raspi/QtProjects`. You can set the directory either by typing it in or using the **Browse...** button.

To make our lives simple, set `~/raspi/QtProjects` as the default location to put all of our projects in and check **Use as default project location** to make it so:

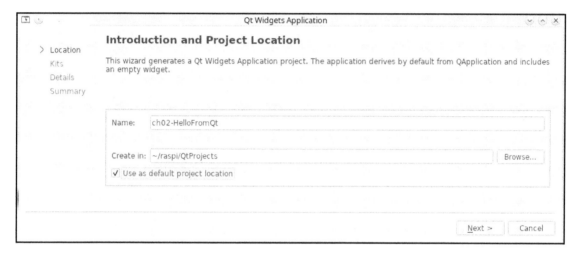

Then, click on **Next**, which will take you to the **Kit Selection** page where you will choose how you build the project.

Selecting a kit

The next widget page allows you to choose what kit(s) you want to use to build your application. *Kit* is the term Qt uses for a configured set of tools (compiler or debugger), Qt version, and target type.

Since we are only building an application for Qt 5.12.0 running on our 64-bit host, we will choose only one target, **Desktop Qt 5.12.0 GCC 64bit3**:

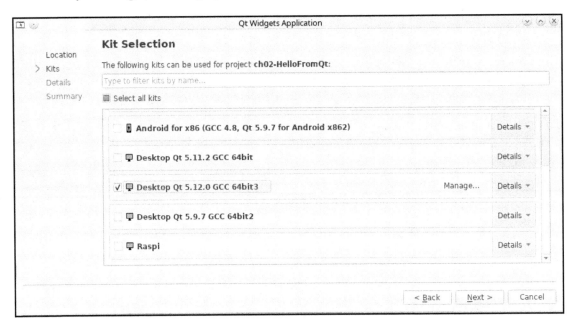

 Unless you have been either reading ahead or playing with other Qt versions, you probably won't have nearly as many choices.

When you click on **Next >**, you will be presented with a page where you can choose the name of the `MainWindow` class for your project.

Defining the main window class

Everything displayed in a Qt Widgets Application is implemented as a C++ class. To make life simple, most custom widgets are built by inheriting from another class. This includes the main window for the application.

Classically, the main window of a Qt Application is a custom widget that inherits from the `QMainWindow` class. `QMainWindow` implements all of the major features of a main window in an application. It includes support for a menu bar, tool bars, dockable widgets, and even a status bar.

If you want to learn more about the QMainWindow class, click on the **Help** icon in the left icon bar to open the **Help** screen. Next, select **Index** from the contents or search pull downs and fill in **QMainWindow** in the **Look for** box. When the results come back, double-click on **QMainWindow**, and then (if prompted) select **QMainWindow** class | Qt Widgets 5.12 from the popup.

This wizard page allows us to define the class for the main window. To keep things simple, let's accept the default settings:

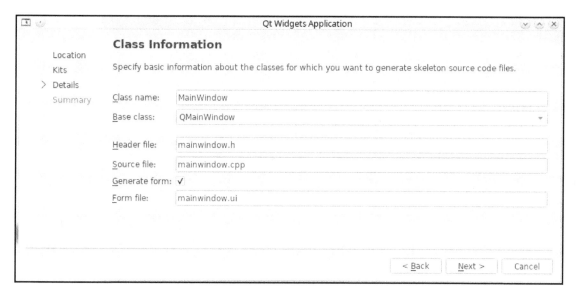

We are almost done with the wizard. Clicking **Next >** takes us to what I have found to be the most important page in the wizard—the page where you choose what source control system you want to use with your project.

Selecting a source control system for your project

I wrote my first program while in high school several decades ago. I spent weeks writing a text-based game for an Apple][+ computer. Whenever I made a change, I would carefully save the program on my one disk. Once in a very long while, I would abuse the printer and print a listing of the code in case something happened.

Then, one day, something happened. I was testing out new code that cleared the program from memory when it exited so that it couldn't be easily copied. I ran the code and it exited, just like it was supposed to. I then carefully saved that update to the disk.

Now, if you have been following along, you will realize what I just did. The program wiped itself out when it exited, and I just saved an empty program to my one copy of the code on the one disk that contained it. I had, in a very sophisticated manner, erased the only electronic copy I had of several weeks of work. If it wasn't for the printout (which was missing some changes), I would have lost everything.

If only I had known about and used a software **Version Control System** (**VCS**), I could have easily gone back to my last change. VCSes keep track of the changes you make to code and help you to recover from mistakes when they happen—if you use them.

Commit your changes often. If you only commit every month, then you could loose a month's worth of work. If you commit every couple of hours, you can only lose a couple of hours of work!

For our project, we are going to use Git for our VCS:

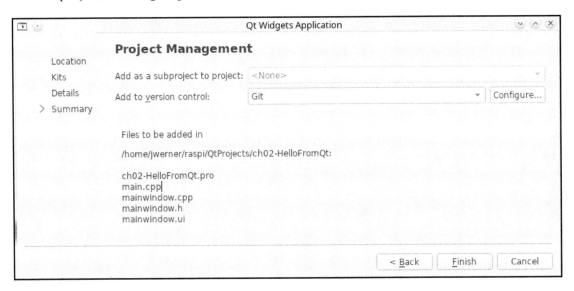

You probably noticed that the **Add as a subproject to project** field is set to **<None>**. The field is used when we create hierarchical projects, but that's a topic for later.

Now, click **Finish** and let the project be created.

Always use a software VCS. I cannot count the number of times I have made a little change to code that completely borked it. Being able to revert back to a previous version has saved me many times.

Examining the Edit screen

Once the project has been created, the C++ source file for our main window class will be opened and the **Edit** screen will be displayed. The following screenshot gives you an overall view of the layout of the **Edit** Screen. We will look at each of the parts individually as we go on:

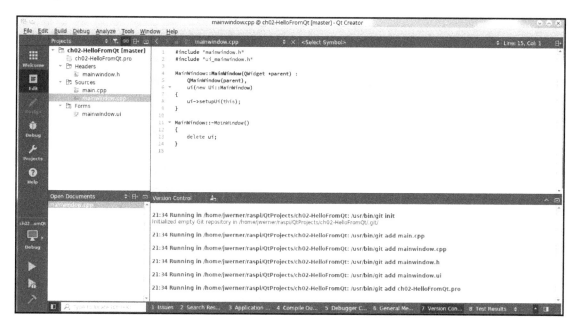

Let's take a look at the parts of the screen as shown.

Viewing projects and open files

The following left column is used to show different views of the project. While the screenshot shows only two sections, you can create as many sections as you want by dividing each pane.

Following is a list of the type of views available:

View	Description
Projects	This is a hierarchical view of the open projects. The current project is in bold. If you are using a VCS, the current branch you are working on is shown in square brackets. Each project is broken down by file types (that is, Headers, Sources, and Forms).
Open Documents	This is a list of all of the files currently open in Qt Creator.
Bookmarks	This is a list of the bookmarks you have made.
File System	This is a view of the computer's filesystem. It centers on the file actively being edited.
Class View	This is a view of all of the classes in the project.
<VCS> Branches	This is a view of the various branches in the selected VCS.
Outline	This is the outline of the file currently being edited.
Tests	This is a view of the supported test tools.
Type Hierarchy	This is a hierarchical view of types in the project.
Include Hierarchy	This is a hierarchical view of the `include` files for the file currently being edited.

A place for editing

The top-right pane is the editing area. This area can be split horizontally and vertically to show more editing screens.

One of the nice features of Qt Creator is the ability to have the same document open in two different sections of the editing area. This enables you to easily work on one portion of a file while referring to information from another place in the same file.

Presenting outputs

The bottom-right pane shown is where the output from various tools can be displayed:

Output section	What it shows
Issues	This shows issues found in the code. These may be warnings and errors from compilation or output of static analysis tools.
Search Results	This shows the results of searches, typically over multiple files.
Application Output	This is the output from a running application.
Compile Output	This is the output from compiling.
Debugger Console	This is the console output from the debugger.
General Messages	This shows messages that don't really fit anywhere else.
Version Control	This shows messages from the selected VCS tool.
Test Results	This shows the results of test code.

In the preceding screenshot, the output from Git is displayed, showing us what Git commands were run.

Designing the UI

Having looked at the editing screen, let's start actually building the GUI for our little application.

In the **Projects** section, double-click on `mainwindow.ui` under the **Forms** section to open up the **Design** screen:

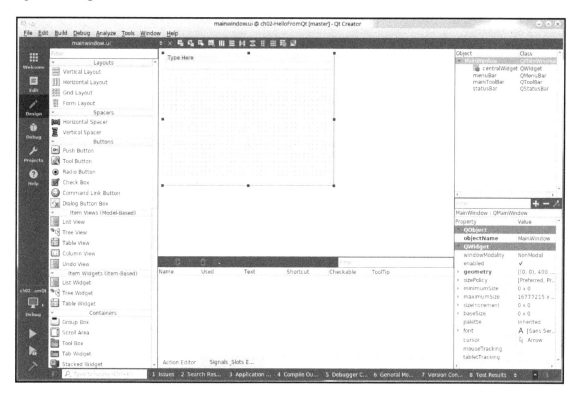

The center of the screen contains the design. The left side contains a list of available widgets that can be dragged onto the design. The top section of the right column shows the design hierarchy. The bottom section of the right column allows editing of various properties of the selected design element.

Placing a text label

Placing things using the designer is a fairly straightforward process:

1. Find the appropriate widget in the left column.
2. Drag the widget from the left column to the design.
3. Edit the widget.

Let's try this with a text label:

1. Scroll down the left column until you find the section called **Display Widgets**. Drag the **Label** to the main window—don't worry about where exactly you drop it.
2. Now, change the text of the widget to read **Hello From Qt!**. One way of setting the text is to double-click on the label and enter new text. The other way is to set the **text** property of the widget (a QLabel) in the bottom section of the right column.
3. You may also want to expand the widget to see all of the text. Do that by dragging the bounding box of the QLabel widget.

You should now have a design that looks something like this:

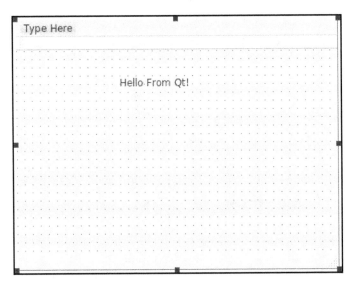

It's time to take our application for a test drive!

Running the code

A project can be compiled and run in a few ways:

- Select **Build** --> and run from the menu bar at the top of the screen.
- Press *Ctrl+R*.
- Click on the run button (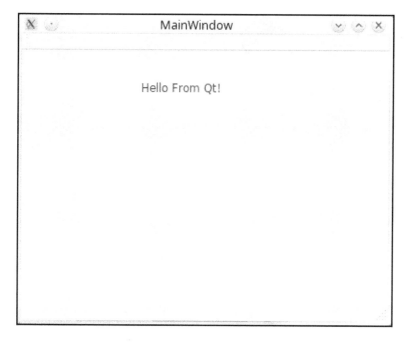) in the left icon bar.

Try it!

Before compiling and running, Qt Creator will prompt to save changes. Save them and, after a few seconds, the application will start:

MainWindow

Hello From Qt!

When you start the application, a window will appear on your desktop and show you something that looks very much like the design you created. It will be decorated with your OS window decorations (borders), but the center should be almost identical, though that really does not help the fact that it is rather boring.

Protecting your work

Now is a good time to save the work you have just done. Most VCSes refer to this as **committing** the code:

1. From the menu bar, select **Tools** | **Git** | **Local Repository** | **Commit** to bring up the **Git Commit** form.
2. Check the files you want to commit.
3. Be sure you fill out **Author** and **Email**.
4. Enter a description.
5. Click **Commit**:

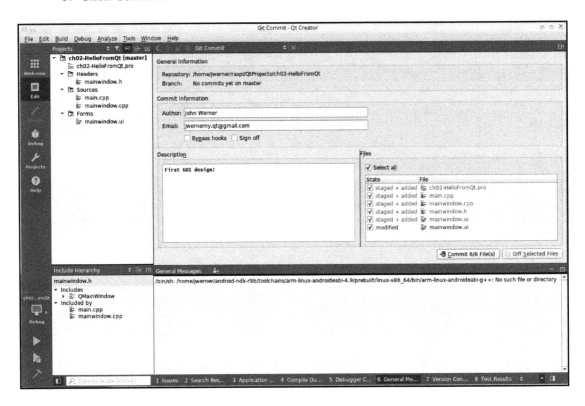

Once you have clicked **Commit**, the process starts and the **Version Control** output window will open up and show the progress.

You have created your first Qt Widget Application! Now, we will take some of the "boring" out of it.

Who are you?

Now that we have created a project, designed a simple UI, built and run the application, and committed our code to a local repository, let's add to the project. As noted before, there really isn't much to make our little application interesting. Why don't we add something to it?

We will start by adding a place for the user to enter their name and then use the name to directly address them in the text.

Adding a place to type your name

For our next trick, let's see whether we can get the application to address us by name. We should have a line editing widget with a label saying **My name is:**.

Before you look further down, why don't you try adding the elements to the design yourself?

The following are some hints:

- You can get back to the design window by clicking on the design icon in the left icon bar or by double-clicking on `mainwindow.ui` again
- You have already found a widget that displays a label
- There is also a widget for editing a single line

Once you have made your changes, save and run the program. You will observe the following screen:

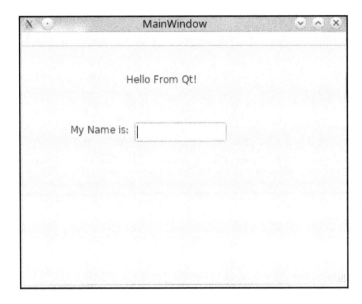

Test the application:

- What happens when you type your name in the box? Try it!
- What happens if you hit *Enter*? Try it!

Nothing seems to happen. We need to do something with the text they input. So, let's move on to the next section!

Causing a response

At this point, you can enter a name, but nothing changes except the text in the edit line. It would be nice if the program did something when we entered our name.

Let's add a button. When the user clicks the button, we will update **Hello From Qt!**.

The first step is to add a push button and change the text to **Enter Name**.

Once the push button is added, we need to make the push button do something. We will be using Qt's signal and slot mechanism to make this happen:

1. Right-click on the button, and select **Go to Slot....**
2. When the popup comes up, select **clicked()** from the **QAbstractButton** section and then click **OK**.
3. As soon as you press **OK**, an editor is opened for mainwindow.cpp and the cursor is placed in a newly added method definition, on_pushButton_clicked(). This is where we will implement the code to fetch the name from the lineEdit box and update label:

```
void MainWindow::on_pushButton_clicked()
{
    QString name = ui->lineEdit->selectedText();
    ui->label->setText(QString("Nice to meet you %1!").arg(name));
}
```

Let's save the code and run it.

Now, try typing a name in the line edit and then click on the **Enter Name** button:

That's not right! The text of the label is cut off. Fix it by changing the size of the label and adjusting the label's horizontal alignment to center. (Hint—**AlignHCenter** is used to specify horizontal center alignment.)

Now, run the code again. Here is what I got:

This is better. The text is no longer cut off, but there is no name. It looks like we need to *debug* the code. Luckily, we can do it right in Qt Creator!

Fixing a mistake

Debugging mistakes is part of developing software. It seems like I have spent at least half of my software development career debugging mistakes in code. I'd like to say that it was other people's code, but it has mostly been in mine. Luckily, I have caught most of them while I was developing the code, but occasionally some slipped past.

Qt Creator comes with built-in C++ and QML (a Qt language) debugging support. Now is a good time to use it to find the mistake in our code.

Launching our application in the Qt Creator debugger

While developing an application in Qt Creator, it is very easy to compile and launch it in the Qt Creator debugger. Like running the application, there are several methods for doing so:

- Click on the debug icon (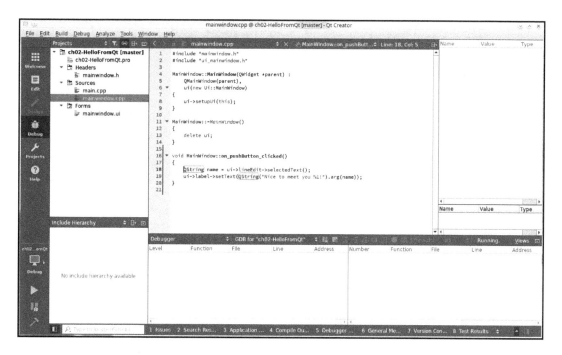) in the left icon bar
- Select **Debug** | **Start Debugging** | **Start debugging** *project_name*
- Press *F5*

Display `mainwindow.cpp` in the editor screen, and then start debugging any way you choose. This will be bring up the **Debug** screen. Notice that the **Debug** icon in the left icon bar is now highlighted and some new panes have opened up.

Examining the Debug screen

This is the **Debug** screen. From here, you can debug on the host and the target. The following screenshot shows you the general layout of the screen. The details are described as follows:

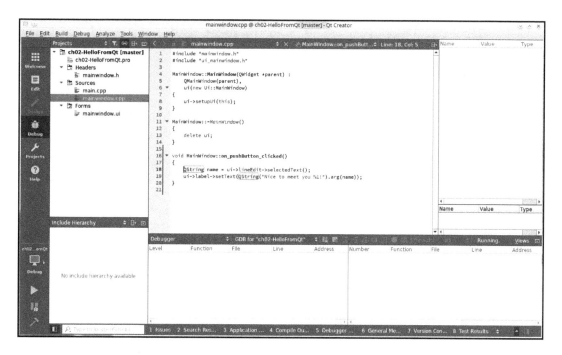

The left side and top-center of the screen look almost identical to the **Edit** screen we saw earlier, but there are some new sections. In the top-right, automatic variables and their values are shown. On the bottom, we have the **Debugger** section. By default, the left side of the **Debugger** section shows the call stack, and the right side shows breakpoints.

Setting a breakpoint

Since we want to debug the `on_pushButton_clicked()` method, find the first line in method and click on the left side of the line number to set a breakpoint. A red dot should appear to the left of the line number and a new breakpoint will be shown in the bottom part of the **Debug** screen:

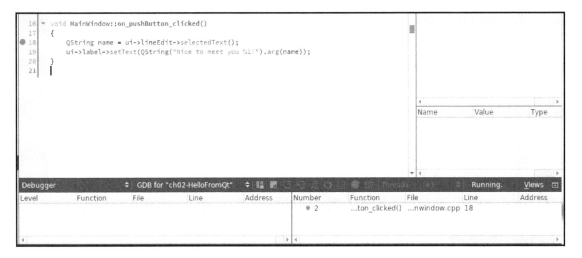

When the code is run in debug mode, the code will stop at the breakpoint so we can see what is happening. We call that *tripping the breakpoint*, and it is what we will do next.

Tripping the breakpoint

Now, go to the running application, enter a name, and press the **Enter Name** button.

The application will stop at the breakpoint we set and the panes will now display some data:

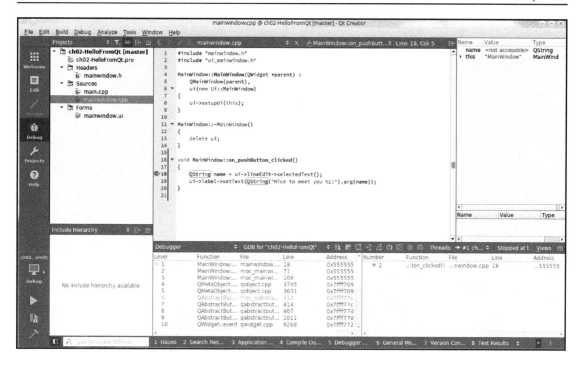

Let's take a closer look at some of the details of the screen:

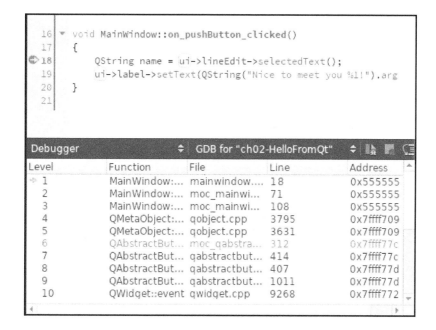

There is now an arrow at the location where we stopped in the code and a corresponding arrow in the call stack showing where we are:

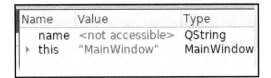

The top-right pane shows the value of all active variables. But wait! It shows the value of **name** is **<not accessible>**. Why would that be?

It is because we stopped before the line was executed, so **name** has yet to be defined. If we click the step over icon ( ) in the **Debugger** section, we will step to the next line of code:

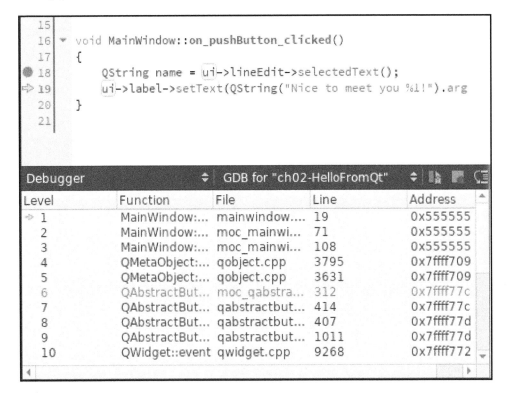

Now, **name** has a value of "":

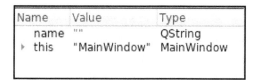

Why? We put text in the line edit box. Why didn't it retrieve it?

I think it is time we get some help to figure out why the value is not what we expected.

Getting some help

Let's go back to the code itself and get some help:

1. In the `mainwindow.cpp` editor screen, double-click on **selectedText** to highlight it and then press *F1*. We are immediately taken to the help page for the **selectedText** method (notice that the **Help** icon is now highlighted in the left icon bar):

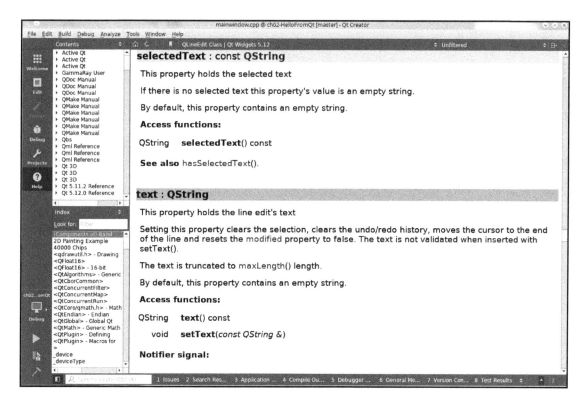

Reading the description, we find that **selectedText** refers to the text selected in the line edit box, and if there is no text selected, we will get an empty string back. That seems to be what is happening. So, what is the right thing to use?

2. Look at the next entry, **text**, and see whether you can figure out what we need to use, modify the code, and test it in the debugger.

Carry out the following in the debugger:

1. Click the **Debug** icon to return to the **Debug** Screen:
    1. To stop the program being debugged, press the **Stop Debugger** icon in the **Debugger** pane. It is the stop button overlaid with a bug.
    2. Pressing the **Continue** button in the **Debugger** pane (⏸) will continue execution of the code.
    3. You can edit the code right in the **Debug** screen.

2. Once you are happy with the code, commit it to the VCS, and then take some time to play around with the code and debugger to see what else it can do. Because you committed your working code, you don't have to worry about breaking it while you play!

Digging deeper

In writing this chapter, I glossed over a few things for the sake of keeping the flow of the lesson. Now is a good time to look at some of them in more depth.

In particular, I want to take a little bit of time to explain the code for the push button, what these *slots* and *signals* are, and to pontificate on testing.

Explaining the push button code

The `on_pushButton_clicked()` handles the user clicking on `pushbutton`. Now, we will go through the method line by line to understand what is happening:

```
void MainWindow::on_pushButton_clicked()
{
```

The naming of this method enables the Qt GUI to automatically connect the signal emitted by the button when it is pressed to a slot in our main window that will handle it. The format is `on_<name_of_widget>_<signal>`. In this case, the name of the widget is `pushButton` and the signal is `clicked`, hence, `on_pushButton_clicked()`. When the GUI starts, it notices the name of the method and connects it to the specified signal in the specified named widget:

```
QString name = ui->lineEdit->text();
```

`QString` is Qt's string type. While similar to `std::string`, it is a bit older and, in some ways, simpler to use. It is also the only string type supported directly by Qt.

When the Qt toolchain creates a UI class (for example, `MainWindow`), the default is to create a pointer named `ui`, through which all of the items in that UI class are accessed by their name.

The name of each item in the UI is specified by the properties of the item. In our application, we left the default name for the line edit box, `lineEdit`, so `ui->lineEdit` refers to the box where we enter the name.

`text()` is a method that returns the content of the line edit box as a `QString`:

```
    ui->label->setText(QString("Nice to meet you %1!").arg(name));
}
```

`label` was the default name given to our **Hello From Qt!** label.

You can probably guess what the `setText(..)` method does by its name, if not by the effect when the code is run.

What about the `QString(..).arg(name)` piece—what does it do? This is really doing two things:

- `QString("Nice to meet you %1!")` defines an unnamed, temporary `QString` with the value: `Nice to meet you %1!`.
- `.arg(name)` is invoking the argument substitution method of `QString`. The passed argument is substituted for the appropriate numbered substitution marker in the `QString`. The first `.arg(..)` function replaces each `%1` in the `QString` with a string representation of the argument. More generally the nth `.arg(..)` function replaces all occurrences of `%n` in the `QString` function. There is an overloaded version of `QString::arg(..)` for most simple types (char, int, float, and so on) and complex Qt types that make sense.

QString::arg(..) is expensive. It makes a copy of the QString and returns it each time it is invoked.

Hence, QString("A").arg(b).arg(c).arg(d) actually creates four QStrings in memory! Because of this, some forms of .arg(..), in particular, .arg(QString), can take multiple substitutions with only one copy being created; for example, QString("A").arg(b, c, d), where b, c, and d are QStrings.

Sending and receiving between objects–signals and slots

Qt uses a very powerful concept to communicate between objects in an application—signals and slots. Objects (like GUI elements) can emit signals that are received by slots.

In HelloFromQt, the **Enter Name** button emits a clicked() signal when the button is clicked. That signal is connected to the on_pushButton_clicked() slot. In the case of our code, the connection is automatically made by Qt based on naming conventions. Later in this book, we will learn how to create our own signals and slots and manually connect them with code.

Although connections are made one at a time, signals and slots can have an *n:n* relation. A signal can be connected to multiple slots, and a slot can be connected to multiple signals.

The other interesting thing about signals and slots is that they can cross thread boundaries. You can use them to communicate progress from a worker thread to a progress indicator in the GUI.

Signals and slots are a very powerful construct that can be easily leveraged to do everything from point-to-point communications between objects to a publish/subscribe messaging system, or even a blackboard design.

Cool things about signals and slots

There are several cool things about signals and slots that are worth noting:

- Signals can cross thread boundaries. If an emitted signal is connected to a slot through a queued connection, the slot will be invoked in the thread of the receiving QObject. That may seem unimportant now, but we will discover later where it can be very important.

- Signal/slot communication can be very fast. When using a direct connection, the slot is invoked directly (called) when the signal is emitted.
- Qt does auto connection of signals and slots in a GUI based on naming rules. We saw this in the code for the push button in `HelloFromQt!`.
- Multiple slots can be connected to one signal, and multiple signals can be connected to a single slot.

Rules of signals and slots

There are a number of important rules to using slots and signals:

- Signals and slots are only used with QObjects.
- If multiple slots are connected to the same signal, the order in which the slots are invoked by the emitted signal is indeterminate.

You will learn more about signals and slots in `Chapter 4`, *Important Qt Concepts*. However, let's turn our attention to one of the topics I have become passionate about—testing.

Testing

Did you notice that we have been interactively testing the application right along? By simply running it the first time, we were able to see that it met a simple, undocumented requirement—display `Hello From Qt!`.

Quick, informal testing during development really isn't that hard unless you make it that way. If we are continually testing our code, even informally, we are more likely to find bugs when we create them, instead of after we have spent weeks writing code and forgotten half of what we have done.

The only difference between our quick test and formal testing really comes down to documentation. In regulated industries, it's all about the documentation of what was tested, how it was tested, and the results of the tests.

Test Driven Development (TDD) is a software methodology in which no code is written unless a test fails. For our simple `HelloFromQt` application, TDD would imply that we would have to first create a test (for example, *Verify that the words* **Hello From Qt!** *are displayed*), run the test, fail it, and then start writing code. While I don't strictly adhere vehemently to TDD, I do like how it forces you to think about writing tests and testing the code from the start instead of waiting until the end.

Summary

Congratulations! You made it! This was a lot of material to cover, but it really forms the basis of working with Qt Creator and developing a widgets-based application. It also got you to write and debug a very simple Qt application.

As we worked our way through this chapter, we covered a fair amount of material. We began by learning how to start Qt Creator. We then learned how to navigate it.

Having learned how to get around Qt Creator, we started to write our first Qt Widget Application. First, we created a Qt Widget project, and then we created the display form. After that, we improved on the application and found a bug in the code during testing. I had not planned to teach debugging yet, but since I made a mistake when I wrote the code, we learned how to debug using Qt Creator and use the help system (like I did) to figure out what the problem was.

In working through this chapter, you were exposed to a couple of very good software development practices that can serve you well in industry. You learned about using a version control system to save your progress, and you learned how easy and important it is to do informal testing as you develop. Perhaps you even found the shared anecdotes useful in understanding what can happen if you don't apply these practices.

The Git repository contains my working example of the application code for this chapter. You can find it in `Chapter02/ch02-HelloFromQt`.

In `Chapter 3`, *Running Your First Application on the Target*, we will configure Qt Creator so that it can build for the target and start running code on the target.

Questions

1. Can Qt Creator interface to version control systems? If so, which ones?
2. Give two ways you can create a new project in Qt Creator.
3. How do you add a C++ class to a Qt Project?
4. Do Qt and Qt Creator only support GUI development?
5. What resources does Qt Creator provide for learning more about a Qt topic?
6. What is the basic process for adding elements to a design?
7. Describe ways in which can you compile and run your application.
8. How can you start debugging an application being developed in Qt Creator.
9. How do you set a breakpoint in the debugger?
10. How often should we test our code, even informally? Why?

Further reading

You may want to look at the following Packt book for more information on the topics covered in this chapter:

- *Application Development with Qt Creator - Second Edition*, by Ray Rischpater

Running Your First Application on the Target

In Chapter 1, *Setting Up the Environment*, we worked through the process of setting up our Host for Qt development and cross-compilation, and we set up our Target. In Chapter 2, *Writing Your First Qt Application*, we wrote a simple Qt program. In this chapter, we will configure **Qt Creator** to work with the Target and run greetings from Qt on it.

In the process, we will be covering the following topics:

- Configuring Qt Creator for our Target
- Building for the Target
- Deploying on the Target
- Running the application on the Target
- Debugging on the Target

By the end of this chapter, you should have learned the following:

- How to configure Qt Creator for cross-compilation builds
- How to transfer an application to the Target
- How to run and debug the application on the Target
- How to use layouts to make flexible displays

Technical requirements

For this chapter, you will need to have finished the setup of your Target, including cross-compiling Qt 5.12.0 and installing it on the Target. You will also need to have a mouse and keyboard hooked up to the Target so you can test our application.

You can find the code for this chapter in the GitHub repository at `https://github.com/PacktPublishing/Hands-On-Embedded-Programming-with-Qt/tree/master/Chapter03`.

Configuring Qt Creator for our Target

Back when I started cross-compiling Qt for embedded QNX devices, Qt Creator was just starting to offer limited support for handing remote Targets. Fortunately for us, a lot of work was put into Qt Creator to make it very easy to implement cross-compilation, remote running, and remote debugging.

The following sections walk you through the process of setting up Qt Creator. These same basic steps can be applied for any supported Targets. The order of the steps is important, as some steps require the previous steps to have been completed first:

1. Tell Qt Creator about the device
2. Tell Qt Creator about the cross-compiler toolchain
3. Configure the debugger for the device
4. Tell Qt Creator about the Qt build for the device
5. Create a Qt Kit with the preceding information

Each step has its own section.

All settings are done through the **Options** dialog. You can access it by selecting **Tools** | **Options...** from the main menu.

Telling Qt Creator about a new device

The first step is to add a new device to Qt Creator:

1. In the left side menu, click on **Devices**.
2. Click on the **Devices** tab on the right half of the screen.
3. Click **Add...**:

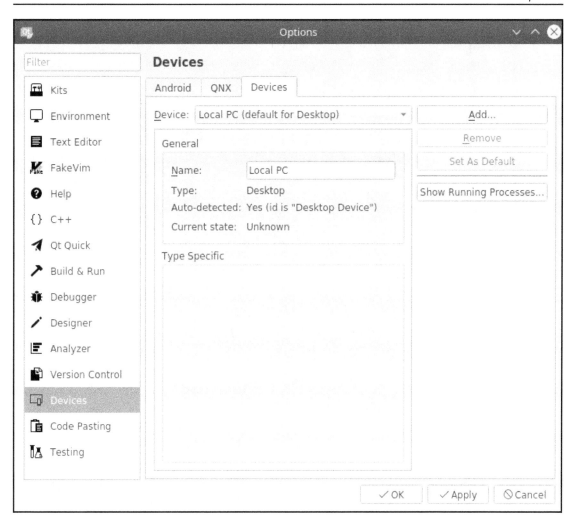

4. In the dialog box, select **Generic Linux Device**, then click **Start Wizard**:

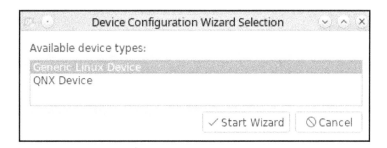

5. On the **Connection** page of the **New Generic Linux Device Configuration Setup** wizard, the steps are as follows:

   1. For the **The name to identify this configuration:** field enter `raspberrypi`.

   2. For the **The device's host name or IP Address:** field enter `raspberrypi` (or use the host name you gave it).

   3. For the **The username to log into the device:** field, enter `root`.

   4. **The authentication type** selection, for now use **Password**.

   5. Enter the password you set up in `Chapter 1`, *Setting Up the Environment:*

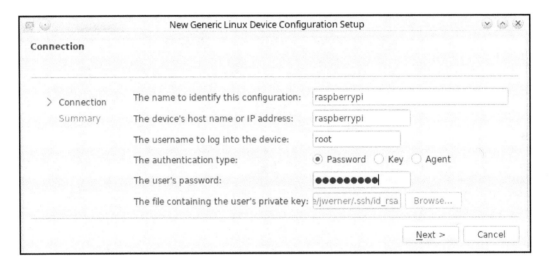

   6. Click **Next >**.

6. On the newly present **Summary** page, click **Finish** to test the configuration.

7. A **Device Test** window will open, run a few tests, and the results will be displayed. If the tests fail, you can edit the device directly on the **Devices** screen:

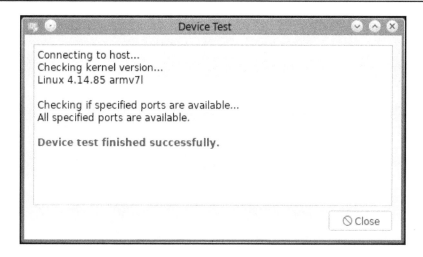

Now that Qt Creator knows about the device, we should tell it about the cross-compiler for the device.

Telling Qt Creator about the cross-compiler

The next step is to inform Qt Creator about the cross-compiler we want to use. This is done from the **Kits** section of the **Options** window:

1. Select **Kits** from the left-hand side list in the **Options** window.
2. Click on the **Compilers** tab.
3. Click on **Add** and select **GCC | C**.
4. Enter the new information on the bottom half of the right screen:
    1. **Name**: Name it something obvious (`Raspi GCC`).
    2. Enter the compiler path (*the* x64 actually refers to the Host OS, not the Target.): `~/raspi/tools/arm-bcm2708/gcc-linaro-arm-linux-gnueabihf-raspbian-x64/bin/arm-linux-gnueabihf-gcc`.

3. The **ABI** should already be set: `arm-linux-generic-elf-32bit`:

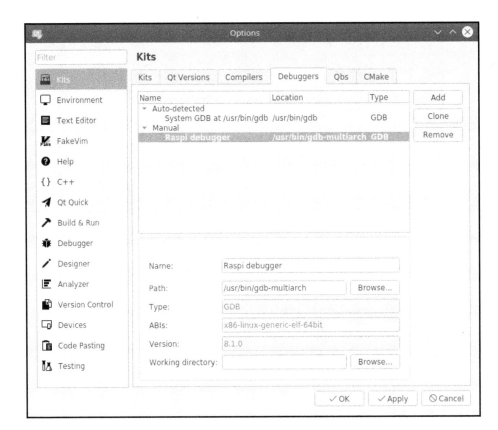

5. Click **Apply**.
6. Repeat the previous steps, but with the following changes:
    1. Select **GCC | C++** under **Add**.
    2. **Name:** `Raspi g++`.
    3. Select the g++ compiler: `~/raspi/tools/arm-bcm2708/gcc-linaro-arm-linux-gnueabihf-raspbian-x64/bin/arm-linux-gnueabihf-g++`.

 Multiple kits can share the same compiler, so you only need to do this for each new cross-compiler you add.

We also need to tell Qt Creator what debugger to use for the Target.

Configuring the debugger for the Target

Now, we need to configure the debugger to use with the Target:

1. Ensure **Kits** is selected in the left menu on the **Options** window.
2. Click on the **Debuggers** tab.
3. Click **Add.**
4. In the bottom section of the window for the newly created debugger entry, do the following:
   1. Enter a name: `Raspi debugger`.
   2. Set the path to the debugger as: `/usr/bin/gdb-multiarch`:

5. Click **Apply**.

Multiple kits can share the same debugger. You only need to do this for each new debugger that you want to tell Qt Creator about.

We are almost there. We still have to tell Qt Creator about the build of Qt that we made for the Target.

Letting Qt Creator know about our Raspberry Pi Qt build

Qt Creator is reasonably smart about finding normal Qt installations for the system you are running. In the following screenshot, you can see that it auto-detected two kits that are installed—**Qt 5.12.0 GCC 64bit2** and **Qt 5.9.7 GCC 64bit**. I had installed both of these using the Qt Installer and Maintenance Tool. Qt Creator did not detect the custom, cross-compiled build we made, so we have to manually configure it. Thankfully, this is very easy because Qt Creator can get everything it needs to know from the version of qmake that was built for it.

We are still working in the **Options** window:

1. Ensure **Kits** is selected in the left menu on the **Options** window.
2. Click on the **Qt Versions** tab.
3. Click on **Add...**:

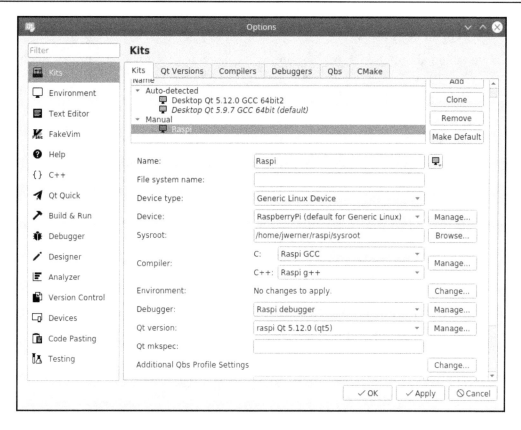

4. In the file selection dialog, navigate to the `qmake` executable in our Qt Raspberry Pi build and select it (`~/raspi/qt5/bin/qmake`).

5. Name it: `raspi Qt ${Qt:Version} (qt5)`.

6. Click **Apply.**

You will need to manually add every custom build of Qt you make, but ones installed with a Qt Installer or maintenance tool should be automatically found.
Like almost everything else in a kit, the Qt version can be shared between multiple kits.

One more step to go—creating a Qt kit we can use.

Creating a Qt kit

Earlier, we talked about Qt kits. A kit is simply a collection of a device, compiler, debugger, Qt build (version), and a Qt mkspec (optional). (A Qt mkspec is a collection of settings for a specific piece of hardware.) In Qt Creator, kits allow you to easily set up builds for different platforms.

Now it is time to configure a kit for use with the Raspberry Pi:

1. Ensure **Kits** is selected in the left menu on the **Options** window.
2. Click on the **Kits** tab.
3. Click on the **Add** button.
4. Fill out the information in the bottom of the page for our Raspberry Pi kit:
    1. **Name**: Raspi.
    2. **Device Type**: Generic Linux Device.
    3. The **Device** is the one created in the previous step: RaspberryPi.
    4. We set the **Sysroot** to where we have the sysroot image: ~/raspi/sysroot.
    5. The two **Compiler** types should be set to what we created previously:
        1. **C: Raspi GCC**
        2. **C++: Raspi g++**
    6. Set the **Debugger** to the one created previously: **Raspi debugger**.
    7. Use the **Qt version** we created previously: **raspi Qt 5.12.0 (qt5)**.
    8. We don't need to set **mkspec**, so leave it empty.
5. Click **OK** to save the changes and close the **Options** window.

Now that we have done all of the setup, we can start building code for the Target. On to the next section!

Building for the Target

Once we have configured a kit for our Qt build for the Raspberry Pi, we can start building Qt applications for the Target. You have already created one Qt application, and you have been told that it is very easy to rebuild a Qt application for different devices. Why don't we prove that? We will start by rebuilding HelloFromQt for the Target.

Open the HelloFromQt project if it is not already open.

Adding a kit to the project

The **Projects** page in Qt Creator allows us to configure a project, including adding a new kit to be built. You can access the **Projects** page by clicking the **Projects** icon (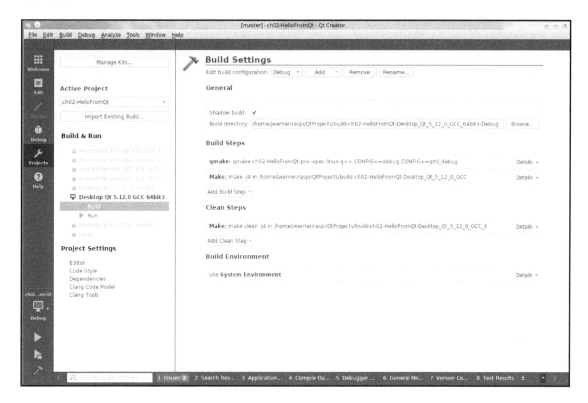) in the left icon bar:

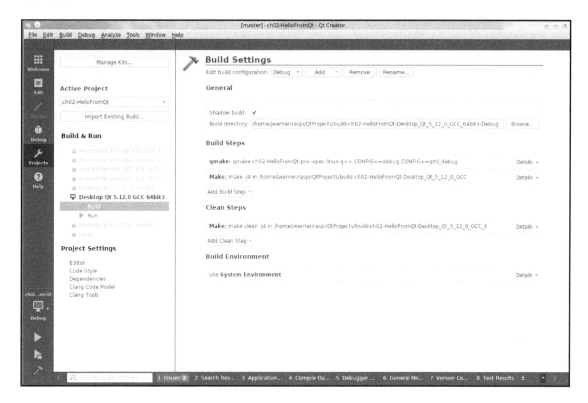

Adding the Raspi kit is very straightforward:

1. Right-click on **Raspi** under **Build & Run**
2. Select **Enable Raspi for Project ch02-HelloFromQt**

Although there are more settings that can be made here, we will leave those for later.

Building the application

Now that the project is configured for the Raspi kit, it is time to build it for the Target.

The first step is selecting the project configuration to build—in this case, Raspi:

- Click on the **Active Configuration** icon (   ) in the left icon bar:
    - Select kit: **Raspi**
    - Build: **Debug**

In `Chapter 2`, *Writing Your First Qt Application*, we used the build and run icon (▶) to do both the building and running in one step. This time, let's just build the application by clicking the **Build** icon (   ) in the left icon bar. In a few seconds, the application should build without errors.

Now that we have built the application, we need to deploy it.

Deploying on the Target

Once built, `HelloFromQt` can be deployed on the Target by selecting **Build | Deploy Project** from the top menu bar. You can verify the successful deployment by looking at the **Compile Output** window. Click on **4 Compile Output** on the bottom bar to open it.

It should look something like this:

```
22:54:10: Running steps for project ch03-HelloFromQt...
22:54:10: Configuration unchanged, skipping qmake step.
22:54:10: Starting: "/usr/bin/make" -j4
make: Nothing to be done for 'first'.
22:54:10: The process "/usr/bin/make" exited normally.
22:54:10: Connecting to device...
22:54:10: The remote file system has 944 megabytes of free space, going
ahead.
22:54:10: Deploy step finished.
22:54:10: Trying to kill "/opt/ch03-HelloFromQt/bin/ch03-HelloFromQt" on
remote device...
22:54:11: Remote application killed.
22:54:11: Deploy step finished.
22:54:11: Uploading file "~/raspi/Hands-On-Embedded-Programming-with-
QT/ch03/build-ch03-HelloFromQt-Raspi-Debug/ch03-HelloFromQt"...
22:54:11: All files successfully deployed.
22:54:11: Deploy step finished.
22:54:11: Elapsed time: 00:02.
```

A couple of the previous lines have been highlighted. The line containing `All files successfully deployed` indicates a successful deployment. In the preceding line, you can find where the application was deployed to, `/opt/ch03-HelloFromQt/bin/ch03-HelloFromQt`, even though it doesn't explicitly say so. The hint is that the deploy process is first trying to kill the application in that place.

With the application deployed, we can now run it.

Running the application on the Target

In `Chapter 2`, *Writing Your First Qt Application*, you learned how to use the **Run** icon (▶) to compile and run the program, but this time, we will use a slightly different way:

1. Open an SSH connection to the Target:

   `$ ssh root@raspberrypi`

2. Execute the application directly from the command line:

   `root@raspberrypi:~# /opt/ch03-HelloFromQt/bin/ch03-HelloFromQt`

3. Using the mouse and keyboard connected to the Target, type in your name and click **Enter Name**:

Once again, we find that the application doesn't display correctly. Apparently, the Target and the host use different sizes for the main window and fonts. That's okay; we can fix it.

Making a more flexible display using layouts

When I first started working with Qt, I would run into the previous problem almost all of the time. When the size of the window changed, everything would break. Things would not be centered or they would go off the screen. Then, I learned about Qt layouts.

In Qt, a layout is flexible way of arranging items onscreen that allows you to specify locations in terms of the size of the containing item. There are several basic types of layouts:

Layout	Description
Vertical	Arranges widgets vertically
Horizontal	Arranges widgets horizontally
Grid	Arranges widgets in a grid
Form	Creates a two-column grid with the first column being a label and the second being an input field

Layouts can contain other layouts, thus allowing some fairly complex arrangements.

Looking at the basics of what we have for a UI so far, it seems we have three vertical sections. That says we will want a vertical layout for the overall layout of the widget, but what about the middle line? The middle line suggests a horizontal or form layout. Since there is only one entry box, we will use a horizontal layout. Had there been more, a grid layout might have made sense.

> There are usually several ways to organize layouts to produce the same result. When designing your own layouts, don't worry too much about how you put it together as long as you get the result you want!

Let's start by making a layout for our line input and its label. Like most things in Qt Creator, there are a couple of ways of doing this. We could drag a horizontal layout from the widget column, drop it in our design, then drop the label and line edit into it, but I like doing things faster:

1. Click in the design window and draw a box around the label and the line edit. This selects both of them.

2. In the tool bar directly above the design, click on the horizontal layout icon (⽥). You will now see the two items surrounded by a red box; this is the outline of the horizontal layout that was just created.

Now it is time to put everything in the main window into a vertical layout:

1. Right-click in the design window (but not on the layout we just created) and select **Lay out | Lay Out Vertically**.

The design should now look something like this:

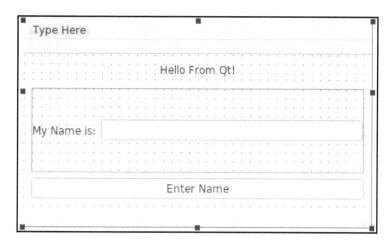

You can test that the layout maintains the relative positions of everything by resizing the design using the blue control points. Try it!

The layout certainly captures everything, but it doesn't really look very good. It is time to start playing with the layout some more.

 Before we start playing with the layout, now is a good point to commit your changes. That way, we have a good fallback point, should we make a mistake.

Try dragging a vertical spacer and dropping it in the bottom of the vertical layout. What happens? What if we add spacers between each line? Experiment a little! You can use *Ctrl +* *Z* to undo your last change, and you should have a good fallback point committed.

Can you drag a horizontal spacer () from the GUI Widget list and drop it to the left of the push button? Try it!

You can't drop the horizontal spacer to the left of the push button, because we only have a horizontal layout. Let's try changing that to a grid layout. (Hint—right-click and then use the **Layou**t option in the popup.)

Now, try dropping the horizontal spacer. What happened?

Everything got moved over because we just inserted a new column! Let's work with that. Drag another horizontal spacer to the right side of the push button.

Now, try dropping some vertical spacers (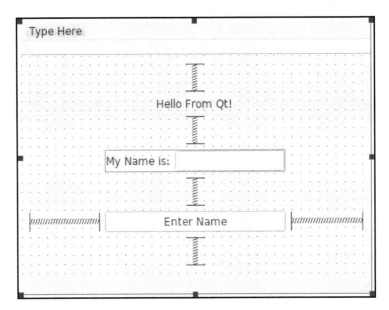) until you get something that looks like the following layout:

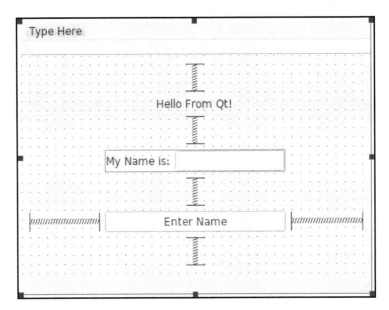

Now, run it on the Target using the **Run** icon (▶) from the left toolbar. It will compile, deploy, then run the application. Now, enter a name and see how it looks:

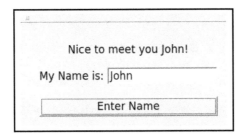

It looks good, so commit the change. Now, try experimenting more with layouts:

- Can you arrange things to the **Enter Name** push button on the same line as the input line?
- Can you make the **My Name is:** label appear above the line edit box?
- Can you make the *Enter* button smaller?

You might also want to try running the application on the Host again:

1. Click on the **Active Configuration** icon () in the toolbar, then select **Desktop Qt 5.12.0 GCC 64bit**.
2. Qt Creator will update its internal project settings.
3. Now click **Run**, and the greetings from Qt will run on the Host.
4. Try changing the size of the Window. What happens? How big can you make it? How small can you make it?
5. Is the application still running on the Target?

But what if I need to debug my code? I'm glad you asked...

Debugging on the Target

If you are expecting a really long and complex answer to *How do I debug code running on the Target?*, then you are going to be very disappointed. Qt Creator makes it incredibly easy. Are you ready?

To debug your code on the Target, simply make sure you have selected the Target build profile, then click the **Debug** icon () in the left toolbar.

Troubleshooting debugging

While developing this chapter, I ran into a small problem. I kept having issues with Qt Creator connecting to the debug program on the Target. After a few failed attempts, and a complete rebuild of my Target image for other reasons, I found the answer. The Yocto image we started with comes with a firewall installed. The firewall prevented the remote debugger from connecting!

Hopefully, you followed the setup procedure correctly in Chapter 1, *Setting Up the Environment*, and disabled the firewall on the Target. If not, I will repeat it here.

To permanently remove the firewall as of the next reboot, use the following:

```
[On Target]$ update-rc.d firewall remove
[On Target]$ rm ./rcS.d/S60firewall
```

To stop the firewall right now, use the following:

```
[On Target]$ /etc/init.d/firewall stop     # stop/disable the firewall

[On Target]$ /etc/init.d/firewall start    # start/enable the firewall
```

The final version of the code, as I developed it, can be found in the GitHub repository at https://github.com/PacktPublishing/Hands-On-Embedded-Programming-with-Qt/tree/master/Chapter03/ch03-HelloFromQt_Final.

Summary

The goal of this chapter was to run our application on the Target. Hopefully, you were able to run it successfully.

The first thing we learned was how to configure Qt Creator for cross-compilation. This process can be applied to any system where you need to do cross-compilation, not just with our Target. We then learned how to deploy (or transfer) our code to the Target.

Once we had deployed our code, we learned another way of starting the code on the Target that did not require Qt Creator. We also saw how easy it was to start debugging code on the Target.

Finally, we learned a little about Qt's layout system for GUIs. It allowed us to make the display look good both on the Host and the Target, even though they had different screen sizes.

You should now know enough to be able to run some of the examples that came with Qt 5.12.0 on the Target. Try it!

In the `Chapter 4`, *Important Qt Concepts*, we will learn about some importance QT concepts that you will use throughout your Qt development. Among these are signals and slots, how Qt does introspection, the model/view architecture, and how Qt can so easily support multiple hardware and OS platforms.

Questions

1. What is a Qt Creator kit?
2. Where are kits configured?
3. How do you add a new device to Qt Creator?
4. How can you tell where the application is deployed to on the Target?
5. What is a layout?
6. If you are designing a form, what kind of layout would you use?
7. How can you space things out in a layout?
8. How can you switch layout types for the main window?
9. How do you switch between different configurations for a project?
10. In Qt Creator, how do you start debugging an application on the Target?
11. How would you configure Qt's Analog Clock Window Example to run a build for and then run on the Target?

2
Section 2: Working with Embedded Qt

Having set up Qt, our host development system, and our target, we can now start exploring Qt itself. In Chapter 4, *Important Qt Concepts*, we will learn some of the core, basic concepts on which Qt is based.

We will then explore a modern development workflow and start working on a long-term project, the BigProject, in Chapter 5, *Managing the Overall Workflow*. This project will accompany us through most of the remainder of this book as we learn new things about Qt and add them.

We will then explore Qt's GUI technologies in Chapter 6, *Exploring GUI Technologies*, and conclude this section with Chapter 7, *Adding More Features*, where we will be exploring more Qt features. In each of these chapters, you will be adding more to BigProject.

The following chapters will be covered in this section:

- Chapter 4, *Important Qt Concepts*
- Chapter 5, *Managing the Overall Workflow*
- Chapter 6, *Exploring GUI Technologies*
- Chapter 7, *Adding More Features*

4
Important Qt Concepts

In Section 1, *Getting Started with Embedded Qt*, we covered the setup of our Host and Target environments, built an application and ran it on the Host, and then recompiled the application for the Target and ran it there.

Now is a good time to pause and take a look at some important Qt concepts:

- Communicating effectively—signals and slots
- Looking inside—the Qt introspection support
- Differing views—model/view architecture
- Keeping it portable—the Qt platform abstraction

When you have finished this chapter, you should have learned the following skills:

- How to use signals and slots to talk between Qt objects (QObjects)
- How to use introspection with Qt objects
- How to separate the GUI presentation and application logic layers using model/view architecture
- How to use Qt's *generic* methods for working with files, hardware, and so on, so they can easily run the code on new platforms

Technical requirements

We are starting to get a little more technical, and, as such, our code is getting a little more advanced. Having knowledge of the following concepts will help you:

- C++11 lambda functions
- C++11 auto keyword (it changed in C++11!)

This chapter does not require the use of the Target. You can go through it without the Target being set up.

The completed code for this chapter can be found at the following GitHub repository: https://github.com/PacktPublishing/Hands-On-Embedded-Programming-with-Qt/tree/master/Chapter04.

Communicating effectively – signals and slots

In Chapter 2, *Writing Your First Qt Application*, I provided a very brief introduction to slots and signals, and talked about how clicking on the **Enter Name** button is communicated to MainWindow. That should have been just enough to whet your appetite to know more.

Signals and slots are one of the fundamental building blocks of Qt. They are used to connect GUI elements to code. They are also used to talk between objects in an application. They form the basis of communication within a Qt application. Therefore, we should spend a little time learning about them.

We will start with a quick overview. Then we will look at how they can be used outside of the GUI. After that, we will see how we can use lambda functions with them. Finally, we will learn about direct and queued connections between signals and slots.

Quick info – Signals and slots

Why don't we start with some quick information about signals and slots? Take a look at the following items:

- Signals and slots work with classes inherited from QObject.
- Signals and slots are defined in the class header.
- A signal is emitted by QObject.
- A signal may send parameters.
- The Qt build system generates the C++ implementation for the signal. You don't implement it.
- Slots may receive parameters.
- You must provide the implementation for the slot.
- A signal can be connected to multiple slots.
- A slot may have connections from multiple signals.
- Only signals and slots with the same signatures (parameter count and types) can be connected.

Having read that, we shall see how signals and slots work together. We will do this in the context of non-GUI code (a console application) so as to get a basic understanding of signals and slots.

Signals and slots in non-GUI code

We already know that Qt widget GUI elements make heavy use of signals and slots, but did you know that you don't even need a GUI to use them? Any class derived from QObject can use signals and slots. One good example of a non-GUI class that uses signals and slots is QTimer, the Qt Timer class. QTimer emits a signal when it expires. Let's experiment a little with QTimer and see what it does.

Start by creating a project for a Qt console application in Qt Creator (refer to Chapter 2, *Writing Your First Qt Application*, if you need a reminder on how to do it). Name the project ConsoleTimers, select the qmake build system, and select at least the Desktop Qt 5.12 GCC kit. We will concentrate on using it on the Host for now, but using what you learned in Chapter 3, *Running Your First Application on the Target*, you can easily try it on the Target. As with all of the examples, I encourage you to select a version control system for the project. It's a good habit to get into, and could just save you time if you make a mistake.

The first thing we will want is a class that can inherit from QObject:

1. Right-click on the name of the project (ConsoleTimers) in the left-hand column. Then select **Add New...**.
2. Select **C++ Class** from the center section and click **Choose...**:

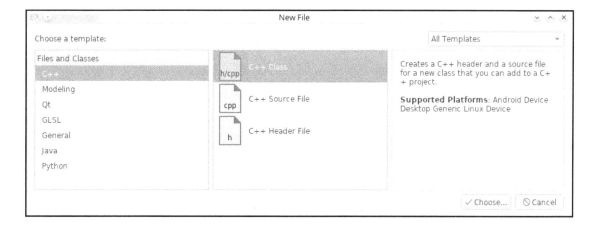

3. Give the class the name `TimeCatcher`.

4. Select **QObject** as the base class:

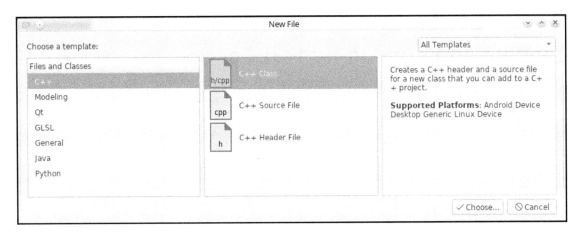

5. Click **Next >**.

6. Ensure `ConsoleTimers.pro` is specified as the project to which we will be adding the class.

7. Ensure that it is added to version control:

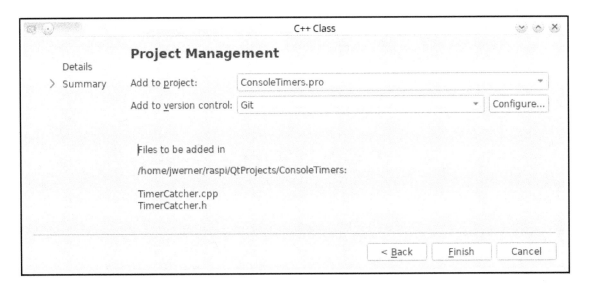

8. Click **Finish.**

`TimeCatcher.cpp` should now open in the editor, but we want to start by adding to `TimeCatcher.h`. We could open the headers section under `ConsoleTimers` in the projects bar and find the file, but instead we'll try another way:

1. Select `TimerCatcher.h` in the source code for `TimerCatcher.cpp`.
2. Press *F2*.
3. `TimerCatcher.h` is opened.

Preparing the header

Pressing *F2* in an editor window tells Qt Creator to find the definition of the selected item. In this case, it looked for `TimerCatcher.h` and opened it for us. Let's stop and look at the definition of `TimeCatcher`:

```
class TimerCatcher : public QObject
{
    Q_OBJECT
public:
    explicit TimerCatcher(QObject *parent = nullptr);

signals:

public slots:
};
```

`Q_OBJECT` is a macro that tells the Qt build system that we are using features from `QObject`. It is required for all classes that inherit from `QObject`, including QWidgets (UI elements).

The `signals` section defines the signals that will be emitted by `TimeCatcher`.

The `public slots` section defines the publicly accessible slots. You may also have protected and private slots that are used internally in the class.

Let's define an instance of `QTimer` for us to use. After **public slots,** add the following code:

```
private:
    QTimer  m_timer;              ///< my timer
```

Depending on how you entered the word `private:`, you may have started typing it indented, but when you hit :, it realigned itself. Qt Creator is good like that.

At this point, you probably have a warning showing up on the QTimer line—*unknown type name* QTimer. That makes sense; we haven't defined it or included its header. Let's let Qt Creator fix the problem:

1. Right-click on **QTimer.**
2. Select **Refactor.**
3. Select **Add #include <QTimer>.**

The include file for QTimer is added to the top of the header for us, and the cursor is right where it was. This works for many classes, but not all.

Now let's add a slot to receive a signal from m_timer when it expires. Under public slots: , add a new method definition:

```
void catchExpiredTimer();    ///< called when m_timer timesout
```

This defines a slot that takes no parameters and returns nothing. Typically, slots do not return any values. What they take as parameters depends on the signal that is sent to them. In this case, the QTimer::timeout() signal sends no parameters, so we receive no parameters.

 By now, you probably noticed that I am using some fancy comments. I strongly believe in commenting even obvious things, as six months after I have coded something, it probably isn't obvious to me anymore, and surely isn't obvious to the next developer who has to fix my code. The comments starting with ///< are a form that tells a very useful package called **Doxygen** that I am providing a short description of the thing I pointed to. If you have never used or seen Doxygen, look it up! It's great for generating code documentation.

We need to define what happens in catchExpiredTimer, so we will again use a Qt Creator shortcut:

1. Right-click on **catchExpiredTimer.**
2. Select **Refactor.**
3. Select **Add Definition in TimerCatcher.cpp.**

Nice, that works with any method definition. It's especially good when you have lots of parameters.

Using the QTimer

We need to do something when the timer expires. Let's keep it simple, but do it the Qt way as follows:

```
void TimerCatcher::catchExpiredTimer()
{
    QTextStream(stdout) << "Got Timeout!" << endl;
}
```

Did you right-click and select **Refactor** to add the appropriate header?

QTextStream is a Qt class for streaming text. In this case, we create it pointing to stdout, then endl simply ends the line.

There's still a couple of steps we need to do before we can see anything.

Setting up the timer

We need to actually set up our timer to do something. To make life interesting, let's create a repeating timer that triggers every five seconds. We will add this to the instantiation of TimeCatcher:

```
TimerCatcher::TimerCatcher(QObject *parent) : QObject(parent)
{
    m_timer.setSingleShot(false);   // repeating, not single shot
    m_timer.start(5000);            // 5000 msec = 5 sec
}
```

That looks good, but there is still something left to do in TimerCatcher.

Connecting the QTimer signal

The way the code stands now, m_timer will generate a timeout() signal every 5000 milliseconds, but no one will receive it. We need to explicitly connect the signal before we start, it as follows:

```
TimerCatcher::TimerCatcher(QObject *parent) : QObject(parent)
{
    // connect the time of m_timer to our catchExpiredTimer
    connect(&m_timer, &QTimer::timeout, this,
        &TimerCatcher::catchExpiredTimer);

    m_timer.setSingleShot(false);   // repeating, not single shot
```

```
        m_timer.start(5000);               // 5000 msec = 5 sec
    }
```

The `connect(..)` method connects a signal to a slot. It has many overloads. We are using one of the new ones introduced in Qt 5 that allows the compiler to make sure we are sending the correct number of arguments instead of waiting for the code not to run correctly. The first argument of this version of `connect(..)` is a pointer to the sender object, `&m_timer`. The second is the name of the signal. The third is the receiving object (`this`), and the last is the name of the slot.

Finishing the code

So far we have given `TimerCatcher` a `QTimer` and a slot to receive it. We also connected the required signals and slots and told `TimerCatcher` what to do in the slot. But, we don't ever create a `TimerCatcher` object. Since there is no GUI, we will need to do that in `main`.

Open `main.cpp` and instantiate an instance of `TimerCatcher` called `tc`, right before `return a.exec();`. This makes sure we have `TimerCatcher`:

```cpp
int main(int argc, char *argv[])
{
    QCoreApplication a(argc, argv);

    TimerCatcher    tc;

    return a.exec();
}
```

Running our application

Save the code and run it using the Run button.

After compilation, a console window should pop up and the program will start printing out `Got Timeout!`:

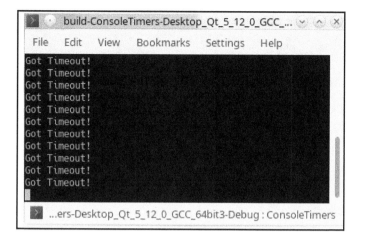

Since we never specified a way to end the program, we can either click on the stop button in the application output area or press *Ctrl+C* in the console window.

The completed code for this part of the example can be found at `https://github.com/PacktPublishing/Hands-On-Embedded-Programming-with-Qt/tree/master/Chapter04/ConsoleTimers_1`.

Next, we will learn about using lambda expressions with signals and slots. *What is a lambda?* I'm glad you asked...

Signals and slots using lambdas

With Qt 5 and C++11, it is now possible to connect signals to lambda functions. A lambda function is a function that is defined at the point of use. It is sometimes called an anonymous function, because it does not have a name. `CProgramming.com` has a good introduction to lambdas at `https://www.cprogramming.com/c++11/c++11-lambda-closures.html`.

Why would you use a lambda instead of a slot? Maybe you have something really simple you want to implement without having to create a class and a slot. Let's expand `ConsoleTimers` a little bit.

Although it is nice to see the message come every five seconds, I would like to output `tic` every second, but I don't want to change `TimerCatcher` to do it or use the space to create a new function. Instead, a lambda function will be employed:

```
int main(int argc, char *argv[])
{
    QCoreApplication a(argc, argv);

    TimerCatcher    tc;

    QTextStream a_cout(stdout);          // create a stream to stdout
    QTimer tocTimer;                     // our timer
    tocTimer.setInterval(1000);
    tocTimer.setSingleShot(false);

    // connect to the lambda function
    QObject::connect(&tocTimer, &QTimer::timeout, [&a_cout]() {a_cout
        << "tic " << endl;});
    tocTimer.start();                    // start the timer

    return a.exec();
}
```

Most of the new section (bold) should be self-explanatory, but the `QObject::connect(..)` line looks a bit different.

Since we are not inside `QObject`, we need to explicitly tell Qt we wish to use the static `connect(..)` method from the `QObject` class.

The next two elements, `&tocTimer` and `&QTimer::timeout`, should be familiar as the sender object and the signal we want to connect to.

The last part is the lambda function. Basically, `[&a_cout]` tells the compiler that we want to capture (make available to the function) the `a_cout` variable by reference. Note that `()` describes the arguments for the method (`void`). Finally, `{a_cout << "tic " << endl;}` is the contents of the function. It should look familiar from `TimerCatcher::catchExpiredTimer()`.

Lambda functions are very powerful constructs. In C++11, you can drop them almost anywhere a functor (pointer to a function) is used. They are also easily misused. As a general rule, if you need more than a couple of statements or plan to use the contents of the lambda in multiple places in the code, you will be better off creating a static method and using it.

I'll leave it to you to fix up the includes (hint—start with a right-click), and then run it:

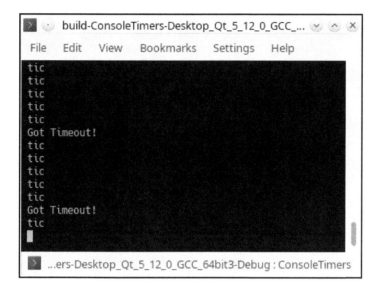

Code for this example can be found at `https://github.com/PacktPublishing/Hands-On-Embedded-Programming-with-Qt/tree/master/Chapter04/ConsoleTimers_2`.

 One often overlooked feature of `QTextStream::endl` is that it causes the text stream to be flushed. Everything that is being buffered is written to the stream. In the preceding code, it was needed to make sure that the tics were output before `Got Timeout!` was output.

Sometimes we want to immediately send a signal; sometimes we want it to wait until we are finished with something else, that is, we want to queue the signal. We will learn more about that in the next section.

Queuing things up

Signals can be delivered to a slot in two different ways—directly and queued. When a signal is connected to a slot through a direct connect, emitting the signal causes the code for the slot to be immediately invoked in the signal's thread. When a signal is connected to a slot through a queued connection, the signal is queued and eventually invoked on the slot's thread.

How the connection is made is determined when making the connection. The generalized form of the connect (..) method between two QObjects is as follows:

```
QMetaObject::Connection QObject::connect(const QObject *sender, const
    char *signal, const QObject *receiver, const char *method,
    Qt::ConnectionType type = Qt::AutoConnection)
```

The last argument, the Qt::ConnectionType type, determines how the connection is made:

Qt::DirectConnection	Immediately invokes the slot in the signal emitter thread when the signal is emitted.
Qt::QueuedConnection	Queues up the signal and returns control to the emitter thread. The receiver slot will be invoked the next time its event loop executes.
Qt::BlockingQueuedConnection	Queues up the signal, but doesn't return control to the emitter thread until the slot has been invoked and finishes. The receiver slot will be invoked the next time its event loop executes.
Qt:AutoConnection	(default) If the receiver is in the same thread as the sender when the connection is created, it makes a direct connection, or else it makes a queued connection.
Qt::UniqueConnection	This is a flag that can be or'd with other connection types. It tells connect (..) to only make the connection if it will not result in a duplicate connection.

For Qt::AutoConnection, note that the choice is made when the connection is made. If you create two QObjects, connect them, and then move one QObject to its own thread, the connection will already be a *direct* connection. Always move QObject to its own thread before making the connection!

You may be wondering why you would use a queued connection. We examine that next.

When should I use a queued connection?

We already know that we should use a queued connection with dealing with multiple threads, but do you ever use one in a single-threaded application? Yes. Let's make yet another change to our `ConsoleTimers` application. This time we are going to add a new signal and slot to `TimeCatcher`:

1. Add a private integer value, `m_count`, to `TimerCatcher` and initialize it to `0` in the constructor.

2. Under `public slots:`, In `TimeCatcher.h`, prototype a slot called `printCount` that takes an integer value, `count`. Then implement it to use a `QTextStream` class to `stdout` to output the count as follows:

```
void TimerCatcher::printCount(int count)
{
    QTextStream(stdout) << "count = " << count << endl;
}
```

3. Under `signals`: Define a new signal, `newCount`, that sends an integer value called count as follows:

```
signals:
    void newCount (int count);
```

4. In the constructor, before we connect the timer, `connect` `TimerCatcher::newCount` to `TimerCatcher::printCount` using `DirectConnection` as follows:

```
connect(this, &TimerCatcher::newCount, this,
    &TimerCatcher::printCount, Qt::DirectConnection);
```

5. In `TimerCatcher::catchExpiredTimer()`, increment `m_count` and then emit it before printing out `Got Timeout!`:

```
emit newCount(++m_count);
    QTextStream(stdout) << "Got Timeout!" << endl;
```

Now compile and run the code. Where does the count get displayed? Before `Got Timeout!` with the direct connection, `printCount(..)` is invoked where the signal is emitted.

Now change the connection to a queued connection and run it. Where does count display now? After `Got Timeout!`, the signal is queued, and `printCount(..)` is not invoked until the event loop for `TimerCatcher` is re-executed (that is, after `catchExpiredTimer()` has exited).

The following is the output of a version of the code that uses two different slots, one connected to `newCount(..)` directly and one connected through a queue. You can see the difference when they are invoked as follows:

```
build-ConsoleTimers-Desktop_Qt_5_12_0_GCC_...

 File   Edit   View   Bookmarks   Settings   Help

d count = 11
Got Timeout!
tic
q count = 11
tic
tic
tic
tic
d count = 12
Got Timeout!
tic
q count = 12
tic

...ers-Desktop_Qt_5_12_0_GCC_64bit3-Debug : ConsoleTimers
```

The code for this can be found in `https://github.com/PacktPublishing/Hands-On-Embedded-Programming-with-Qt/tree/master/Chapter04/ConsoleTimers_3`.

Are you still waiting to see how we implement the code for a signal? Well, I am not going to tell you because we *never* implement. Let me explain that to you next.

Implementing Signals Not Needed

Did you notice? We never actually implemented the contents of our signal. Was that a mistake? No, it was on purpose. The implementation of signals is done for us by the **meta-object compiler (moc)**, which is a Qt tool that generates the code that makes slots and signals work.

When we define a signal, moc generates all of the needed code to implement that signal. Similarly, the **emit** keyword is also processed by moc, and the correct code for emitting the signal is generated.

> Never write your own implementation for a signal. That's moc's job, and we don't want to start a Qt union action against us!

We come to one of the most powerful aspects of Qt, its introspection support. Once you read the next section, I think you will understand why I like it so much.

Looking inside – Qt's introspection support

Several years ago I was tasked with writing a C# based application. My pride as a C++ programmer of over two decades at that point told me two things—firstly, I won't like a *petty* Microsoft(tm) language like C#, and secondly, if I were to write a C# program, it would be very easy to learn as it must be like C++. I was wrong, on both counts. C# is much more like Java than C++, and it has become a feature-packed language with lots of cool things.

One of the things I enjoyed the most was introspection, or the ability to look into a class at runtime and find out what attributes and methods it has. That is something not even C++17 has, and this lowly C# language already had it! (There is a good chance we will see some introspection support directly in C++20, but it's not final yet.)

The trolls that developed Qt must have known how powerful introspection can be because Qt has had the concept of properties of QObjects for almost a couple of decades, since Qt 3!

> The developers of Qt, pronounced *cute*, are sometimes called **trolls** because Qt was originally developed and maintained by a company called **Trolltech**. Since then, it has changed hands a couple of times, but *trolls* still may be heard from those who remember its origin.

Properties

In the Qt world, a property is a special attribute of QObject or Q_GADGET that can be accessed by generic methods. A property is defined by using the Q_PROPERTY(..) macro.

Consider the following incomplete definition of QObject, Person that defines two properties, name and birthdate:

```
class Person : public QObject
{
    Q_OBJECT

  Q_PROPERTY(QString name ...)
  Q_PROPERTY(QDate birthdate ...)


    ...
};
```

To get either name or birthdate, I can use one method, property(property_name), to retrieve the value. Similarly, I can use one method, setProperty(property_name, value), to set the value of the property. Consider the following code:

```
Person p;
p.setProperty("name", "John");
p.setProperty("birthday", QDate(2000, 9, 24)); // September 24, 2000

QTextStream(stdout) << p.property("name") << ": " <<
p.property("birthday");
```

You are probably thinking, that looks interesting, but why not just define the class attributes and getter and setter methods for them (that is, QString a_name, QString name(), setName(QString n), and so on)? The truth is you still have to define them. The definition of Q_PROPERTY is a little more than I showed previously. Here is the definition that includes specifying the read (getter) and write (setter) methods that are used for the properties:

```
        Q_PROPERTY(QString name READ name WRITE setName)
        Q_PROPERTY(QDate    birthdate READ birthday WRITE setBirthday)

   public:
        QString name()              {return m_name;}
        void    setName(QString n) {m_name = n;}
        ...

   private:
        QString    m_name;
```

While Qt Creator will automatically generate the definitions for the getter and setters for the class attributes (right-click and select **Refactor**), we still have just added more code with no real benefit other than having a generic interface to data. Why bother? Here are the reasons you want to use Q_PROPERTY:

- QML objects can only access attributes stored as a Q_PROPERTY from a C++ class. (We'll see this later.)
- You can ask QObject to disclose all of its properties and their values.
- An instance of QObject can be given new properties at runtime. These are called **dynamic properties**, and they are accessed the same way as properties defined at compile time. Only that instance will have the property—no other instances will. The following would add a new dynamic property, sex, with the male value to Person p:

```
p.setProperty("sex", "male");
```

Let's learn a little more about using the compile-time property definition, Q_PROPERTY.

Q_PROPERTY

You have seen examples of Q_PROPERTY, but we should formalize things a bit.

The simplest definition of Q_PROPERTY is for a read-only property:

```
Q_PROPERTY(type property_name READ getterMethod)
```

For a read/write property, we just add the setter:

```
Q_PROPERTY(type property_name READ getterMethod WRITE setterMethod)
```

Let me explain what you see in the code snippet above:

- type is any type that Qt can handle as QVariant.
- property_name is the name by which the property is accessed. It is usually the name of the class attribute as, by convention, getterMethod shares its name with property_name.
- getterMethod is the name of the method that returns the value of the property. Convention has it that it is the same as the property name. It must take no arguments and have a return type of type.
- setterMethod is the name of the method that is used to set the value property. It must take exactly one argument of type *type* and have the return type of void.

We have only scratched the surface of what Q_PROPERTY has to offer. You can find more out by looking up *property system* on the Qt Creator help screen.

> With a little creative macro writing, it is possible to create a macro that takes a type and name and defines all of the required methods and attributes for a read/write property.

Another very powerful concept in Qt is QVariant. Like signals, slots, and Q_PROPERTY, it is one of the backbones of Qt. We will learn about it in Chapter 5, *Managing the Overall Workflow*.

QVariant

QVariant is one of Qt's most interesting features. It is a generic container for any type that the Qt meta-object system knows about, including types that you define and tell Qt about. Qt's meta-object system is what allows signals, slots, properties, and many other features of Qt to work.

Sometimes the best way to explain things is through an example. Take a look at the following code, found in main.cpp at https://github.com/PacktPublishing/Hands-On-Embedded-Programming-with-Qt/tree/master/Chapter04/QVariantExample:

```cpp
#include <QVariant>
#include <QTime>
#include <QDebug>

int main(int argc, char *argv[])
{
    QVariant    v;                  // define v as a QVariant
    v.setValue(10);                 // set the v to hold an int value
                                    // of 10

    int y = 41 * v.toInt();         // get the value of v as an int
    qDebug() << v.toString() << " * 41 = " << y;
    qDebug() << "v as a bool = " << v.toBool();
    qDebug() << "v as a list = " << v.toList();

    qDebug() << "-------------------";

    QList<QVariant> l;
    l << v;                         // append v to the list
    l << QVariant(1);               // append the int 1 to list
    l << QVariant(2.3);             // append the double 2.3
```

```
        l << QVariant("Hello World!");   // append "Hello World!"

        qDebug() << "The List: " << l;
    }
```

There is a lot going on in here, but let's focus on the key ideas:

- The first thing we do is to create a QVariant class called v and assign it an int value of 10. We don't need to explicitly set the type because the C++ compiler can infer it from 10.
- Next, we try to retrieve the value of v as different types:
    - int
    - A string (QString)
    - bool
    - A list (QList)
- Finally, we demonstrate the ease with which we can store a random collection of different data types in a list (QList) using QVariant:
    - Another QVariant class, v
    - An int, 1
    - A double, 2.3
    - A QString class, Hello World!

I also introduced QDebug and qDebug(), new ways of generating output. They are specifically designed for debugging output, but are useful for us as they show in a bit more detail what QTextStream normally does. This is the output that the code produces:

```
"10"  * 41 =   410
v as a bool =   true
v as a list =   ()
--------------------
The List:  (QVariant(int, 10), QVariant(int, 1), QVariant(double, 2.3),
QVariant(QString, "Hello World!"))
```

In the first line, we see v.toString() produced a string containing 10, in the second line we see that v.toBool() produced a Boolean value of true (qDebug() translated that to true for display), and in the third line we find that trying to convert v to a list produced () or an empty list. Why? Because a single integer is not a list of unspecified type.

The last line shows us how multiple *QVariants* are stored internally in a list (QList). Note that each item we added to the list is a QVariant class with a type and a value, and qDebug() outputs it in a way that shows that.

You probably noticed that Qt calls its string class `QString`. `QString` is older than `std::string` and was supported across multiple compilers back when each had its own way of doing strings. It is not as insanely flexible as `std::string`, but it is much easier to use and has built-in support for multi-byte encodings.

The example only looked at data types that Qt already knows about. If you want to add your own, you can use `Q_DECLARE_METATYPE(..)` to declare them during compilation, and `qRegisterMetaType(..)` at runtime to let the meta-object system know about it.

Signals and slots use `QVariant` behind the scenes. You must use `Q_DECLARE_METATYPE(..)` and `qRegisterMetaType(..)` to tell Qt about any custom data types you want to use when emitting signals and receiving slots. We will see these later in the book.

We now know that the Qt meta system can handle new data types. Next we will learn how it can handle enumerations and even make it easy to convert them to and from strings at runtime!

Enums

Qt's introspection support also supports enumerations. `Q_ENUM(..)` is used to tell Qt about an enumerated type. Once Qt knows about `Q_ENUM`, the value of a `Q_PROPERTY` macro of the enumeration type can be set using the enumeration name for the value. Similarly, the value of the `Q_ENUM` can be easily converted to a string representation.

Let's add *sex* as a property of the `Person` class we looked at earlier. We will be generous and allow for more than just `male` and `female`:

```
class Person : public QObject
{
    Q_OBJECT

    Q_PROPERTY(QString name READ name WRITE setName)
    Q_PROPERTY(QDate   birthday READ birthday WRITE setBirthday)
    Q_PROPERTY(Sex     sex READ sex WRITE setSex)

public:
    explicit Person(QObject *parent = nullptr);

    ...

    enum Sex    {male, female, other, unspecified};
```

```
Q_ENUM(Sex)

    ...
}
```

We now have a property, sex, that is a known enum, Sex, so we can set the enumeration simply by the string version of the enumeration value:

```
p.setProperty("sex", "male");
```

As of Qt 5.12, there are actually two different ways of dealing with enumerations in Qt—the new way is to use Q_ENUM. The old, deprecated, less capable way is to use Q_ENUMS. (Note the added S.) You want to use the new way—Q_ENUM. I would like to give you something easy to remember, but the best I can come up with probably only works for English—Q_ENUMS *is Superceded*.

Here is the tip:

Since Qt now knows of the enum type, we can also use it in signals and slots!

A complete, worked example can be found at `https://github.com/PacktPublishing/ Hands-On-Embedded-Programming-with-QT/tree/master/Chapter04/ CompletePersonExample`.

From learning about Qt's introspection support, we now turn to learning about the architectural style best suited for Qt, the model/view architecture.

Differing views — model/view architecture

A consistent theme between Qt Widgets and QML, the two GUI technologies Qt offers, is the use of the model/view architecture.

Simply put, the model/view architecture separates the data (model) from the display (view) of the data. This allows you to separate how the data is updated from how the UI designer presents the data. Should the UI designer change how the data is viewed, the code that puts the data in the model doesn't have to be changed.

A quick dive

For whatever reason, the concept of a model/view architecture was one of the harder ones for me to understand. It is really straightforward, but I had a mental block. Finally, I wrote some sample code to help me understand it, and this is what it produced:

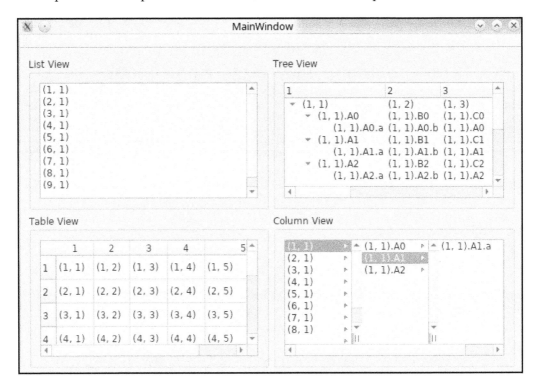

The top left presents some data in the form of a one-dimensional list, the bottom left presents the same data in a two-dimensional table, the top right presents the data in the form of a tree, and the bottom right shows it in a series of columns. Each quadrant presents a view of the same data model.

That's the quick explanation of a model/view architecture.

The code for this example can be found at `https://github.com/PacktPublishing/Hands-On-Embedded-Programming-with-Qt/tree/master/Chapter04/MVExample`. I will warn you, the code is very brute force, but it does show you how things are connected.

Formalizing Qt's model/view

At the highest level, there are two pieces to the model/view architecture:

- The *model*, abstracted by `QAbstractItemModel`
- The *view*, abstracted by `QAbstractItemView`

Consider the following diagram:

The model contains the structured data. The view contains code to display the structured data. When the model is changed, the change is reflected in the view. Similarly, when data is edited in a view, it is reflected in the model.

Customizing how model data is viewed

The view actually knows very little about how to present the data, other than which data from the model to put where. Qt uses a **renderer** to render the data for the view. With simple data, such as text and dates, the default renderer will work well. For more complex or custom data, you can write your own renderer. Consider the following diagram:

Filtering and sorting what's viewed

What would happen if we created something that looked like a model but was actually just a proxy for another model? We could use the **proxy model** anywhere we used a model:

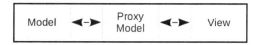

Filtering and sorting of the model data that is displayed can be easily accomplished using proxy models. This is such a fundamental concept that Qt already provides sort/filter proxies to handle the basics of sorting and filtering. Like most Qt things, you can also create your own proxies to do custom or more complex filtering and sorting.

Since a proxy model presents a model, it is possible to chain more than one proxy model. Sometimes it is quicker to chain more than one standard proxy model instead of coding a custom one.

Keeping it portable – Qt's platform abstraction

Qt has been around for a very long time. Work on it started in 1991. Back in the early 1990s, standardization of compilers was basically non-existent. There was Microsoft C, Turbo C, Watcom C, AT&T's C implementation for their flavor Unix, BSD's implementation for their flavor Unix, GNU C, C for the Mac, and so on. Each had some basic core functionality, and each saw the need to extend the core to handle basic things such as strings instead of just a group of characters. But, they all did it a little differently.

Because of this, many people working on Unix machines resorted to GNU C. Since GNU C was freely available as a source, it could be installed (with a bit of tinkering) on almost any machine. When I encountered a new system, the first thing I did was download, configure (by hand), and build GNU C. (Next, I downloaded and built my favorite editor, GNU Emacs.)

The developers of Qt wanted to provide a toolkit that could work on multiple systems without having to force the users of Qt to know all of the ins and outs of the various systems and compilers. So, they did something smart. They abstracted away the details and created their own common sets of useful constructs. This allowed them to focus their work on building a powerful framework without getting caught in the low-level implementation details.

Much of this work was done before the C++ standards became well accepted, so now you will see some overlap in some of the functionality of Qt and the standard libraries of C++11 and C++17.

It is because of all of the work Qt put into abstracting away the hardware and underlying OS that you can so easily write a Qt application on a Host machine running Linux (or even Windows), test and debug most of it on the Host, and then simply recompile/retarget it for another system (for example, Raspberry Pi) and find it works there. Yes, you may encounter UI issues like we did in Chapter 3, *Running Your First Application on The Target*, but that more exposed a design problem (or a better way of setting up the UI) than a bug in the code.

Qt's OS and filesystem abstractions

These are some of my favorite Qt classes for handling file and OS type functions:

QDir	A class for working with directories, including finding what's in them and creating them. It also takes care of the path.
QFile	A class for reading and writing files.
QFileInfo	A class for handling information about a file.
QPath	A class for handling filesystem paths. Along with converting between relative, absolute, and canonical paths, it can also pull out parts of a path, such as a filename or extension, and the attributes of a file.
QUrl	A class for handling URLs.
QThread	One of several classes for handling threading. It could be considered the lowest Qt level.
QThreadPool	A class for handling pools of threads. We will talk more about this later.
QtConcurrent	This is actually a collection of classes for using threads without having to worry about low-level threading details.
QStateMachine	This allows you to easily implement state machines in your code.
Qt SCXML	This is another collection of classes and tools. This allows you to graphically design state machines and use them in your code. We will see how powerful this is, later in this book.

All of the file- and directory-related classes try to solve the directory path separator problem (\ versus. /) for you. Typically, Qt developers always use / when they are developing code, even if it is primarily targeted to Windows systems.

Qt's container class abstractions

If you are a hardcore developer, you will recognize some of the classes as being very similar to those found in the Boost libraries and/or in the new C++17 and C++20 standard libraries. That's because they are. Many of these were developed long before there were standard libraries:

QList<>	A generic list template class, which we already saw an example of in this chapter.
QVector<>	A template class for an array of items.
QStack<>	A template class for a stack of items.
QQueue<>	A template class for a queue of items.
QMap<>	A collection of *1:1* mapping between items.
QMultiMap<>	A collection of *1:n* mapping between items.
QPair<>	A pair of items.
QHash<>, QMultiHash<>	Very similar to QMap<> and QMultiMap<>, but they use hash tables to speed up lookups.
QVariant<>	Arguably not a *container* as normally talked about, but it can contain anything. We saw this earlier in the chapter. It is also probably my favorite class.

Most of these are implemented without using the standard libraries, but there is talk of that changing in future releases that require C++17 or 20. The good news is that the classes themselves are not planned to go away so your code should be future-safe.

Taking a closer look at building and Main

Part of the job of both teaching and writing is to try to keep a good flow over the main material you want to cover. With that in mind, I only gave a brief mention to some subjects. In this section, we will look at two of those—the build systems supported by Qt Creator, and the reason Main() looks like it does.

Qt Creator's supported build systems

Signals, slots, and properties don't just happen because you declare them in your code. The declarations are processed by a special *moc* compiler that takes your C++ code along with the Qt-specific commands and generates pure C++ code that can be handled by a C++ compiler. Similarly, the UI description files are processed to generate C++ code and headers that can be compiled.

In order to do all of this, magic has to happen. This magic is done by a makefile. Thankfully, you don't have to write the makefile yourself. There are several supported build systems that will do it for you. Let's look at the major ones.

QMake

QMake was developed by Qt as a way to simplify the description of how to build Qt applications.

QMake project (`.pro`) files are processed by qmake to generate makefiles, which then must be run by **make** (or **nmake** when generating for Microsoft Visual Studio).

For our projects, we will be using QMake files. Why? Because they are well supported by Qt, easy to understand and very powerful when used to the fullest, many projects in the wild use them, and—well—I have been using them for over a decade and really like them. QMake strikes a good balance between flexibility and needing a doctorate degree to understand them.

Qbs

Qbs (pronounced *cubes*) was developed at Qt to be a replacement for QMake. It is a very powerful build description that uses an ECMAScript-like language based on QML to describe a project.

As of October, 2018, Qbs has been deprecated.

CMake

CMake is a well-known build system. It is very powerful, but with that power comes more complexity in setting it up.

What's all that in main(..)?

I glossed over some of the stuff in main(..) from our first piece of code. Let's take a look at what is really happening here:

```
int main(int argc, char *argv[])
{
    QCoreApplication a(argc, argv);

    TimerCatcher    tc;

    return a.exec();
}
```

QCoreApplication a(argc, argv) instantiates the core of Qt. The core is responsible for handling signals and slots along with supporting other Qt features including QTimers. Without it, Qt doesn't do anything.

One of the cool things that QCoreApplication can do is handle command-line argument parsing, and that's why we are passing argc and argv to it.

Signals and slots require Qt to run an event loop. For the most part, we don't worry about it and let it just run itself. Furthermore, a.exec() starts the event loop and stays in there while the application is running.

Summary

We have covered a lot of ground in this chapter in an effort to understand some basic principles of Qt applications. Hopefully, you did not find it too dry.

We started with a more in-depth look at signals and slots and discovered that Qt can be used to write console (non-GUI) applications. We also saw hints that Qt supports threading.

Next, we took a look at the Qt introspection support, which is one of the most powerful features of Qt. Once again, we uncovered another Qt gem, QVariant.

Not happy stopping there, we looked at the model/view architecture.

We also looked at how Qt abstracts file and platform considerations, thereby making it easier for us to write cross-platform applications.

Finally, we took a close look at the different build systems supported by Qt Creator and the contents of main().

That really is a lot, but in some ways we only scratched the surface.

In Chapter 5, *Managing the Overall Workflow*, we will look into the overall development paradigm of embedded Qt projects, and start building a project to use for most of the rest of the book.

 Even though this chapter was technically very heavy, it only scratched the surface. Feel free to look up and explore the Qt classes and concepts mentioned in the Qt help system.

Questions

1. If a signal is emitted, when is a slot connected by a direct connection executed?
2. Can console-only (non-GUI) applications be written in Qt?
3. Can a signal with two parameters (int and QString) be connected to a slot that accepts one parameter (QString)?
4. What must be defined for Q_PROPERTY when creating a property?
5. Can properties be added to QObject at runtime instead of when the class is defined?
6. What is QVariant?
7. Which Qt class would you use to find out if a file is read-only?
8. What is one advantage of the model/view architecture?
9. Is it possible to link more than one proxy model?

Managing the Overall Workflow

5

In this chapter, we will look at modern software development practices that allow us to test and debug code, both on the host and target platforms. We will even look at how we can develop and test sections of code before target hardware ever becomes available.

As we cover these items, we will start working on our `BigProject`, a project that will follow us and grow throughout the rest of this book.

The main sections of this chapter are as follows:

- Falling down the development cycle
- Starting our `BigProject`
- Mocking the hardware

As a result of reading this chapter, you should have learned about the following:

- The host/target development cycle, and when the code can be tested on the host
- How to deploy, test, and debug on the host (before the hardware is ready!)
- How to create stand-ins (m*ocks*) for hardware devices to facilitate testing without real hardware

Technical requirements

This chapter assumes that you have a Qt 5.12 environment set up on both your host and target. It also assumes that you have basic C++ comprehension.

You may need to refer back to earlier chapters in order to complete some of the work in this chapter.

A reference to the final implementation of the code is given in the summary. Try to complete this chapter without looking at it, but if you get stuck, it's there to guide you.

Modernizing software development

I started doing embedded programming in 1992. In those days, spirits were brave, the stakes were high, men were real men, women were real women, small furry creatures from Alpha Centauri were real small furry creatures from Alpha Centauri, and programmers knew the source of the misquote (Douglas Adams' *The Hitchhiker's Guide to the Galaxy*). Writing embedded code usually meant coding in assembly language, counting bytes, and working with hardware emulators, oscilloscopes, and maybe even a logic analyzer if you were lucky. It might take a couple of hours to trace a simple problem and another hour to fix the assembly code.

By the turn of the century, we had readily available cross-compilers, from C++ to multiple embedded microprocessors and micro-controllers. We even had debuggers that let us step through the code and check the contents of registers and memory. Still, debugging was something that was only done on the target hardware.

We have come a long way. We now write in object-oriented languages, use modern debuggers, and it still takes several hours to find a simple mistake. But, with Qt, we have a new tool—debugging on the host. We have already looked at this in previous chapters, but let's extend the development process that's typified in modern software development practices.

Falling down the development cycle

Many people who are familiar with the waterfall model of software development do the following:

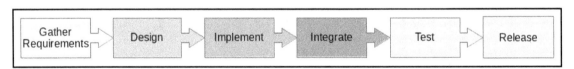

In real life, it is a little different:

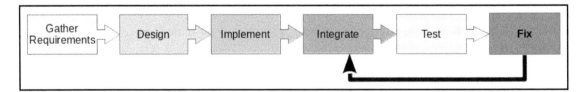

We start by gathering requirements, designing the software, breaking up the design into pieces, individually implementing all the pieces, integrating everything at once, testing it, discovering problems in integration, fixing things, reintegrating, testing again, and finally explaining to management why it is taking so long to release the product.

What if we did things differently?

Continuous Integration

Most of the issues that are found in the integration process could have been found much sooner if the software had been integrated earlier. Why wait until you are looking at shipping in one week to find out that the small change you made to your piece of code over two months ago broke someone else's code? What if you could know immediately?

Continuous Integration (**CI**) is a development process that's designed to find issues earlier. Simply put, whenever code is committed to the repository, the code is integrated with everyone else's code, built, and tested. If every developer on the project is doing that, bugs, misunderstandings, and other code issues are found out much sooner while they are easier to fix.

How often should a developer commit code? On the projects where I have established CI, we found that every time you got to a place where your code compiled and passed your own tests, it was the right time to commit the code. On one project, we moved from developers committing code every three weeks to a month to developers committing code multiple times a day and complaining when they didn't get the results of the tests back in 15 minutes! (That project was also the first one that the developers had worked on that went into testing with every defect already known and accounted for. There were no surprise bugs from the testing group!)

Unit testing

You may not be ready or able to implement CI, but you can implement your own unit testing. In the case I noted previously, the reason we were aware of every bug the testing group found is that we were pedantic with testing. We set a goal of 100% of the code to be executed during tests, including the error paths, and we were able to hit 99%. (Corporate IT would not allow us to change the time on their server to test our clock correction algorithm.) The remaining 1% was code reviewed by all the members of the software team.

Modern development cycle

Modern software development really comes down to a set of small, iterative cycles. Instead of looking at one monolithic set of features, features are broken up into manageable sets. Each of these goes through its own development cycle, and integration with the entire software is a constant part:

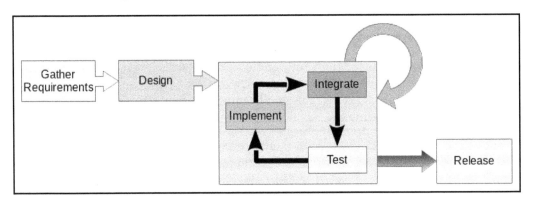

Moving ahead without hardware

By the time I had been writing embedded code for 15 years, I had found one thing that always irritated me – software was always the last step and the one that got blamed for late deliveries. It didn't seem to matter if the embedded hardware was late: since we were last on the schedule, we got the pressure to make the delivery on time.

Qt is one of the companies that helped change that. By being able to write the code once and then simply recompile it for a different target, it is now possible to do much of the development, testing, debugging, and integration right on the host computer. We no longer have to be the last team done. We can start before the hardware is finished.

There is one more thing that really aids development—a layered architecture.

Layering the problem

The model/view architecture that's used by Qt is an example of a layered architecture. The view only needs to know how to display the data in the model, not how the data is fetched. Similarly, we can extend this down a level.

Consider a model that holds temperature readings. The model doesn't need to know how the temperature readings are made as long as something (let's call it the **Hardware Layer**) can retrieve the temperature readings and send them (signals/slots) to the model:

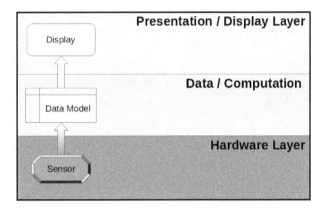

In a layered architecture, each layer is loosely coupled with other layers. In other words, each layer knows how interface to its neighboring layers, but not the details. Changes inside a layer that do not affect the interface do not affect other layers.

Starting our BigProject

Everything we have done has led to this point—we now have a basis to start a project that we will be building on and learning with for the rest of this book.

All projects start with a set of requirements. So, let's see what we can come up with.

BigProject customer requirements

After a five-minute meeting with the product and sales managers, I was able to confirm these requirements. It's not much, but it is all that we have for now, and we already have a completion date (yes—once again, the sales manager already told a key customer that it is available, so now we have to make him look good):

- **Customer Requirement 1**: The device shall display the current date and time
- **Customer Requirement 2**: The device will be run on simple hardware
- **Customer Requirement 3**: We must develop using Qt

I'm sure we will uncover more requirements once we start implementing and testing.

Starting the Qt project

You already learned how to create a Qt project in Chapter 2, *Writing Your First Qt Application*, so go ahead and create a Qt widgets application called BigProject:

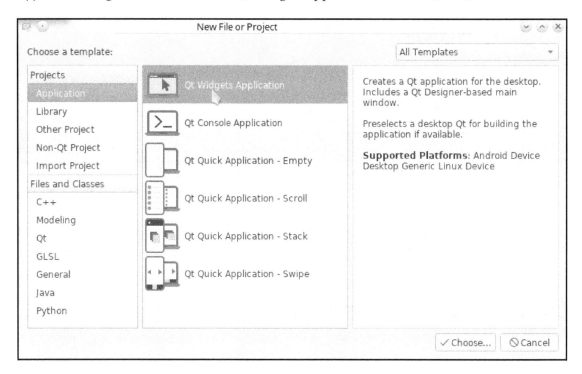

Be sure to select Qt 5.12.0 desktop and Raspberry Pi for targets. Use MainWindow for the QMainWindow class, and use a Git repository to store the code in.

Initial main window design

Once you have created BigProject, start building out the main window.

It looks like we will need something to display the date and time. Create a label named currentDateTime to display the date and time in the center of the window. You may also want to change the **font** property of the label to a larger point size and maybe even a nicer font. Just make sure that you pick a font the target supports.

You should also make sure that the central widget is using a grid layout. It will make life easier:

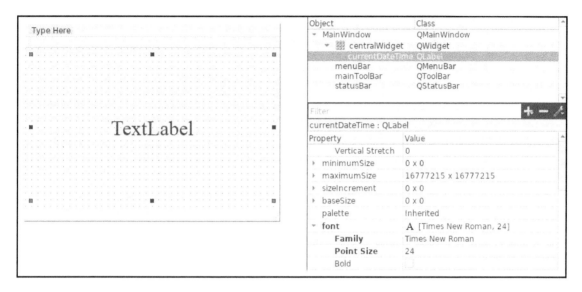

Now that we have a place to display the time, we need to actually put a time on the display.

Wiring up the time display

You have already been introduced to the `QTimer` class. Now, I want to introduce you to the `QDateTime` class. You can probably guess what it does.

Go to the `MainWindow.h` file and add a private `QTimer` to the `MainWindow` class. We will be using this to update the time display. Call it `m_updateTimer`.

One C++ convention I have fallen in love with and which is well supported by Qt Creator, is prefixing private member variables with `m_`. Using this convention helps us know where the variable was defined when reading the code. Qt Creator can also automatically generate nice getter and setter names from member variables that are named this way.

Next, add a new void private slot called `updateDisplay()` to the class. It should take no parameters. This will be used to do the actual update of the display. Then, add the implementation. You probably want to right-click and select **Refactor | Add definition** to get `MainWindow.cpp` to start.

The QDateTime class is used to store a date/time value and do the math on it. It can also be used to retrieve currentDateTime() and convert a date/time toString():

```
void MainWindow::updateDisplay()
{
    QDateTime   now = QDateTime::currentDateTime();
    ui->currentDateTime->setText(now.toString());
}
```

Finally, we need to periodically call updateDisplay() from our QTimer class. If you don't remember how to connect(..) the QTimer's timeout() to the updateDisplay() slot and start the timer to repeat 1-second signals, refer back to the section, *Communicating effectively – signals and slots*, in Chapter 4, *Important Qt Concepts*, on signals/slots.

Testing

Now, run the code on the host and look at how it works. We will consider this the first test of our code:

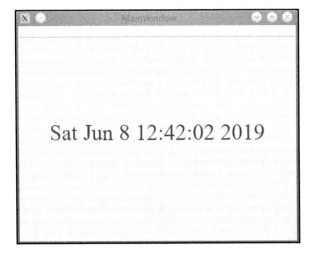

Does it meet requirements?

Update it as required until it satisfies requirements when run on the host.

When you are happy with how it runs on the host, run it on the target.

Does it still meet requirements?

Did the display change?

Again, update the code until you are happy.

Commit it

Once you are happy with how it runs on both the target and host, commit the code to the Git repository.

Mocking the hardware

So far, everything we need to do can be done on both the host and target without any changes, but what if we need a special sensor, say a temperature sensor, that was only available on the target and not on the host? How could we check our code on the host?

The answer is **mocking**. You may have heard of a Mockingbird, or Mockingjay. They are birds that repeat what they hear. They *mock,* or pretend to be something else. We can do the same thing in software. If we can specify the interface (what inputs and outputs it uses), we can create something that acts just like the real thing for a controlled set of inputs.

Once we have a mock, we can test the rest of our system against the mock and verify whether the rest of the system sends the expected signals and handles the responses correctly. We could even generate error or fault responses without having to create the real condition.

Mocking allows us to do development and automated testing on single units of the code (that is, the display) independently of the development of other modules. The only real concerns to be managed are that all the signals are tested and that the mock and the actual implementation continue to present the same interface.

A new requirement

We just got a new requirement for our `BigProject`:

- **Customer Requirement 4**: The device must display the current ambient temperature.

The problem is that we don't have the hardware to do that on the target yet, let alone something on the host to handle it.

If we didn't know about mocking, we might get stuck, but since we know about mocking, we will use this to our advantage.

Defining the interface

The first step is having a defined interface, so let's make the first attempt:

- The temperature sensor will periodically emit a signal, newTemperature, that contains a date/time stamp and a floating-point temperature in degree Celsius.

It's a simple interface, so let's code it up. We will create a base class called TemperatureSensorIF to do so. This will declare our **Interface (IF)**:

1. In the projects list on the left of the Qt creator screen, right-click on **BigProject** and select **Add New...**.
2. Add a C++ class called TemperatureSensorIF. Since it will emit a signal, it should inherit from QObject.
3. Make sure it is part of the Git repository.
4. Add a new signal to the class definition, newTemperature(..), that takes a QDateTime called timestamp and a float called degreesCelsius:

```
class TemperatureSensorIF : public QObject
{
    Q_OBJECT
public:
    explicit TemperatureSensorIF(QObject *parent = nullptr);

signals:
    void newTemperature(QDateTime timestamp, float degreesCelcius);

public slots:
};
```

Now that we have defined the interface, we need to provide an implementation for it.

Implementing the mock

Once again, we will add a new class, but this time, we will call it `MockTempSensor` and it will inherit from `TemperatureSensorIF`. It will not inherit from `QObject` again since `TemperatureSensorIF` already does that for us.

When you create the class and look at the header file, you will find that although you specified a custom base class, Qt creator did not automatically add a reference to the correct `include` file. You have to do that for yourself. Luckily, that is little more than a right-click away.

If you look at `TemperatureSensorIF`, you will see that the constructor takes a `QObject` *parent. We will need to modify the constructor for `MockTempSensor` to do the same. Be sure to change both the header and `.cpp` files!

We want to periodically emit a signal. It sounds like we need a `QTimer`, so let's add `m_sendTempTimer` to the class.

While we are at it, let's create a float to store the last temperature we sent. Call it `m_lastTemp`.

Now, let's do something with the variables so that we can see the temperature being sent:

```
MockTempSensor::MockTempSensor(QObject *parent) :
    TemperatureSensorIF (parent)
{
    m_lastTemp = 20.0;
    m_sendTempTimer.setInterval(4000);
    m_sendTempTimer.setSingleShot(false);
    connect(&m_sendTempTimer, &QTimer::timeout, this, [this]() {
        QDateTime now = QDateTime::currentDateTime();
        // create a temp change of -4 to 5 based on the time
        float change = static_cast<float>(now.time().second() % 5 -
            10);
        m_lastTemp += change;
        emit newTemperature(now, m_lastTemp);
    });
    m_sendTempTimer.start();
}
```

Looking at the code, you can see that everything is done in the constructor for `MockTempSensor`. The *timeout* signal from our timer is connected to a lambda function that handles the calculation of a new temperature and emits the signal with the new value.

Injecting the mock

The last thing we will do is inject the mock so that it will be used by `MainWindow`.

Dependency Injection (DI) is a technique where you inject dependencies into a class that will use them. This allows you to test a class using a mock without hardcoding the mock into the class under test. To do this, we will add a pointer to `TemperatureSensorIF` as one of the constructors of `MainWindow`:

```
public:
    explicit MainWindow(TemperatureSensorIF *tempSensor, QWidget
        *parent = nullptr);
```

> As you add *TemperatureSensorIF * tempSensor*, you will notice a light bulb appear at the end of the line. Clicking on the light bulb will automatically update the `.cpp` file, and vice versa.

You will also need to add a place to store the pointer to `TemperatureSensorIF`. Let's call it `m_tempSensor`. Then, you need to initialize it as part of the constructor.

Finally, we need to actually inject an instance of `MockTempSensor`. This will be done in the `main()` function where `MainWindow` is created:

```
int main(int argc, char *argv[])
{
    QApplication a(argc, argv);
    MockTempSensor  mockTemp;
    MainWindow w(&mockTemp);

    w.show();

    return a.exec();
}
```

Since `MainWindow` requires that we inject (pass) `TemperatureSensorIF`, we defined an instance of `MockTempSensor` called `mockTemp` and passed a pointer to it into the constructor of `MainWindow`.

Wiring up the temperature display

We now have a temperature signal that is generated every few seconds, but we can't do anything with it. We need to update the UI to display the temperature.

Add a new label called `tempDisplay`. Once you have created `tempDisplay`, make a slot called `updateTempDisplay` that will update the label with the temperature. It should take the same parameters as the `newTemperature` signal sends. The display should only show the temperature in degree Celsius.

Test it!

Now, let's test it! Here's what we get:

Does it work as expected?

Does it meet requirements?

If you did everything as specified, it shouldn't. The display should still show **TextLabel** where the temperature should be. That's because a step was left out. The signal emitted by `m_tempSensor` was **never** wired to `updateTempDisplay`!

Fix that and try it again! Now look:

Once you are happy that it works, commit your code to the Git repository you created for the project.

 There's another mistake in `MockTempSensor`. Try debugging the value of *change*. Does it really do what the comment says it does?

Summary

In this chapter, we looked at the modern software development cycle and learned about CI and unit testing. We also talked about developing on the host before we have the target hardware available and how we can architect our software into layers to make that easier.

In this chapter, we started to develop our `BigProject`. This project will be followed through the majority of this book and provide the framework to which we will apply the topics we learn about.

Finally, we looked at how we can mock units of the software to allow us to test individual pieces. We also learned about DI, one of the tools that's used to make easily testable code.

The full code for this chapter's incarnation of our `BigProject` can be found at https://github.com/PacktPublishing/Hands-On-Embedded-Programming-with-Qt/tree/master/Chapter05/BigProject.

In the next chapter, we will look at the two GUI systems, Qt widgets and QML/QtQuick, which are supported directly by Qt. We will also discover another requirement or two for the `BigProject` and look at ways to implement them.

Questions

1. What is the name of the process where software is continuously integrated, built, and tested is called
2. Why should code be integrated often and as soon as possible?
3. What kind of software architecture can be used to separate the display of data from the code that provides the data?
4. Why do all the code examples use m_ as the prefix to class member variables?
5. How do you run code on the target instead of the host?
6. What is Dependency Injection?
7. What is mocking?
8. Why is testing and debugging at an early stage important?
9. Does the author's source listing always execute as expected?
10. How well does the implemented code fit into the Presentation-Data-Hardware layer model?

Further reading

CI is one of the concepts that has been brought to just about every project I have worked on in the last 10 years. This includes Qt, .NET, QNX, and Visual C++-based applications and toolchains. In each case, I have turned to Jenkins when it came to set up a CI server.

As a starting point with Jenkins, I suggest that you take a look at the following items in Packt's library:

- *Jenkins Fundamentals,* by Joseph Muli and Arnold Okoth (`https://www.packtpub.com/in/networking-and-servers/jenkins-fundamentals`)
- *Learning Continuous Integration with Jenkins – Second Edition,* by Nikhil Pathania (`https://www.packtpub.com/in/virtualization-and-cloud/learning-continuous-integration-jenkins-second-edition`)
- *Hands-On Continuous Integration and Automation with Jenkins* [Video], by Sandro Cirulli (`https://www.packtpub.com/virtualization-and-cloud/hands-continuous-integration-and-automation-jenkins-video`)

If you are interested in learning more about software architecture, the following Packt resource may come in handy:

- *Software Architect's Handbook,* by Joseph Ingeno (`https://www.packtpub.com/in/application-development/software-architects-handbook`)

6
Exploring GUI Technologies

Qt has two different technologies that support the creation of GUI objects—widgets and QML. In this chapter, we will take a look at these technologies and how they compare. We will also look at how both technologies can be used together. In the process, we will discover and implement more requirements in our `BigProject`.

The main sections of this chapter are as follows:

- Two roads diverge
- Revisiting some old friends
- Comparing technologies
- What if you didn't have to choose?

While going through these sections, you will learn about the following:

- The two basic GUI technologies that are supported by Qt
- How Qt Widgets and QML differ
- How to develop both Qt Widget and QML applications
- How to combine both Qt Widgets and QML into the same application

Technical requirements

This chapter builds on what we learned and developed in Chapter 4, *Important Qt Concepts*, and Chapter 5, *Managing the Overall Workflow*. Make sure you have read them. You will also want to have make sure that your Target is connected and working.

The code examples in this chapter can be found in this book's GitHub repository for this chapter, at https://github.com/PacktPublishing/Hands-On-Embedded-Programming-with-Qt/tree/master/Chapter06.

Two roads diverge

In his 1916 poem, *The Road Not Taken*, Robert Frost ponders having to decide which way to go at a fork on a wooded trail. In a sense, Qt offers the same dilemma.

For the most part of two decades, Qt had only one technology for GUI development—Qt Widgets. Qt Widgets are built and coded in C++. If you wish to create a custom version of a widget, you are forced to use C++. In 2011, a new method of developing UIs was introduced with the goal of making GUI development, especially on mobile devices, easier and quicker. Instead of coding in C++, a JavaScript-like language (QML) was used and a graphics framework, Qt Quick, was developed.

In this section, we will look at how to create both widget and QML-based GUIs and look at an overview of how they are coded.

Let's start exploring the two technologies by looking at Qt Widgets.

Qt Widgets

Rumors of the death of Qt Widgets have been greatly exaggerated. (Apologies to Mark Twain.)

A couple of years ago, it seemed like Qt Widgets were going to go the way of vinyl LP records. That hasn't happened. Qt Widget-based applications are still being developed. The Qt company recognizes widgets as first-class citizens of the Qt ecosystem. They are even planning to release a couple of new widgets in future Qt releases.

We have already seen and developed a few Qt Widgets applications. The test program we ran to verify the setup of the Raspberry Pi in `Chapter 1`, *Setting Up the Environment*, and the first program we wrote, *Hello from Qt!* in `Chapter 2`, *Writing Your First Qt Application*, were both implemented in Qt Widgets. Even our `BigProject`, which was started in `Chapter 5`, *Managing the Overall Workflow*, has thus far been a Qt Widgets application.

So, what does that mean? In this section, we will look a little deeper into Qt Widgets, their advantages and disadvantages, and see what kind of applications they are well suited for.

Programming widgets

In their basic form, Qt Widgets are implemented in C++. A widget receives window events (mouse events, touch events, keyboard events, and so on) and paints itself on an *output device* (screen, printer, image file, or within another widget). Most of the time, you won't have to worry about events and painting because every widget inherits directly or indirectly from the QWidget base class, and somewhere in the inheritance tree the events and painting are handled for you. That doesn't prevent you from implementing your own event and painting algorithms.

A widget can be as simple as a letter or image, or as complex as a collection that contains a table, some labels, a picture, and a few buttons.

A common practice in Qt is to develop a complex widget and reuse it in multiple places. In one application I wrote, I created a custom widget that allowed you to display about 30 different checkbox options to the user to . I used that widget in several different screens. By doing this, I only had to develop and test the options widget once.

Remember the **Don't Repeat Yourself** (**DRY**) principle in software development. The idea is that you should implement something only once and reuse it. Don't copy the implementation in several places. Why? Because if you use the copy approach, you will invariably end up fixing a bug or making a change in one place and not in another.

So, how do you create a widget?

Creating a widget with Qt Creator/Designer

When we started working on *Hello From Qt!* in Chapter 2, *Writing Your First Qt Application*, we created our first widget, MainWindow:

MainWindow inherited from QMainWindow, which traces its ancestry back to QWidget. The Designer screen allowed us to populate MainWindow with different predefined widgets.

There are actually three files associated with `MainWindow`:

- `MainWindow.h` defines the `MainWindow` C++ class
- `MainWindow.cc` (or `.cpp`) provides the implementation of `MainWindow`
- `MainWindow.ui` defines the graphic elements (widgets) that make up the display of `MainWindow`

What if we want to add a custom widget to our code? The process of creating a custom widget using Qt Creator's Designer is straightforward:

1. Right-click on the project you want to add the widget (also called a *form*) to.
2. Select **Add New...**
3. Choose **Qt** from the left selection pane, then choose **Qt Designer Form Class** and click **Choose...**:

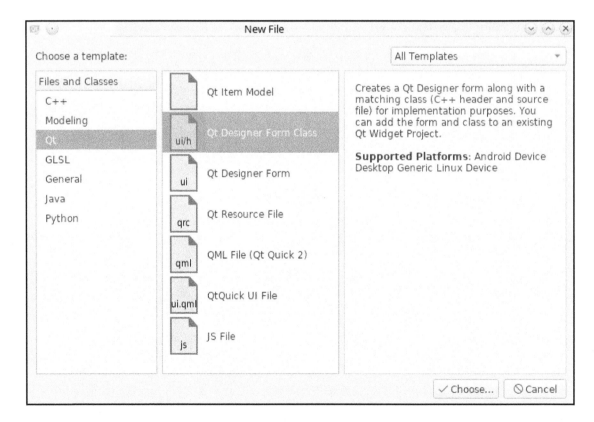

4. Select the type of widget. You can use a template/form or inherit from an already-defined widget. Then, click **Next**:

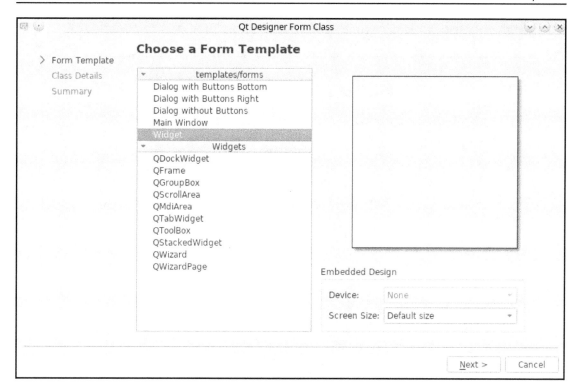

5. Define the name of the class and click **Next:**

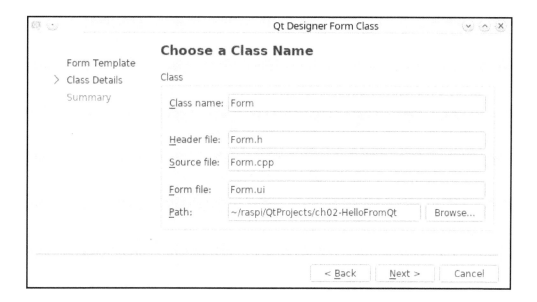

6. Verify the Qt Project and version control system to use:

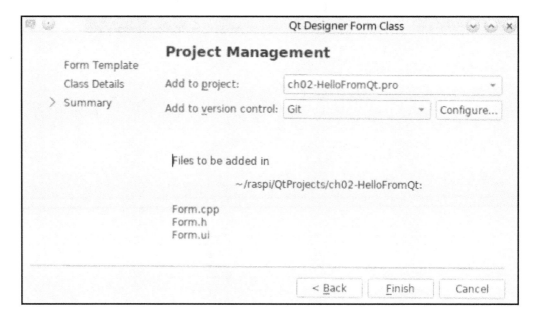

7. Click Finish.

Like before, you will now be presented with a form to which you can start adding other elements, and you will have three files—the a.h file for defining the widget class; the a.cpp file for implementing the class; and the a.ui file, which contains the definition of the elements of the widget.

The .ui file is just an XML file. It's very unlikely that you will ever need to manually edit the .ui file, but to give you some idea of what it is, here is an excerpt:

```
<?xml version="1.0" encoding="UTF-8"?>
<ui version="4.0">
(1)
 <class>MainWindow</class>
 <widget class="QMainWindow" name="MainWindow">
  <property name="geometry">
   <rect>
    <x>0</x>
    <y>0</y>
    <width>400</width>
    <height>300</height>
   </rect>
  </property>
```

```
  <property name="windowTitle">
   <string>MainWindow</string>
  </property>
(2)
  <widget class="QWidget" name="centralWidget">
   <layout class="QGridLayout" name="gridLayout">
    <item row="4" column="1">
     <spacer name="verticalSpacer_2">
      <property name="orientation">
       <enum>Qt::Vertical</enum>
      </property>
      <property name="sizeHint" stdset="0">
       <size>
        <width>20</width>
        <height>40</height>
       </size>
      </property>
     </spacer>
    </item>
    <item row="3" column="1">
     <layout class="QHBoxLayout" name="horizontalLayout">
(3)
      <item>
       <widget class="QLabel" name="label_2">
        <property name="text">
         <string>My Name is:</string>
        </property>
       </widget>
      </item>
(4)
      <item>
       <widget class="QLineEdit" name="lineEdit"/>
      </item>
     </layout>
```

There are a few things that are worth pointing out, as follows:

- (1) is where the definition of the MainWindow starts.
- (2) is where the definition of the central widget (the main area of our UI) begins.
- (3) is where the definition of the My Name is: label starts.
- (4) is where the definition of the input box for the name starts.

Creating a widget by hand

It is also possible to create a widget purely by writing C++ code and without a .ui file.

In the case of a Qt Designer-made widget, the .ui file defines the graphical elements of a widget. During the build process, a Qt tool called **uic** compiles the .ui into a C++ include file. Qt Creator is smart enough to insert the include statement for the file at the top of the C++ source file:

```
#include "mainwindow.h"
#include "ui_mainwindow.h"
```

The bold line in the preceding code is the generated file. If we look at the contents of the file, we can see how MainWindow is actually created in the setupUI(..) method, which is where all of our UI elements are defined:

```
class Ui_MainWindow
{
public:
    QWidget *centralWidget;
    QGridLayout *gridLayout;
    QSpacerItem *verticalSpacer_2;
    QHBoxLayout *horizontalLayout;
    QLabel *label_2;
    QLineEdit *lineEdit;

...

    void setupUi(QMainWindow *MainWindow)
    {
(1)
        if (MainWindow->objectName().isEmpty())
            MainWindow->setObjectName(QString::fromUtf8("MainWindow"));
        MainWindow->resize(400, 300);
(2)
        centralWidget = new QWidget(MainWindow);
        centralWidget-
            >setObjectName(QString::fromUtf8("centralWidget"));
        gridLayout = new QGridLayout(centralWidget);
        gridLayout->setSpacing(6);
        gridLayout->setContentsMargins(11, 11, 11, 11);
        gridLayout->setObjectName(QString::fromUtf8("gridLayout"));
        verticalSpacer_2 = new QSpacerItem(20, 40,
            QSizePolicy::Minimum, QSizePolicy::Expanding);

        gridLayout->addItem(verticalSpacer_2, 4, 1, 1, 1);
```

```
        horizontalLayout = new QHBoxLayout();
        horizontalLayout->setSpacing(6);
        horizontalLayout-
            >setObjectName(QString::fromUtf8("horizontalLayout"));
(3)
        label_2 = new QLabel(centralWidget);
        label_2->setObjectName(QString::fromUtf8("label_2"));
        horizontalLayout->addWidget(label_2);

(4)
        lineEdit = new QLineEdit(centralWidget);
        lineEdit->setObjectName(QString::fromUtf8("lineEdit"));
        horizontalLayout->addWidget(lineEdit);
...
}
```

I put the same markers in this code so that you can see how the `.ui` file is translated:

- `(1)` is where the definition of the `MainWindow` starts.
- `(2)` is where the definition of the central widget (the main area of our UI) begins.
- `(3)` is where the definition of the `My Name is:` label starts.
- `(4)` is where the definition of the input box for the name starts.

As you can see, it takes a good amount of C++ code to create a widget, but it can be done. In the widget I created with the checkbox options, the checkboxes were generated with C++ code because the options were read from a file at runtime, not hardcoded before compilation.

Doing something new – QML

In 2008, Nokia was looking for a quick path to upgrade the UI on their phones. Nokia decided that, rather than develop another technology in-house, they would buy it. Looking around, they found what they wanted in another firm called **Trolltech**. Trolltech offered a framework for developing applications and GUIs. Thus, Qt was bought by Nokia and soon, the focus of Qt's GUI work would change from desktop applications to phone-based applications. It is important to understand that the phone GUIs we see in today's Android and iOS phones were still yet to come. Most mobile GUIs then were little more than a small screen on a flip phone.

Nokia really wanted to jump-start the development of new GUIs, and felt that having to learn C++ in order to create UI applications was a deterrent to developers wanting to use Qt for phone applications. Out of their desire to make it easy for developers who already knew JavaScript to pick up Qt, QML and Qt Quick were born.

In this section, we have a quick overview of QML and `QtQuick`. We will start by looking at what QML is.

What is QML?

QML is a declarative language that somewhat resembles JSON.

The general format of QML is as follows:

```
<TypeName> {
    <attributes>
}
```

For example, to define a simple Qt Quick `Label` with `text`, `Hello from QML!`, and an `id`, `greetings`, we would use the following:

```
Label {
    id: greetings
    text: "Hello from QML!"
}
```

You could also add other attributes to `Label`:

```
Label {
    id: greetings
    text: "Hello from QML!"
    color: "red"
}
```

As you will see later, objects in QML may contain other objects. A common example of this is when we're creating a `Window` instance:

```
Window {
    id: myWindow

    Label {
        id: greetings
        text: "Hello from QML!"
        color: "red"
    }
}
```

We will look at these in more detail later in this chapter.

One area of minor confusion I have seen (and experienced) is the difference between QML and Qt Quick. QML is the Qt modelling language. Qt Quick is a toolkit for developing UI applications in QML. The Qt documentation provides a good idea of the differences in its introduction to QML applications, available at `https://doc.qt.io/qt-5/ qmlapplications.html`.

Developing a UI in QML

Like C++ with Qt Widgets, UI applications can be developed in QML using Qt Quick. This can be done either programmatically or through the use of a designer.

We'll look a little more at how they are developed in the next two sections, where we will revisit some Qt Widgets applications we have already created and add a new feature to our `BigProject`.

Revisiting some old friends

Up until this point, we have talked about Qt Widgets and QML, but so far we haven't really done much in the way of a direct comparison. Let's take a look at one of the applications we have already developed in Qt Widgets and consider how it might look if we were to rewrite it in QML.

Hello from Qt!

The first project we did was *Hello from Qt!* You probably still remember it:

The program simply presented a screen where you could enter your name and it would reply with **Nice to meet you** and your name. We started developing it on the Host in Chapter 2, *Writing Your First Qt Application*, and then finished its development in Chapter 3, *Running Your First Application on the Target*, when we ran it on the Target and cleaned up the formatting on the screen.

 The final version of the Qt Widgets code can be found at https://github.com/PacktPublishing/Hands-On-Embedded-Programming-with-Qt/tree/master/Chapter03/ch03-HelloFromQt_Final.

There were no fancy visual effects—just a simple, straightforward display. Simple, straightforward displays, especially on desktop-sized monitors, are something that Qt Widgets does very well.

Now, let's rewrite this application using Qt Quick and QML!

Hello from QML!

Hello from QML! will be a reimagining of *Hello from Qt!* It will be written purely in QML and will use Qt Quick. For this code, we will hand-code the UI. Don't worry—QML and Qt Quick are much easier to hand-code than Qt Widgets.

Creating the project

Start by creating a new *Qt Quick Application—Empty* project called HelloFromQML:

- Select qmake for the build system
- Select Qt 5.12 for the *Minimal required Qt version*

For the kits, make sure that both Desktop Qt 5.12 and Raspi are selected, and once again choose Git for version control.

When you have done that, you will be presented with main.qml in the editor portion of Qt Creator. You can safely ignore any warnings on the screen at this point:

```
     ⟨ ⟩  ▢ ▦  main.qml                    ⇕ ✕
   1     import QtQuick 2.12
 ○ 2     import QtQuick.Window 2.12      ○ QML module not found
   3
   4  ▾  Window {
   5         visible: true
   6         width: 640
   7         height: 480
   8         title: qsTr("Hello World")
   9     }
  10     |
```

Before we go further, let's change the title of the window from `Hello World` to `Hello from QML!`. Edit line **8** and replace `Hello World` with `Hello from QML!`.

 `qsTr(..)` tells Qt Quick that you plan on eventually providing translations for the string in other languages. You can read more about this at `https://doc.qt.io/qt-5/qtquick-internationalization.html`.

The next step will be defining the contents of the main window.

Defining the window

In our Qt Widgets application, we used a `QGridLayout` to hold all the items in the GUI. For the QML version, we will use a combination of column (vertical) and row (horizontal) layouts. These layouts work very similar to their Qt Widgets counterparts, `QHorizontalLayout` and `QVerticalLayout`.

Vertically, we have three sections:

- The greeting—this is a `Label`.
- The name entry area. This is divided horizontally into two sections:
    - The text prompt (`My Name is:`) – a `Label`
    - The input field for the name – a TextField
- The *Enter* button—a **Button**.

For the vertical sections, we use a `ColumnLayout`. For the horizontal sections, we use a `RowLayout`.

There is one more piece we will need before we can write our code. We need to make sure that we tell QML what definitions we need to import (include). We have already been given the first two, `QtQuick` and `QtQuick.Window`. The other pieces we will need are `QtQuick.Layouts` and `QtQuick.Controls`. For each of these imports, we need to specify the version. Luckily, Qt Creator will help you with this.

Now, let's look at the *finished* code:

```
import QtQuick 2.12
import QtQuick.Window 2.12
import QtQuick.Controls 2.4
import QtQuick.Layouts 1.11

// (1) We are defining a Window
Window {
    visible: true                  // the window is visible on start
    width: 640
    height: 480
    title: qsTr("Hello from QML!")   // define the Title for the Window

    // (2) In the window, we have a column layout (QVerticalLayout in
        QWidgets)
    ColumnLayout {
        id: gridLayout          // the "id" we refer to the
            ColumnLayout by
        anchors.fill: parent    // fill the parent (the Window)

        // (3) The first row in the ColumnLayout is a Label called
        //  "greetings"
        Label {
            id: greetings
            text: qsTr("Hello from QML!")

            Layout.alignment: Qt.AlignHCenter | Qt.AlignVCenter
        }

        // (4) The next row in the ColumnLayout is a RowLayout
        RowLayout {

            // center this row vertically and horizontally
            Layout.alignment: Qt.AlignHCenter | Qt.AlignVCenter

            // (5) the leftmost item in the row is a label, "My Name
            //  is:"
            Label {
                id: nameLabel
                text: qsTr("My Name is:")
```

```
            Layout.alignment: Qt.AlignRight | Qt.AlignVCenter
        }

        // (6) The next item in the row is a TextField referred to
        // by "nameField"
        TextField {
            id: nameField
            text: qsTr("")

            Layout.alignment: Qt.AlignLeft | Qt.AlignVCenter
        }
    }   // End of the RowLayout

    // (7) The next Row contains a Button, called "button" with
    // text "Enter Name"
    Button {
        id: button
        text: qsTr("Enter Name")

        Layout.alignment: Qt.AlignHCenter | Qt.AlignVCenter

        onClicked: {
            greetings.text = "Nice to meet you " + nameField.text +
                "!"
        }
    }
    }   // End of ColumnLayout
}   // End of MainWindow
```

You will notice that some additional attributes have been added, so let's take a look at them:

- `anchors.fill: parent`: This instructs the renderer to make the element fill its parent
- `Layout.alignment: ....`: This specifies how the element should be aligned in its section of the Layout

`Button` has a very interesting new attribute:

```
onClicked: {
    greetings.text = "Nice to meet you " + nameField.text +
        "!"
}
```

onClicked is used to specify the action that should be taken by the button when it is clicked. Within the curly braces ({ . . }) appears some simple, JavaScript-like code. The code simply says, find the element with the greetings ID and set its text attribute to the specified value. If you were thinking that nameField.text refers to the value of the text attribute of the element with the nameField ID, then you are absolutely correct.

Now is a good time to test the code and verify that it works.

Once you are happy that it works, commit the code to your local Git repository.

Customizing the display

When we first talked about how QML is coded, I mentioned the idea of setting a Label to color: "red". Try doing the same now and see what the effect is.

There are many attributes that a Label can take. Why not try some?

- color : color (use double quotes around SVG color names)
- contentHeight : real
- contentWidth : real
- font.bold : bool
- font.family : string
- font.italic : bool
- font.pixelSize : int
- font.pointSize : real
- font.strikeout : bool
- font.underline : bool

What would happen if you changed Button to RoundButton? Try it!

Did the button become rounded? It should have.

What if we could make it so that pressing the *Enter* key while in the nameField automatically worked like clicking on **Enter Name?** Make one more change to the code:

```
TextField {
    id: nameField
    text: qsTr("")

    Layout.alignment: Qt.AlignLeft | Qt.AlignVCenter
    onAccepted: {
```

```
greetings.text = "Nice to meet you " +
    nameField.text + "!"
}
}
```

The final implementation of *Hello from QML* can be found on GitHub at `https://github.com/PacktPublishing/Hands-On-Embedded-Programming-with-Qt/tree/master/Chapter06/HelloFromQML`.

Using the Designer

Since we already have the `main.qml` file open, let's take a look at editing it with the

Designer. In the left-hand tool button column, click on the **Design** (Design) icon. The QML Designer will open up and your Qt Creator window should now look something like the following:

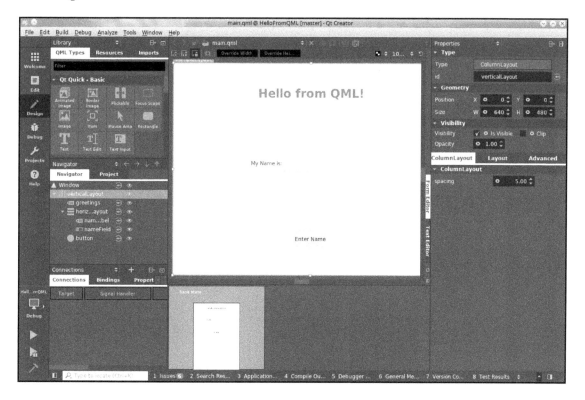

We should examine these sections in a little detail.

The Form Editor

Since we are working with our *Hello from QML* form, you can clearly see it displayed in the **Form Editor**. The **Form Editor** is selected by clicking the vertical tab labelled **Form Editor** on the right-hand side of the center section:

The **Form Editor** allows you to drag and drop form elements from the **QML Types** section of the **Library** window onto the form like you would in the Qt Widgets Designer.

The Text Editor

If you want to work with the actual QML for the form, you can use the **Text Editor** window. The **Text Editor** window is selected by clicking on the **Text Editor** tab of the central window:

```
         main.qml                              ↕ × 📑 🖼️ 🗔 🗔
 1   import QtQuick 2.12
 2   import QtQuick.Window 2.12
 3   import QtQuick.Controls 2.4
 4   import QtQuick.Layouts 1.11
 5   import QtQuick.VirtualKeyboard 2.4
 6
 7 ▼ Window {
 8       visible: true
 9       width: 640
10       height: 480
11       title: qsTr("Hello from QML!")
12
13 ▼     ColumnLayout {
14           id: verticalLayout
15           anchors.fill: parent
16
17 ▼         Label {
18               id: greetings
19               text: qsTr("Hello from QML!")
20
21               Layout.alignment: Qt.AlignHCenter | Qt.AlignVCenter
22               color: "red"
23               font.bold: true
24               font.pointSize: 20
25           }
26
27 ▼         RowLayout {
28               id: horizontalLayout
29               Layout.alignment: Qt.AlignHCenter | Qt.AlignVCenter
30
31 ▼             Label {
```

Notice that the **Text Editor** and **Form Editor** are mutually exclusive. You cannot display both at the same time.

The Library window

The **Library** window allows you to choose QML Types, add resources (such as pictures) to be used in the form, and select the libraries to import. You can choose which of these from the top tabs of the **Library** window:

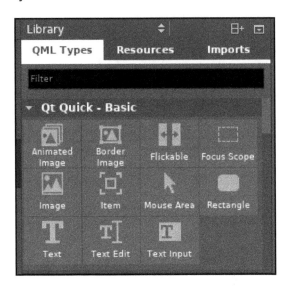

You will probably find the **QML Types** tab to be the most useful, as it is here where you drag elements from and drop them on the form. You will find that the **QML Types** tab is separated into different sections. The preceding screenshot shows the basic Qt Quick items.

Don't be afraid to scroll down the **QML Types** section.

The Navigator window

The **Navigator** window shows you an outline of the structure of the form:

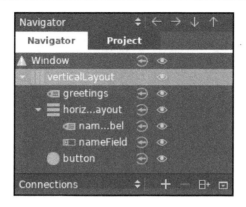

In the preceding screenshot, you can see that we have a window that contains an element called **verticalLayout**. Inside the **verticalLayout** element, there is a label (notice the icon) called **greetings**, a horizontal layout, and a button called **button**. Inside the horizontal layout is a label called **nam...bel** and a text field called **nameField**.

If you want to move elements to a different container (for example, layout), just click and drag them into the **Navigator**. You can also change the default visibility by clicking on the eyeball icon.

The Connections window

The **Connections** window allows you to look at the **Connections**, **Bindings**, **Properties**, and **Backends** associated with the QML form:

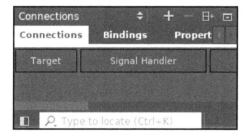

We will leave the discussion of these to other sources, but I will give you some foreshadowing—if we were to have something that responded to a signal called `NewReading` from something called `temperatureData`, we would see it listed under the **Connections** tab, along with the action that is performed when the signal is caught.

The Properties window

The **Properties** window allows you to control the properties of elements in the form:

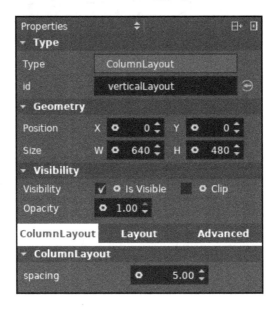

As you can see from the preceding screenshot, it is the equivalent of the **Properties** section of the Qt Widgets Designer.

Experimenting with the QML Designer

Now that we have discussed the various areas on the QML Designer screen, why not experiment with what you can do with it?

Try adding an image to the form:

1. First, add an image resource using **+ Add New Resources** from the **Resources** tab of the **Library**.
2. Drag an **Image** element from the Qt Quick—Basic elements in the **QML Types** list to the form.
3. Change the **id** of the image in the **Properties** window.
4. Set the image source to the image resource you just added using the Source field in the **Image** tab of the **Properties** window (try hitting the ellipsis, **...**).
5. Resize the image by dragging the corners of the image box.

Is the image in the layout? Take a look at the Navigator and you will see that the image is not part of the **verticalLayout** item. Let's fix this:

1. Try moving the image into the layout using the **Navigator.**
2. Adjust where the image is placed in its section of the layout using the **Layout** tab of the **Properties** window.

Can you change the size of the image? Try it!

You will find that there are no longer controls in the corners of the image to allow you to resize it, but you can resize the image in the **Geometry** section of **Properties** (on the right).

Click on the **Text Editor** tab on the right of the central design to take a look at the code.

Here is the final layout I came up with by trying these things about and setting the colors for a few items. The code for this can be found at https://github.com/PacktPublishing/ Hands-On-Embedded-Programming-with-Qt/tree/master/Chapter06/HelloFromQML-Final. I encourage you to take a look:

I find that I learn the best when I use something. Feel free to experiment some more with what QML Designer can do. As long as you are regularly committing your changes to version control, you can always go back.

Now is a good time to compare the different technologies.

Comparing the technologies

Now that we have looked at both technologies, let's compare them side by side:

	Qt Widgets	Qt Quick (QML)
Advantages	• Mature technology • Very customizable • Fast • Easily interface to C/C++ libraries • Lower **hardware** (**HW**) requirements (don't need OpenGL, and so on)	• Easy to learn • Based on ECMASCRIPT (JavaScript) • Easy to implement flashy GUI • Already contains support for modern UI concepts (flick scroll, slide in from side, and so on)
Disadvantages	• Steep learning curve • Need to know how to use C++ • Hard to implement flashy UIs because more custom coding is required • *Cannot be used for WebGL interfaces*	• Not easy to interface to C/C++ libraries • Can be slower • *Higher HW requirements (requires OpenGL, and so on)*
Typical Applications	• Desktop applications • Applications where large datasets must be viewed • Image capture and processing applications where controls need to be easy to use and interfacing to C/C++ image processing libraries is very important • Spreadsheet and word-processing types of applications	• Mobile applications • Games • Graphically heavy applications • Process monitoring • Dashboards • In-car infotainment systems

Using the information in the preceding table, you can begin to make a decision as to which you wish to use. Typically, mobile designs use `QtQuick` as that is what it is designed for, and desktop designs use Qt Widgets; but as you have and will continue to see with our `BigProject`, that doesn't always apply.

The only firm rules in the choice of which (or both) technologies to use comes down to the two *italicized* disadvantages in the preceding table. If your hardware does not support OpenGL, you cannot use `QtQuick`. If you wish to provide full remote GUI access through a WebGL interface (see the *Remote GUI* section of `Chapter 10`, *Using More Qt-Related Technologies*), you cannot use Qt Widgets.

However, I have some questions for you – what if you could have the best of both worlds? What if you didn't have to choose one or the other? That is exactly what we will look at in the next section.

What if you didn't have to choose?

When we looked at the QML application, we focused purely on the QML side of things, but if you look at the HelloFromQML project and expand the sources area, you will find that there is a main.cpp file. Let's take a look at its contents:

```
#include <QGuiApplication>
#include <QQmlApplicationEngine>

int main(int argc, char *argv[])
{
    QCoreApplication::setAttribute(Qt::AA_EnableHighDpiScaling);

    QGuiApplication app(argc, argv);

    QQmlApplicationEngine engine;
    engine.load(QUrl(QStringLiteral("qrc:/main.qml")));
    if (engine.rootObjects().isEmpty())
        return -1;

    return app.exec();
}
```

That looks a lot like the standard main.cpp file for a Qt Widgets application, but instead of a MainWindow class being instantiated, a QQmlApplicationEngine is being created.

QML code is run in a QQmlEngine. QQmlApplicationEngine is a specialization of QQmlEngine that provides an easy way to create QML only applications. With a little imagination, it seems like there should be a way incorporate QML into a widgets-based application.

New requirements for BigProject

We started our `BigProject` in `Chapter 5`, *Managing the Overall Workflow*. Since then, we have received a couple of new requirements from marketing:

- Requirement 5: The user shall be able to see a historical table of temperature readings.
- Requirement 6: The user shall be able to see a scrolling, real-time graph of temperature readings.

It makes sense to use the `QTableView` and a Model/View architecture to implement the historical temperature readings, but we will use `QtQuick.ChartView` to implement the scrolling real-time graph.

Designing the UI

Before we get too far, we need to figure out what the UI for these two new features is going to look like.

After much consideration, we've decided that we will create a new *form* to show the graph and the table, and that we will use *tabs* to change between the old display and the new historical data display.

Creating the historical data form

For the historical data display, we will create a new *form* out of a generic `QWidget` and call it `TemperatureHistoryForm`.

Add the new widget to the `BigProject` by doing the following:

1. Right-click on `BigProject` in the **Projects** list.
2. Select **Add New...**.
3. Select **Qt** in the left column and then **Qt Designer Form Class** in the right column:

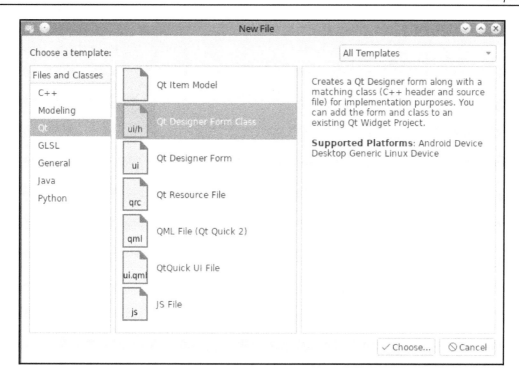

4. Click **Choose...** to move to the next page of the wizard.
5. For the template, select a generic **Widget**:

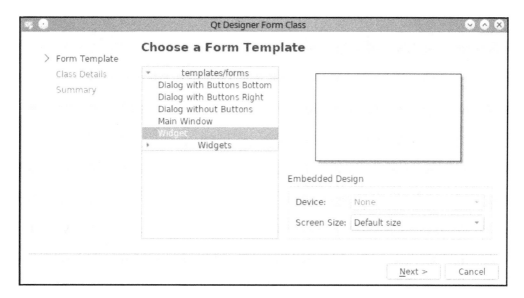

6. Click **Next >**.
7. Name the form `TemperatureHistoryForm`. The other fields on the page will be updated automatically:

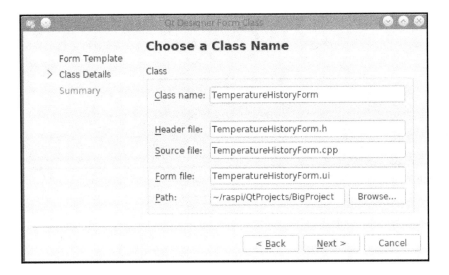

8. Click **Next >**.
9. Make sure that you are adding it to `BigProject.pro` and using Git for version control.
10. Click **Finish**.

Just like when we created other widgets-based applications, we are dropped into the Designer so that we can start adding widgets.

We are going to use two widgets that we can change the size of, so let's add them now:

1. Grab a **Table View** from the left column and drop it toward the bottom of the new form. This is where we will display the table of values.
2. Now, scroll the left column to the bottom, grab a `QQuickWidget`, and drop it toward the top of the form. This is where we will display `QtQuick.GraphView`.
3. Select both widgets (using *Ctrl*+ left-click for the second one).
4. Right-click on one of the selected widgets.
5. Choose **Layout | Layout Vertically** in Splitter.
6. Right-click on the form but not on a widget, and select **Layout | Layout Vertically**.

Your form should now look like this:

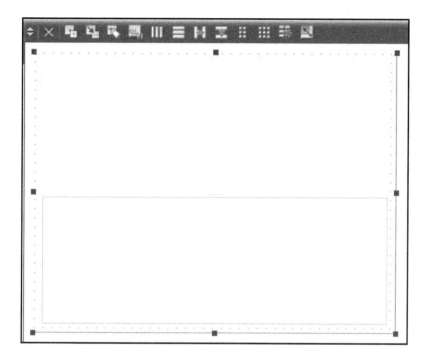

Now, we need to turn our attention to implementing the form.

Implementing the historical table

To keep a record of the temperatures, let's use a `QStandardItemModel` much like the one we used in `Chapter 4`, *Important Qt Concepts*. Let's also add a `QSortFilterProxyModel` to allow us to sort the data. We will call `QStandardItemModel m_tempRecord` (see note 1 in the following code). Then, we will call `QSortFilterProxymodel m_tempProxy` (see note 2).

To receive the new temperature data, we will create a new slot, `temperatureUpdate` (see note 3), which takes `QDateTime` and `float`, just like `MainWindow::updateTempDisplay(..)`.

We will do this in the newly created `TemperatureHistoryForm.h` file:

```
...
#include <QWidget>
#include <QStandardItemModel>
#include <QSortFilterProxyModel>
```

```
...

class TemperatureHistoryForm : public QWidget
{
...
public slots:
    /// (3) The slot to receive the temperature update
    void temperatureUpdate(QDateTime timestamp, float temperature);

private:
    Ui::TemperatureHistoryForm *ui;

    QStandardItemModel      m_tempRecord;  ///< (1) a record of time &
      temperature
    QSortFilterProxyModel   m_tempProxy;   ///< (2) a way to sort/filter
      m_tempRecord
};
```

We need to do some implementations, so let's get started:

1. Right-click on `temperatureUpdate(..)` and use refactor to add start adding the implementation to `TemperatureHistoryForm.cpp`. Once you're there, store the data in the model we created:

```
void TemperatureHistoryForm::temperatureUpdate(QDateTime timestamp, float
temperature)
{
    // ** update the table **
    // create a row with the timestamp and temperature.
    auto time = new QStandardItem; // a place for the timestamp
    auto temp = new QStandardItem; // a place for the temperature

    // set the displayable data (Qt::DisplayRole)
    time->setData(timestamp, Qt::DisplayRole);
    temp->setData(temperature, Qt::DisplayRole);

    // create the row
    QList<QStandardItem *> row;
    row << time << temp;

    // add the row to the model
    m_tempRecord.appendRow(row);
}
```

The `QTableView` needs to know about the data model (`m_tempRecord`). This is usually done in the class constructor, so we will implement it there. We are using a `QFilterProxyModel` to allow us to do some filtering and sorting if we want, so there is an extra step in the wiring. The wiring of the model to proxy model to view will be done in the constructor for `TemperatureHistoryForm`. I've highlighted the lines you need to add to your code in the following snippet:

```
TemperatureHistoryForm::TemperatureHistoryForm(QWidget *parent) :
    QWidget(parent),
    ui(new Ui::TemperatureHistoryForm)
{
    ui->setupUi(this);

    // tell the sort filter proxy what model to data from
    m_tempProxy.setSourceModel(&m_tempRecord);
    // tell the table view what model to use
    ui->tableView->setModel(&m_tempProxy);
}
```

Now, it is time to turn our attention to the chart.

Adding the QtQuick (QML) chart

We will start by adding a new Resource file (`qml.qrc`) to hold the QML file. A Resource file is simply a file where we define resources (such as images, QML code, icons, other files, and so on) that we want to package and use in the application.

We can add `qml.qrc` the same way we add any new file. The only difference is that we will create a Qt Resource file:

1. Select `BigProject` from the **Projects** window.
2. Right-click and select **Add New...**.

3. Select **Qt Resource File**:

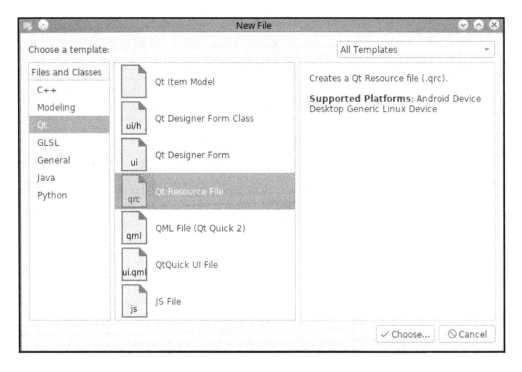

4. Then, continue as normal, using the name qml.qrc for the file.

Now that we have a resource file, we can add something to it:

1. Right-click on qml.qrc in the **Projects** window.
2. Add a new **QML File (Qt Quick 2)** called TemperatureChart.qml:

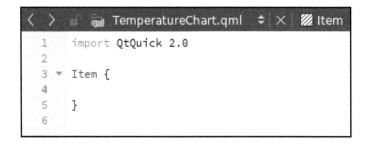

While we have the start of a QML form, it doesn't do anything yet. We need to define a simple `ChartView`. To do that, we need to start by importing `QtCharts 2.0` and then start the definition of our `ChartView`:

```
import QtQuick 2.0
import QtCharts 2.0

ChartView {
    height: 480
    width: 640
    antialiasing: true

    title: "Temperature History"
    theme: ChartView.ChartThemeQt
}
```

Since we want a line chart, we need to include it as part of the `ChartView`. To do this, we will define a `LineSeries` with an ID of `temperatureSeries` and a name of `Temperature` within the `ChartView`:

```
ChartView {
...
    title: "Temperature History"
    theme: ChartView.ChartThemeQt

    LineSeries {
        id: temperatureSeries
        name: "Temperature"
    }
```

With that done, we will need to provide data for `temperatureSeries`, but first we need to add the temperature history form to the `MainWindow` UI.

Adding the temperature history form to the UI

There are many ways we can add `TemperatureHistoryForm` to the UI. After playing around with some ideas, I think the best way is to use a tab widget. One of the tabs will show the current data, while the other will show the historic data:

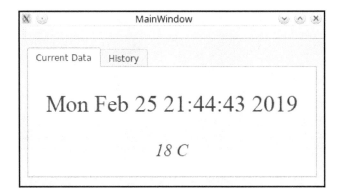

To do this, you will have to open up `MainWindow.ui` and do some editing:

1. Put our old display in the first (leftmost) tab.
2. From the left-hand tools, find the tab widget in the **Containers** section and drop it into the Main Window.
3. Select the first (left most) tab in the tab widget.
4. Grab the top **TextLabel** in the Main Window and drop it into the tab widget.
5. Grab the other **TextLabel** and drop it below the first one in the tab widget.
6. Right-click in the tab and set the layout to be vertical.
7. Set the **currentTabText** property to `Current Data` (the text in the UI should change).
8. Set the **currentTabName** property to `currentDataTab`. This identifies the tab for easy access.
9. Select the second tab.
10. Set the **currentTabText** property to `History` (the text in the UI should change).
11. Set the **currentTabName** property to `historyTab`.
12. Drop the widget control from **Containers** in the second tab.
13. Set the **Layout** of the second tab to vertical.
14. Click on the widget and set its **objectName** to `historyForm`.
15. Right-click on the widget and select **Promote to...**. This will allow us to specify our own widget here.

16. Enter `TemperatureHistoryForm` for the promoted class name.

17. Click **Promote**. Now, a `TemperatureHistoryForm` will be placed in that widget position.

18. Reselect the **Current Data** tab.

When you work with a Tab Widget in Designer, when you save the UI, the selected tab is the one that will be the active tab when the code is run. Always make sure that you reselect the one you want to display first before you compile your code.

Providing data for the chart

As you may recall from Chapter 5, *Managing the Overall Workflow*, temperature data is provided to our C++/Qt Widget MainWindow by a signal from `TemperatureSensorIF`. A slot captures the data reading and then displays it in **MainWindow**. To get it to the **Temperature History Form**, we can use the same mechanism. Since `TemperatureHistoryForm` is now contained in the Main Window, we can simply provide a slot in `TemperatureHistoryForm` and connect it to `TemperatureSensorIF`.

To get data from the C++ **Temperature History Form** and into the **QML Chart**, we are going to use a signal from the **Temperature History Form** and connect it to the `ChartView` defined in `TemperatureChart.qml`. When the **Temperature History Form** receives a `temperatureUpdate(..)`, we will store the new value as `m_lastReading` and then emit a `newReading` signal. The `ChartView` will receive that signal, retrieve the `lastReading` value, and add it to the chart:

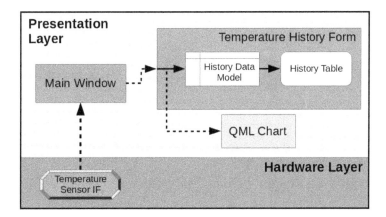

Simple? Yes, but it will still take some code.

Storing the last reading

In `Chapter 4`, *Important Qt Concepts*, we introduced the idea of `Q_PROPERTY` and mentioned that it is useful for many things, including as a way to provide data to QML objects. In order to make the last reading available to `TemperatureChart.qml`, we will define a `Q_PROPERTY`, along with the supporting code and storage for it. The QML code will reference the data using the name specified for the `READ` parameter of the property:

```
    ...
    Q_PROPERTY(QPointF lastReading READ lastReading WRITE setLastReading
NOTIFY newReading)

public:
    ...
    QPointF lastReading() const;
    void setLastReading(const QPointF &lastReading);

signals:
    newReading();
    ...
private:
    ...
    QPointF m_lastReading;
```

Remember that if you first define `QPointF m_lastReading`, you can generate basic getter and setter methods by right-clicking on `m_lastReading` and using the **Refactor** menu.

We will need to adjust `setLastReading(..)` so that it emits the `newReading()` signal. Go to the implementation of `setLastReading(..)` and update the code to add the `emit` statement, as follows:

```
void TemperatureHistoryForm::setLastReading(const QPointF &lastReading)
{
    m_lastReading = lastReading;
    emit newReading();
}
```

Did you use *F2* to jump from the header to the implementation of `setLastReading(..)`?

Updating temperatureUpdate(..)

We need to modify `temperatureUpdate(..)` to set the last reading:

```
void TemperatureHistoryForm::temperatureUpdate(QDateTime timestamp, float
temperature)
{
...
    // add the row to the model
    m_tempRecord.appendRow(row);

    // ** update the m_lastReading **
    double xVal = timestamp.toSecsSinceEpoch();
    setLastReading(QPointF(xVal, temperature));
}
```

We use `setLastReading(..)` to make sure that we emit the required notification signal.

Catching newReading in the chart

We are using a signal to send the data to `ChartView`, so we will need to do some setup work and connect it.

On the C++ side, we need to tell the QML engine about `temperatureData`. We can do that as part of the constructor for `TemperatureHistoryForm`, along with other initialization of the QuickWidget:

```
TemperatureHistoryForm::TemperatureHistoryForm(QWidget *parent) :
    QWidget(parent),
    ui(new Ui::TemperatureHistoryForm)
{
...
    //** setup the QtQuick Chart **
    ui->quickWidget->resize(QSize(640, 480));
    ui->quickWidget->engine()->rootContext()-
        >setContextProperty("temperatureData", this);
    ui->quickWidget->setSource(QUrl("qrc:/TemperatureChart.qml"));
    ui->quickWidget->setResizeMode(QQuickWidget::SizeRootObjectToView);
}
```

The call to `setContextProperty("temperatureData", this)` tells the QML engine that the QML code will be referring to `this` instance of `TemperatureHistoryForm` using the `temperatureData` ID.

On the QML side, we need to establish the connection:

```
ChartView {
. . .
    Connections {
        target: temperatureData
        onNewReading: {
// (1)
            if (temperatureSeries.count > 120)
                temperatureSeries.remove(0);
// (2)
            temperatureSeries.append(temperatureData.lastReading.x,
        temperatureData.lastReading.y)

// (3)        // adjust time axis
            timeAxis.min = temperatureSeries.at(0).x
            timeAxis.max = temperatureSeries.at(temperatureSeries.count
                -1).x

// (4)        // adjust temperature axis
            if (temperatureData.lastReading.y < temperatureAxis.min)
                temperatureAxis.min = temperatureData.lastReading.y;
            if (temperatureData.lastReading.y > temperatureAxis.max)
                temperatureAxis.max = temperatureData.lastReading.y;
        }
    }
}
```

`Connections` allows us to define connections to the containing object (`ChartView`). In this case, we are expecting a connection for the *target* called `temperatureData` (in our C++ world, we know this as our instance of `TemperatureHistoryForm`), and we are connecting to a signal called `newReading`. In the QML code, we want to perform an action when `newReading` is emitted, so we want to do it `onNewReading` (that is, on the receipt of `newReading`).

The code that is executed when the signal is received does a few things:

- It makes sure that we only keep the last 120 readings.
- It retrieves the *x* and *y* values of `temperatureData.lastReading` (the `lastReading` property of our instance of `TemperatureHistoryForm`) and adds the point to the QML chart line series, `temperatureSeries`.
- It adjusts the `time` axis for the times.
- It adjusts the *temperature* axis for the temperature readings.

Now is probably a good time to define the axes:

```
LineSeries {
    id: temperatureSeries
    name: "Temperature"

    axisX: timeAxis
    axisY: temperatureAxis
}

ValueAxis {
    id: timeAxis
}

ValueAxis {
    id: temperatureAxis
    min: 15
    max: 25
}
```

Adjusting the .pro file

Before we can compile things, we need to make sure that we can support QtQuick (QML). Therefore, we need to adjust `BigProject.pro` and tell it that we are using `quick` and `quickwidgets`:

```
QT       += core gui

greaterThan(QT_MAJOR_VERSION, 4): QT += widgets quick quickwidgets
```

We are ready to test our code! Build and run it on both the Host and the Target.

Reformatting the History page

When you ran the code on the Target, you probably noticed that the vertical layout of the **History** tab doesn't work well. The table is too wide and the chart is too short. Changing the splitter to a horizontal layout should solve this problem:

1. Open `TemperatureHistoryForm.ui`.
2. Select **splitter** from the top-right Object list.
3. Under **Properties**, change **orientation** in the **QSplitter** section to be **Horizontal**.

4. Rebuild and run the program on the host and the target:

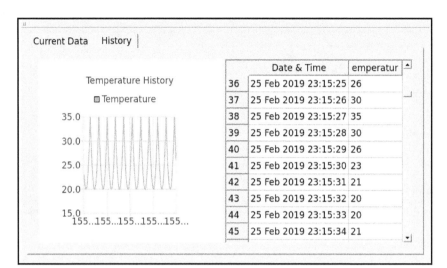

Be sure to commit your changes to Git. The final implementation of `BigProject` for this chapter can be found at `https://github.com/PacktPublishing/Hands-On-Embedded-Programming-with-Qt/tree/master/Chapter06/BigProject`.

We have covered a lot of material in this chapter. Now, it is time to summarize what we have learned.

Summary

Wow! This has been a long chapter. Here, we looked at how Qt has come to have two graphics technologies—Qt Widgets and QML/QtQuick. We explored how to use both technologies, and how UIs are created both with code and with the Designer in Qt Creator. Next, we looked at a comparison between the two technologies.

We also uncovered two new requirements for our `BigProject` and used them to explore how we can combine both Qt Quick and Qt Widgets in the same program. We even learned one way to pass data from C++ into QML objects, something that will serve us well as we interface our embedded code with C and C++ device drivers and display the UI using Qt Quick.

In `Chapter 7`, *Adding More Features*, we will discover more requirements for `BigProject` that will require us to learn about using databases in Qt, designing with state machines, using web sockets, and even adding a virtual keyboard. Keep reading—it is going to be fun!

Questions

1. What is the difference between QML and Qt Quick?
2. Why were QML and Qt Quick originally developed?
3. Are Qt Widgets a dead-end technology?
4. What types of application are best suited for Qt Widgets?
5. What types of application are best suited for Qt Quick and QML?
6. How do we expose data stored in a C++ QObject to QML code?
7. What keystroke can be used to go from a C++ method declaration in a class to its implementation?
8. What language or data format is QML based on?

Further reading

This chapter has covered a lot of ground and only skimmed the surface of several topics. Luckily, Packt offers some great books that you can refer to so that you can learn more:

- *Mastering Qt 5 - Second Edition*, by Guillaume Lazar and Robin Penea, will help you learn more about Qt Widgets and Qt Quick.
- *End to End GUI development with Qt5*, by Nicholas Sherriff *et al.* also looks at Qt Widgets, Qt Quick, and even Qt 3D.
- If programming games is more interesting to you, check out *Game Programming using Qt 5 Beginner's Guide - Second Edition*, by Pavel Strakhov, Witold Wysota, and Lorenz Haas.

7
Adding More Features

In the previous chapters, we have been building a `BigProject` while learning about some of the features that Qt offers. In keeping with that spirit, we will be exploring a few more features as we gather more requirements for our `BigProject`. To do that, we will be looking at the following:

- Keeping records
- Designing with state machines
- Searching for a keyboard
- Weaving a web of sockets
- Considering IoT security

When you have finished this chapter, you will have learned about the following:

- How to interface a Qt application to a SQL database
- Easily going from a graphical state machine design to an executable state machine
- How to add a virtual keyboard for use in the project
- How to communicate between IoT devices using WebSockets
- What cybersecurity is and why it is important for IoT devices

Technical requirements

In this chapter, we will be working with SQL databases. While you will not be required to write your own queries, having a basic understanding of SQL (in particular, the SQLite 3 variant) will help you to understand the queries that are used.

This chapter also assumes that you have successfully gotten Qt running on your target, and that you have been updating your `BigProject` along with this book. This chapter builds more features into `BigProject`. The source code for the examples and projects in this chapter, including this chapter's end implementation of `BigProject`, are available at `https://github.com/PacktPublishing/Hands-On-Embedded-Programming-with-Qt/tree/master/Chapter07`

Keeping records

In this section, we will look at how we can store and retrieve data in Qt. In particular, we will work out a solution for yet another requirement.

Management has taken a look at what we have done so far with our `BigProject`, and they like it. Mostly. They did find something to ask about—*Where is the old data? When you start the program, there is no history. Why don't we keep the old data so that we can see it?* From that, and the conversations that followed, comes a new requirement:

Req. 7: The system shall maintain a history of readings across power cycles.

There are a lot of ways we could store data, but we are here to learn about how to use a database and Qt's database access methods. `QSqlDatabase` provides a generic interface to several database backends, including MySQL (and MariaDB), SQLite, IBM DB2, PostgreSQL, and generic ODBC (for example, Microsoft SQL Server).

We have chosen SQLite 3 for our database. It's a lightweight solution that supports both file-based and in-memory databases. Since the data must be maintained across reboots, a file-based solution seems appropriate.

In the following subsections, we will learn how to create the structure of the database and interact with the database through `QSqlDatabase`. In the process, you will learn about different ways of retrieving and working with data in the database.

Defining the database structure

We will start by defining the database schema or structure. Our first table will be for our temperature history, so we will call it `TemperatureHistory`. It will have two columns: timestamp and temperature. Here is some SQL to define it:

```
create table TemperatureHistory (
    timestamp   datetime primary key,
    temperature float
);
```

We can either create a database file and copy it, or we can create the database programmatically in Qt. Since this is a book about developing with Qt, it only seems appropriate to create the database programmatically. However, before we can create the database, we need to have an interface to it.

Interfacing to the database

In `Chapter 5`, *Managing the Overall Workflow*, in the *Injecting the Mock* section, we introduced dependency injection and interfaces for reading the temperature sensor. While it would be nice to create another interface, this time, we are going to just plunge directly into an implementation.

We will start by defining a class to hold a single temperature reading. We will then define a class that can store those temperature readings and slowly work through building the data and saving and retrieving methods. Finally, we integrate the temperature reading storage into the rest of the program.

Simplifying handling readings

So far, in the `BigProject`, we have always stored temperature readings as `QPair<QDateTime, float>`. That gets a bit awkward to type and it is easy to forget what the two parts are. Since we are going to be working more with readings, we will define a simple class, `TemperatureReading`, to store them:

1. Start by creating a new class called `TemperatureReading`. It doesn't inherit from any other classes.
2. Define two private attributes, as follows:

```
float      m_temperatureC; ///< the temperature in C
QDateTime m_timestamp;     ///< the time of the reading
```

3. Use the Refactor menu to create getter and setter methods for both attributes. (Do you remember the *Refactoring trick?*)

4. Add initialization of the attributes to the constructor, as follows (see the bolded lines in the following code):

```
TemperatureReading::TemperatureReading() :
 m_temperatureC(0.0),
 m_timestamp(QDateTime())
 {
 // nothing to do here
 }
```

5. Create a new public `bool` method to check whether there is valid data stored in the reading, as follows:

```
bool TemperatureReading::isValid() const
{
    return m_timestamp.isValid(); // timestamp init'd to non-valid
}
```

Now that we have a simpler way of handling the readings, it is time to define the storage class.

Defining the TemperatureStorage class

The `TemperatureStorage` class will take care of persisting our `TemperatureReading` by using a SQL database.

Before we can code the header, the Qt project (`BigProject.pro`) needs to know that we plan to use a SQL database in our project. We do that by adding `sql` to the `QT +=` line (I've also simplified the old multiline statement into one line since we will not be supporting Qt 4):

```
QT += core gui widgets quick quickwidgets sql
```

Once you save the project, Qt Creator will reevaluate it and find that we will be using Qt's SQL support. Qt Creator will recognize the classes and their methods.

Knowing the class and methods for Qt SQL will make it easier to write the code. Why don't we starting coding the class definition for the class that provides storage for `TemperatureReading` and `TemperatureStorage`:

1. Create a C++ class, `TemperatureStorage`, that does not inherit from any other class.

2. Give the class a database, `QSqlDatabase`, to use. We don't need getters and setters for this attribute:

```
private:
    QSqlDatabase m_db;  ///< the database
```

3. Add the public method definitions for working with the temperature readings to the public section of the `TemperatureStorage` class definition:

```
void AddReading(const TemperatureReading &reading);
QList<TemperatureReading> GetAllReadings() const;
QList<TemperatureReading> GetLastNReadings(int n) const;
TemperatureReading GetLastReading() const;

void ClearAllReadings();
int NumberOfReadings() const;
```

4. We will need public methods for opening and closing the storage. I have added the concept of `id` so that we can store more than one set of readings in the future:

```
bool OpenStorage(const QString &id = "readings");
bool CloseStorage();

QString id() const; ///< retrieve storage id
```

That completes the rough class definition for `TemperatureStorage`.

Feel free to take a look at `TemperatureStorage.h` in this chapter's Git repository for BigProject, `https://github.com/PacktPublishing/Hands-On-Embedded-Programming-with-Qt/tree/master/Chapter07/BigProject`, to see my complete class definition.

Now that the class definition is complete, we will implement the pieces in `TemperatureStorage.cpp`.

Opening (and creating) the database

Let's start by defining our database opening and closing methods.

Before we can open the database, we need to make a connection to it using `QSqlDatabase`. This is done with the `addDatabase(..)` static function. The function needs to know the database driver (`QSQLITE`) and the connection name. The connection name is only a reference name, so we can find it again from within our code. We also need to provide the name that the system knows the database as. For SQLite databases, this is the filename that contains the database:

```
QString dbName = QString("ReadingStore_%1").arg(id);
QString dbFileName = QString("%1.sqlite").arg(dbName);

m_db = QSqlDatabase::addDatabase("QSQLITE", dbName);
m_db.setDatabaseName(dbFileName);
```

Now that the database connection is set up and associated with a SQLite database filename, we need to open the database using the `open()` method. `open()` returns true if the database was successfully opened; otherwise, it returns false and sets `m_db.lasterror()` appropriately:

```
bool result = m_db.open();
```

For the purposes of this design, it has been decided that the `OpenStorage()` method will take care of creating the database if it hasn't been created already. We need to add code to do that, but only if the database has been successfully opened. This is done by executing `QSqlQuery` on the database.

There are two ways of executing a query in SQL. Directly executing a query causes the passed string to be interpreted and executed in one step. We can also prepare a query with placeholders for the data and then execute it. During the prepare stage, the query is interpreted and staged for execution. You can then bind data to the query and execute it. To use different data, you can simply bind other data and re-execute it without having to prepare it again.

First, we create a `QSqlQuery` object associated with our database (`m_db`), and then we execute the query string. We could have also prepared the query and then executed it, but for our purposes, it is just as easy to do it in one step:

```
if (result) // if the db was opened
{
    // create the table if it does not exist
    QSqlQuery query(m_db); // build query
```

```
result = query.exec("create table if not exists
TemperatureHistory ("
                    " timestamp datetime primary key,"
                    " temperature float"
                    ");"
                    );
}
```

Using the preceding fragments, implement `TemperatureStorage::OpenStorage(..)`.

My final implementation of `TemperatureStorage::OpenStorage(..)` returns the result of trying to open the database, along with printing a debug message on a database failure. It also initializes `QSqlQueryModel`, which we will talk about when we look at ways to retrieve data. You can look at the code in `TemperatureStorage.cpp` from the repository to see how close you came.

How about closing the database?

Closing the database

Looking at the method that's used to open the database, what do you think we would use to close the database? If you guessed you use a method called `close()` to close the database, then you are correct. The method takes no arguments and acts on a `QSQLDatabase` object `m_db`.

Here is the implementation for closing the storage. Add it to `TemperatureStorage.cpp`:

```
void TemperatureStorage::CloseStorage()
{
    m_db.close();
}
```

Now that we can open and close the database, let's put some data in it.

Saving data

Saving data is simply a matter of adding it to the database. For the `AddReading(..)` method, we will use a simple insert query using another form of `QSqlQuery`: the prepared statement. Use the following code for the implementation of `AddReading(..)`:

```
void TemperatureStorage::AddReading(const TemperatureReading &reading)
{
    QSqlQuery query(m_db);
    query.prepare("insert into TemperatureHistory values (:timestamp,
```

```
          :temperature);");
    query.bindValue(":timestamp",    reading.timestamp());
    query.bindValue(":temperature", reading.temperatureC());
    query.exec();
}
```

One of the nice things that QSqlQuery allows is using real names for the placeholders in prepared queries. This allows explicitly bindings values to a name. It is still possible to use question marks (?) for placeholders, but then the binding is by position in the query. The placeholder names start with a colon (:), see the bolded text in the listing. From the preceding code, you can see how easy it is to bind values and then execute the query.

We can now add data, but we can't retrieve data for it. Shall we change that by implementing our data retrieval methods?

Retrieving readings

There are several methods that we declared in our header file for retrieving the data:

- QList<TemperatureReading> GetAllReadings() const;
- QList<TemperatureReading> GetLastNReadings(int n) const;
- TemperatureReading GetLastReading() const;

If you think about it, GetLastReading() is really a specialization of GetLastNReadings(n) with $n = 1$, so that should be a very quick method for you to implement.

The other two could be implemented with almost identical code that only differs in the actual SQL query, but where would the fun be in that? Instead, we are going to use two different implementations so that we can look at two different ways of retrieving data from a SQL database.

Using a QSqlQuery

We have already seen how to use QSqlQuery to create the database. Now, we will use it to retrieve data for GetLastNReadings(..) using a simple query with a couple of modifiers so that we can get the last *n* entries in the database:

```
select * from TemperatureHistory order by timestamp desc limit n
```

In order to fill in *n*, we can use `QString(..).arg(n)`:

1. Start the implementation of `GetLastNReadings(..)` by adding the creation of `QSqlQuery` on the database (`m_db`). This can be done in one statement:

```
QSqlQuery    query(qStr, m_db);
```

2. Now, use `exec()` with no arguments to execute the query.

Once the query has been executed, data must be retrieved from it. `query.next()` fetches the next result row if it can. It returns `true` if a row was fetched. When it returns `false`, no more data is available.

If a row is fetched, `query.value(column_name)` can be used to retrieve the value stored in `column_name` of the row.

3. Using these pieces, write the rest of the method. The code should fetch all of the rows returned by the query and store the temperatures and timestamps into `QList` of `TemperatureReading` and return it.

 Feel free to look at the code in this chapter's implementation of `BigProject`, `https://github.com/PacktPublishing/Hands-On-Embedded-Programming-with-Qt/tree/master/Chapter07/BigProject`, to see how I implemented it.

As for another method of retrieving data from a SQL database, continue reading to learn about `QSqlTableModel`.

Using QSqlTableModel

`QSqlTableModel` provides a `QAbstractTableModel` (remember those from our table view?) connected to a specific table in a database:

```
QSqlTableModel   model(nullptr, m_db);      // create the model
model.setTable("TemperatureHistory");       // choose the table
model.select();                             // select the data
```

Once the model is associated with the database table, it is a simple matter of going through the table and building `QList` of `TemperatureStorage` records:

```
for (int row = 0; row < model.rowCount(); ++row)
{
    auto rec = model.record(row);
    data << TemperatureReading(rec.value("timestamp").toDateTime(),
                               rec.value("temperature").toFloat());
}
```

Using the pieces presented in this section, implement the following:

```
QList<TemperatureReading> GetAllReadings().
```

You can view my implementation in the `BigProject` repository at `https://github.com/PacktPublishing/Hands-On-Embedded-Programming-with-Qt/tree/master/Chapter07/BigProject`.

So, how do we use the data?

Integrating the storage

I have a confession to make—I had originally planned to pass data to the table view using the lists of `TemperatureRecords`, then I realized that I was missing an opportunity to show off one of the easiest ways to display data from a SQL database in a table view—using `QSqlQueryModel`. Like `QSqlTableModel`, `QSqlQueryModel` presents `QStandardItemModel` filled with data in a SQL database. The difference is that instead of being connected to a single table, `QSqlQueryModel` is connected to a query.

To do this, `TemperatureHistoryForm` was modified to use `temperatureModel` provided by `TemperatureStorage`. `temperatureModel` provides the model that's used for the history table in the form. When a temperature reading is added to `TemperatureStorage`, the temperature model is updated, which causes the table view to be updated.

You can take a look my implementation in this book's Git repository at `https://github.com/PacktPublishing/Hands-On-Embedded-Programming-with-Qt/tree/master/Chapter07/BigProject`.

This concludes our overview of using Qt's SQL database classes for data storage. In the next section, we will look at another very powerful feature that Qt provides: the ability to draw state machines and easily produce executable code.

Designing with state machines

For all of my professional career, I have been working with state machines in one form or another, and I used to hate implementing them. Since most of the code in my early career was done on a true microcontroller in a single thread, implementing a state machine meant having a state variable that indicated the current state and a giant case statement for each state. The state machine was easy to draw, but quite painful to implement and even worse to change.

Still, for some things, state machines really are the right way to go—especially when you're implementing a control system.

 A finite-state machine (or state machine for short) is a model of a system with a finite set of conditions (states) and rules or events that cause a transition between conditions. I'll explain them more in the next section.

In this section, we will implement some new requirements for `BigProject` using a state machine. We will start by developing the state machine model, and then learn how we can implement it in Qt just by drawing it in Qt Creator!

Guess what marketing wants now?

Marketing has determined what they really want us to build is a thermostat to control heating and cooling. To that end, marketing has created some new requirements:

- **Requirement 9**: The user shall be able to set a minimum acceptable temperature
- **Requirement 10**: The user shall be able to set a maximum acceptable temperature
- **Requirement 11**: If the temperature falls below the minimum acceptable temperature, the heater must be turned on
- **Requirement 12**: If the temperature is above the minimum acceptable temperature, the heater must be turned off
- **Requirement 13**: If the temperature rises above the maximum acceptable temperature, the cooler must be turned on
- **Requirement 14**: If the temperature falls below the maximum acceptable temperature, the cooler must be turned off

Requirements 9 and 10 are simple UI items that we will address a little later. For now, let's look at the control system for the thermostat. After reading through the rest of the requirements, we can develop a simple state machine.

To develop the state machine, we will go through three steps:

1. Determining the states (conditions) that are needed
2. Determining the transition events
3. Drawing it out in picture form

Determining the states

The first step is to determine what states (or conditions) are mentioned in our requirements. By reading through them, I've come up with two of them directly related to parts of an HVAC system—*Heating* and *Cooling*.

Looking closer, there seems to be another state, doing neither Heating nor Cooling. Let's call that *Idle*. As a side note, we will assume that the system starts in the *Idle* state (neither *Heating* nor *Cooling*).

The following table maps the states to the requirements that they came from:

State	Requirement
Heating	11, 12
Cooling	13, 14
Idle	12, 14 (heating/cooling turned off)

With the states identified, we can look at what causes us to move between them.

Determining the conditions that cause transitions

Once again, we need to look at the requirements. This time, we are looking for the conditions or events that cause us to move between states. We need to identify the condition, the state it is in before we make the transition, and the state it will be in after the transition.

I will start with the first one. Requirement 11 can be paraphrased into, *If it is too cold, turn on the heat*. From that, I identified `TooCold` as a condition that puts us in the *Heating* state. But where did we come from? Using the dictatorial power of authorship, I will say that we cannot go directly from *Heating* to/from *Cooling,* so I will declare that the transition must come from *Idle.*

We can continue along these lines and work out a table that shows the `From State`, `Destination State`, and the condition that causes state change. For the sake a brevity, I will simply show you the table I generated:

From State	Condition	Destination State	Requirement
Idle	TooCold	Heating	11
Heating	TargetReached	Idle	12
Idle	TooHot	Cooling	13
Cooling	TargetReached	Idle	14

`TargetReached` is the condition where it is neither too hot nor too cold. The target temperature range has been reached. `TargetReached` is used twice in the table as it really is the condition that causes the change. It also means that our code can be easier as we don't need to determine the condition in two places.

Now that we have a state table, we could stop, and for some applications, it makes perfect sense. I personally find that drawing things out helps me to understand things and see opportunities for improvements (including errors I've made).

Drawing it out

State diagrams are a great way to visualize a state machine. The process of drawing one is quite simple:

1. Draw a rounded rectangle for each state and place the state's name in the rectangle.
2. For each transition condition, do the following:
   1. Draw an arrow from the `From State` pointing to `Destination State`.

2. Label the arrow with the name of the condition:

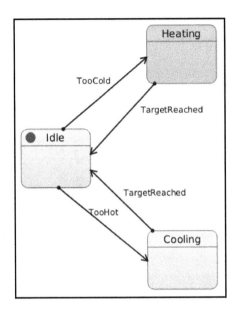

You can draw the state machine on whatever you want, but you already have a tool for doing it in Qt Creator. Before we talk about that, let's step back and see how Qt used to support state machines.

Qt's early state machine support

Qt has had support for state machine programming since Qt 4.6 (~2009). It made programming state machines much easier, but it still wasn't a trivial thing to do. You had to code the states and transitions and then add them to the state machine. Implementing a simple heating-only control would look something like the following, and it doesn't even do anything except change states:

```
QStateMachine    hvacControl;

auto idleState = new QState();
auto heatState = new QState();

idleState.addTransition(sender, signal(TooCold),       heatState);
heatState.addTransition(sender, signal(TargetReached), idleState);

hvacControl.addState(idleState);
hvacControl.addState(heatState);
```

```
hvacControl.setInitialState(idleState);

hvacControl.start();
```

`sender` is just a `QObject` class that emits `TooCold` and `TargetReached` signals when it detects the conditions. When the signals are emitted, the state of `hvacControl` changes to the state specified by `addTransition(..)`.

Being totally honest, I don't know if the preceding code will really work. That isn't how I create state machines in Qt anymore. There is an easier way to do it.

An easier way to make state machines

With Qt 5.7 (2016), a new way to implement state machines was introduced using SCXML and some custom tools. **State Machine XML (SCXML)** is an XML schema for describing state machines. Qt has created tools not only to take SCXML and create an executable state machine from it, but to even allow you to create the SCXML by drawing the state machine diagram!

Let's add an SCXML model for the thermostat controls to our `BigProject`. Assuming that you have `BigProject` open in Qt Creator, do the following:

1. Start by adding a new item to `BigProject`. To do this, right-click on `BigProject` and select **Add New**.

2. This time, we are adding a **Modeling** template for a **State Chart**:

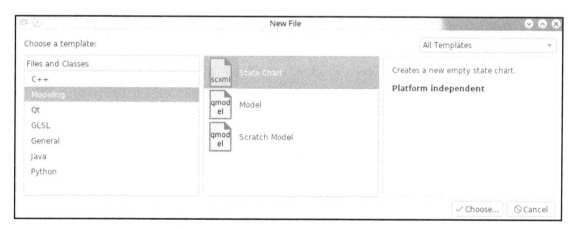

3. Name the model `HVACControl`.

When you complete the wizard, the **State Chart Design** screen will open, as follows:

On the left are the components you can add to the state chart, on the right is information about the state chart, and in the middle is where you will draw the state chart.

The following procedure will walk you through how to draw the state chart:

1. Click and drag the **State** icon from the left and drop it in the state chart.
2. Click on the name of the new state in the diagram and rename it `Idle`. (Be sure to hit *Enter* when you're done changing the text!)
3. Do the same thing to create the Heating and Cooling states. (Try to lay them out like in the diagram we looked at previously.)
4. Now, click on the Idle state and select the arrow icon (left-most). An arrow should now follow your mouse.
5. Right-click on the Heating state. The arrow should turn solid.
6. Now, click on the new Transition name and change it to `TooCold`.

7. Draw a transition named `TargetReached` from Heating to Idle.

8. Now, draw a transition called `TooHot` from Idle to Cooling, and another, `TargetReached`, from Cooling to Idle.

> You can move labels by clicking on them without selecting text. A box will form around the arrow and the mouse pointer will become a move cursor.

You should now have a diagram like the one at the beginning of this section, except for the color.

> For me, the hardest thing is remembering that drawing transitions starts with a left mouse click on the originating state and finishes with a *right* mouse click on the destination click. I usually end up trying to left-click a couple of times, then just right-clicking, deleting the transition, and trying again until I remember *right-click to finish the transition*.

> Above the state diagram are several icons. The icon that looks like a paint bucket allows you to change the color of the state that is currently selected.

Now that we have a state machine, we need to use it. Continue to the next section to read how.

Using the state machine

QMake needs to know that we will be using the `scxml` support in our project. The simplest way is to add it to the `QT` settings in the QMake project file, `BigProject.pro`:

```
QT += scxml
```

The SCXML support will take care of generating C++ code from the SCXML file containing our state machine and compiling and linking the code, but we need to do a little bit of work to use that state machine.

With the change to `BigProject.pro` finished, we can continue with the tasks that will allow us to use the state machine: updating the UI, creating a controller class (HVAC controller), wiring the state machine and controller into our code, and testing it.

Updating the UI

The first order of business is to make some changes to the UI so that we can do the following:

- Enter the min and max temperatures
- See when the system is heating and cooling
- See when the fan is running

Why don't we start with the status indicators? These indicators should be visible on all of the pages, so let's add them to the bottom of `MainWindow.ui`, below the tab widget:

1. Using the Qt Creator Designer, insert a horizontal layout below the tab widget.

   We will keep the three indicators really simple by using labels that change their appearance when heating, cooling, and the fan is on.

2. Create three QLabels and put them in the horizontal layout you just created. From left to right, the labels should read Heating, Cooling, and Fan and have the names `heatingInd`, `coolingInd`, and `fanInd`, respectively.

3. Change the label text to be bold. (Hint: check the label properties.)

4. Set the `QFrame` shape *(another property)* for each label to *panel*. This will generate a nice box around the text.

When you insert a horizontal (vertical) layout, it is often hard to drop widgets into it because it is too small. I solved this by adjusting the top (left) margin of the widget to 5 or more pixels. Just be sure to set it back to 0 once you have dropped stuff into it.

You now have three rather boring looking labels. Let's add some color that will be enabled when the various items are on. We can do this easily using **Qt Style Sheets (QSS)**. QSS is basically standard CSS, but with some special items. It is set using the `stylesheet` property of the element. For our purposes, we want to change the background color of each label when it is enabled so that we can add the following:

```
*:enabled {
  background-color: rgb(rrr, ggg, bbb);
}
```

The values of `rrr`, `ggg`, and `bbb` are different for each label and can be found in the following table:

	rrr	ggg`	bbb
Heating	255	211	212
Cooling	170	255	255
Fan	255	255	171

When you are done, you should get something that looks a lot like this in Qt Creator Designer:

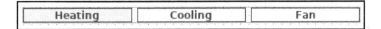

Having created our indicators, we still need a way to set the minimum and maximum values. For this, we will start by creating a third tab in our tab widget, **Settings**, and position it between the **Current Data** and **History** tabs:

1. Select the **Current Data** tab.
2. Right-click on the tab label and select **Insert Page --> After Current Page**.
3. Select that new tab, name its **Settings**, and give it the tab name `settingsTab` in the property menu.
4. Drop a Form widget onto the new tab.
5. Double-click on the form layout to bring up the **Add Form Layout Row** dialog, and enter the following information (the rest will auto populate):
     - Label text: **Max Temperature**
     - Field type: `QSpinBox`
6. Select **Ok.**
7. Double-click on the form layout to add another `QSpinBox` for **Min Temperature**.
8. Right-click on the tab contents, but not the form layout, and select **Layout |** **Vertically**.

That should be all of the UI changes we need, but we still have to wire the state machine into the rest of the code so that it does something.

Creating an HVAC controller

The state machine by itself only advances states. We need to create something that will act on the state machines. To do this, we will create an `HVACController` class.

We have already seen how to create an interface and mock so that we can develop on the Host, so we will simply create a single class. It still won't control hardware—that will come later.

`HVACController` is a very simple class. It just turns things on and off in response to signals. Here is the full definition of this `QObject`:

```
class HVACController : public QObject
{
    Q_OBJECT
public:
    explicit HVACController(QObject *parent = nullptr);

public slots:
    void setHeatingOn(bool on);
    void setCoolingOn(bool on);
    void setFanOn(bool on);
};
```

Using what you have learned about adding a new C++ class to a project, create the `HVACController` C++ class.

After creating the headers, use the refactoring tools to create implementations of the slots. For now, the slots should just send a message to `qDebug()`, indicating what action is being performed.

Now that we have an HVAC controller and indicator lights, let's wire everything up in `MainWindow.cpp`.

Wiring in the HVAC state machine

The first steps in wiring up the HVAC state machine to the HVAC controller is as follows:

1. Allocate member variables for them in `MainWindow.cpp`:

    ```
    private:
    ...
        HVACStateMachine m_hvacSM; ///< state machine for controlling
            hvac
        HVACController m_hvacCtrl; ///< controller or the HVAC system
    ```

2. Once you have done that, connect things up in the constructor for `MainWindow`.

Both the indicators and the controller need to respond to specific states being active. QScxmlStateMachine (the base class of HVACStateMachine) provides a connectToState(..) method that takes a state name and connects it to a slot. For the indicators, we will adjust the Enabled state of the labels so that they change colors. Here is how the connectToState(..) method is used to wire the states to the indicators:

```
m_hvacSM.connectToState("Heating", ui->heatingInd,
    &QLabel::setEnabled);
m_hvacSM.connectToState("Cooling", ui->coolingInd,
    &QLabel::setEnabled);
m_hvacSM.connectToState("FanOn", ui->fanInd,
    &QLabel::setEnabled);
```

The first argument of connectToState(..) is the name of the state in the state machine to connect to. When that state becomes active/inactive, the slot specified by the third argument (QLabel::setEnabled) of the object specified in the second argument will be invoked with true/false. That is a long, complex sentence, so I will provide an example. The first line in the preceding code will cause heatingInd::setEnabled to be invoked with true when the state machine enters the Heating state, and with false when it leaves the Heating state. Because of how we configured the labels, enabling/disabling them will cause them to change colors.

Now that you have seen how the states are connected to the indicators, do the following:

1. Wire up the states to the HVAC controller.

    Last, the most important (and most often overlooked) step is to start the state machine. If you don't start the state machine, it won't run and you will spend a lot of time trying to figure out why nothing seems to happen. (Okay, maybe you will find the cause faster than I did my first time.)

2. Right after all of the connectToState calls, add m_hvacSM.start(); to start the state machine.

I could tell you to check your work against the completed chapter implementation of BigProject, but where would the fun in that be?

Testing our simple thermostat

We have now graphically created a state machine and wired it both to the indicator lights in the GUI and to an HVAC controller. It is time to test the code!

Run the code on the Host and then on the Target and see how it runs!

- Does it work?
- Does it fulfil the requirements?
- Is there anything you would change?

If you answered no to either of the first two questions, or yes to the last question, make some changes to the state machine, UI, and/or code until you are happy with it.

Once you are happy, check your code into your own Git repository.

But wait! There are more requirements!

Handling more requirements!

System engineering has had a look at the requirements and found a problem. Nothing prevents the minimum temperature from being set higher than the maximum temperature. If that happens, both the heater and the cooler will be turned on at the same time! They also noted that the system cannot control temperatures tighter than three degrees:

- **Requirement 15**: The minimum and maximum temperatures must be separated by three degrees.
- **Requirement 16**: The minimum temperature must be lower than the maximum temperature.

These requirements can be handled easily in the UI changes that we developed for requirements 9 and 10, so I am going to leave it to you to work out how you would solve the problem that is going to happen when the *value of the spin boxes changes* so that the conditions are met.

 You can set the value of a spin box in response to the change in another.

As always, you can refer to the `BigProject` final solution for this chapter to see how I implemented it.

The following requirement gets interesting:

- **Requirement 17**: The HVAC Unit needs to wait 30 seconds between activations of either the Heating or Cooling sections.

You are about to learn about the power of using Qt Creator to draw the SCXML when working with state machines! We can do this by adding a new state, moving some transitions, and modifying the new state.

Adding a new state

Luckily, we can quickly update our state machine diagram to add a wait state before we go back to Idle:

1. Drop a new state called **Wait** on the state machine chart.
2. Change both **TargetReached** transitions to go to the **Wait** state by clicking on the arrow then dragging the arrowhead to the **Wait** state.
3. Create a transition from **Wait** to **Idle** and call it **DoneWaiting**.

This is what our state machine will look like:

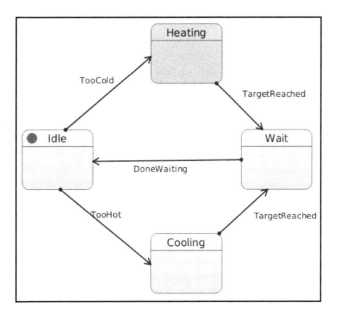

There are a couple of ways we can implement the waiting period. One way would be to catch the transition to the new state in our code and set QTimer to inject the **DoneWaiting** event when QTimer expires. The other way is to have the state machine fire the **DoneWaiting** event itself 300 seconds (minutes) after the **Wait** state has been entered. The first way requires changing both the state machine and the code that it affects. The second requires only changing the state machine (and is more interesting to us), so we will implement it.

Adding an event to a state

Whenever a state is entered, it processes an **onentry** event. Likewise, when the state is left, it processes an **onexit** event. One of the things we can do in an action is send an event either immediately or after a wait period. We are going to use this to make the wait state automatically transition to Idle.

Here is the very simple procedure we will use:

1. Right-click on the **Wait** state and select **onentry | send:**

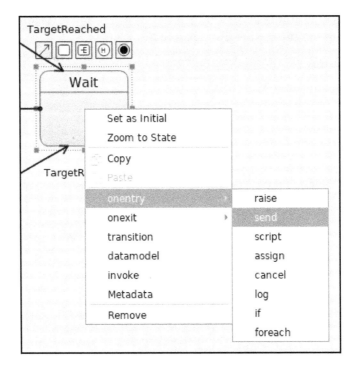

2. In the **Structure** window, we will see the new **onentry** event with a send action, and below it in the **Attributes** window, we will see a table.

3. Set the following attributes:
   - **event**: **DoneWaiting**
   - **target**: **Wait**
   - **delay**: **30:**

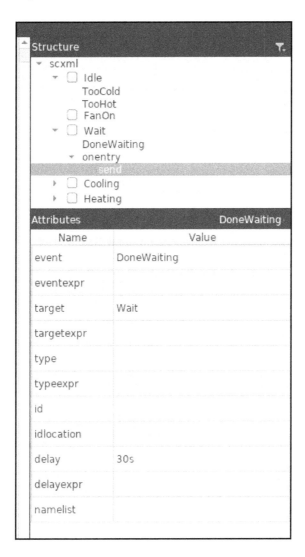

That's it! **Save** the program and test it! When you are happy with how it runs, commit the changes to your Git repository.

Working with embedded states

One more requirement has been added. It is rather obvious, but we missed it:

- **Requirement 18**: When heating or cooling, the fan must be on.

Once again, it sounds like we have a state machine with two states—**FanOn** and **FanOff**, but they are controlled (so far) by the **Heating** and **Cooling** states. Luckily, we can have multiple state machines in a chart, and a state may contain multiple other states.

Using the techniques we learned about previously, we can add the following states and transitions:

- States are: **FanOn, FanOff**.
- Transitions are as follows:
  - **TurnFanOff: FanOn | FanOff**
  - **TurnFanOn: FanOff | FanOn**

 You can change the size of a state by selecting it and using the controls around the outside of the state. (You really want to make sure that **FanOn** and **FanOff** are big!)

By dragging and dropping, we can place **Heating, Cooling,** and **Wait** in the **FanOn** state and **Idle** in the **FanOff** state. By doing this, we get the following:

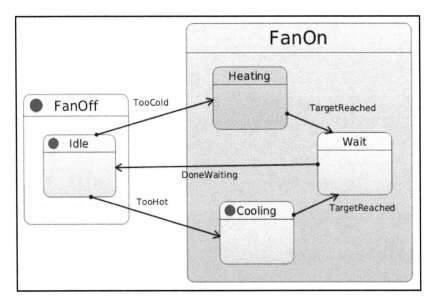

When in the **Idle** state, the state machine is also in the **FanOff** state, and it reports being in both states. When in the **Heating** state, the state machine is also in the **FanOn** state, and hence reports being in both the **Heating** and **FanOn** states.

State machines are a very powerful way of designing systems, but they are often not the easiest to program. Using Qt's SCXML diagramming tool in Qt Creator, along with its ability to translate the diagram directly into code, makes using and even modifying state machines incredibly simple!

State machines are a natural fit for control systems, but did you know that they also are great for designing GUIs? One typical GUI application is changing what is being displayed based on the operating state of the system. Instead of just enabling and disabling text labels, you could hide and show sections of the UI.

Having dealt with state machines, let's see what other *fun* requirements we have waiting for us. I'm guessing it is going to have to do with how values are entered into our UI when there is no keyboard attached to the system. It sounds like we will need a Virtual Keyboard.

Searching for a keyboard

Marketing doesn't like the idea of selling a product with a keyboard:

- **Requirement 19**: The system shall have a Virtual Keyboard for entering text on the screen.

Luckily for us, this is one of the simplest requirements we have to deal with because Qt 5.12 ships with a Virtual Keyboard, licensed both under (L)GPL 3 or commercially, that can be used in a couple of simple steps:

1. In `BigProject.pro`, add another QT component, `virtualkeyboard`:

   ```
   QT += virtualkeyboard
   ```

2. In `main.cpp`, set a couple of environment variables before creating `QApplication` to tell Qt to use the Virtual Keyboard:

   ```
   // virtual keyboard
   qputenv("QT_IM_MODULE", QByteArray("qtvirtualkeyboard"));
   qputenv("QT_LOGGING_RULES", QByteArray("qt.virtualkeyboard=true"));
   ```

Now that you have made those two changes, run `BigProject` on the Host and see whether the Virtual Keyboard works by going to the **Settings** tab and selecting one of the numbers:

- What happened?
- Did a Virtual Keyboard come up?
- Was it where you expected it?

Assuming you are running a setup like mine, the Virtual Keyboard appeared outside the application window. That isn't what we want. We want the keyboard in the application. In fact, if you try to run the application on the Target, you will find that no keyboard appears on the screen. Try it if you like.

So, what happened?

Quite simply, if we want to show a Virtual Keyboard in our application GUI, we need to create a space for it. We do that by instantiating QML `InputPanel` where we want it to appear.

Defining the input panel

Defining the input panel is one of the easiest pieces of QML that you will ever write:

```
import QtQuick 2.0
import QtQuick.VirtualKeyboard 2.3

Item {
    InputPanel {
        id: inputPanel
        anchors.left: parent.left
        anchors.right: parent.right
    }
}
```

Create a QML resource called `InputPanelArea.qml` using the same procedure we used in `Chapter 6`, *Exploring GUI Technologies*, when we created `TemperatureChart.qml`. This time, you want `InputPanelArea.qml` to contain the preceding code.

Now that we have defined our input panel, it needs to be placed on the UI.

Adding the input panel to the GUI

The only place we need text input is in the Settings tab. Since there are only two settings, we can take over the bottom of the tab for our Virtual Keyboard:

1. We have already added a `QQuickWidget` class in which we display the temperature graph, so we know that we just have to drop a `QQuickWidget` class into the vertical layout, below the form layout.

2. Once you have placed `QQuickWidget`, we need to specify the QML file to use by setting the *source* property to `qrc:/InputPanelArea.qml`.

3. Next, we need to adjust the input panel so that it takes as much room as it can by setting the horizontal and vertical size policies to *Expanding*.

> Remember, the default tab on program start is the one you were viewing in the Qt Creator Designer. You will probably want to select **Current Data** before you save the file.

4. Now that you have added the area for the Virtual Keyboard, try running the code on the Host or the Target. The following screenshot was formed from the running the code on the Target:

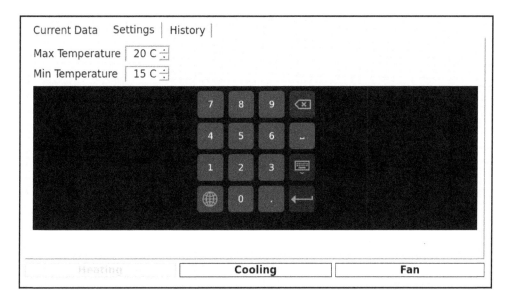

What happens when you click on the **Max Temperature** number and then click on a number? Is it what you expected? Is there a warning message in the application output?

By now, you should have discovered that, when you press a key on the Virtual Keyboard, the key is not sent to the widget and the application output says that there is no place to send the key. That's because touching the Virtual Keyboard changes the focus from the input box to the keyboard. We need to prevent that from happening by adjusting the *focus* policy for `QQuickWidget`. By setting the `focusPolicy` property to `NoFocus`, `QQuickWidget` gets the focus and the input goes to where we expected it to go.

Make the changes and try it!

If you are happy with how it is running, commit all of the changes to your local Git repository. If you aren't happy, feel free to play around with the layouts and other changes until you get it just right.

Solving a crash

Mystery crashes are one of the most frustrating things to solve. As I tested my code, I found a mystery crash that would occasionally happen when I touched the Target screen instead of using the mouse pointer. It took weeks to track down, but I finally did. If you are experiencing it, follow these short steps:

1. SSH into your Target.
2. Edit `/etc/profile` (I use vi; it is installed on the target already) and add the following lines at the end of the file:

```
# fix touchpad issues, and rotate for screen
export QT_QPA_PLATFORM=eglfs
export QT_QPA_EVDEV_TOUCHSCREEN_PARAMETERS=/dev/input/touchscreen0
export TSLIB_TSDEVICE=/dev/input/touchscreen0
```

3. (Optional) You may have noticed that the screen is upside down in the case. By that, I mean when the text on the display is right-side up, the wires come out the bottom of the case and the little feet on the case are on top. If you would like to solve that for Qt applications, do the following in `/etc/profile`:
    1. Add the following lines:

```
# if you want the wires coming out the top of the raspi,
# uncomment this next line.
export QT_QPA_EGLFS_ROTATION=180
```

2. Add `:rotate=180` to the line starting with `QT_QPA_EVDEV_TOUCHSCREEN_PARAMETERS`, as follows:

```
export
QT_QPA_EVDEV_TOUCHSCREEN_PARAMETERS=/dev/input/touchscreen0
:rotate=180
```

4. Reboot the Target.

So, what did we just do? I'll decode the fix for you.

Decoding the fix

The fix does a couple of things:

- `QT_QPA_PLATFORM=eglfs` instructs Qt to use the `eglfs` display
- `QT_QPA_EVDEV_TOUCHSCREEN_PARAMETERS=/dev/input/touchscreen0:rot ate=180` instructs Qt about which device to use as the touch screen, and (optionally) to rotate the input to match the (optionally) rotated screen
- `TSLIB_TSDEVICE=/dev/input/touchscreen0` lets Qt know to use `tslib` for the touchscreen
- `QT_QPA_EGLFS_ROTATION=180` rotates the display by 180 degrees

Now that we have a Virtual Keyboard we can use, we are going to find that there is another requirement that will have us delve into the world of WebSockets in Qt.

Weaving a web of sockets

Never quite happy with what we give them, marketing has decided we need to add yet another feature to the `BigProject`:

- **Requirement 20**: It should be possible to remotely monitor the temperature reading

To implement this requirement, we will use WebSocket. A WebSocket is a bi-directional connection over TCP (the first part of TCP/IP) that is commonly used with web applications. Because we are learning about Qt, we will use Qt's WebSocket support.

Websockets require two halves—a server that provides data and a client that consumes the data. Every time new data is available, the server will send the data down the WebSocket to the client using JSON. The client will then determine how it wants to handle the data.

The more I work with Qt, the more I enjoy it. It feels like the Qt Framework was developed by real engineers who wanted to solve real-world problems as efficiently as possible. The Qt implementation of WebSocket is just one of those things they did well.

When I started looking at adding a WebSocket server to our `BigProject`, I was a bit scared. It seemed like it would be really hard. I expected I would have to do all sorts of low-level socket and network work. Instead, I was pleasantly surprised with just how simple it is. Let me show you.

Implementing the embedded WebSocket server

Like almost everything we do to add to `BigProject`, we will be adding a class to implement, so start by creating a new class based on `QObject`. Call the class `WSReporter`.

Defining the WSReporter class

We will be using the `QWebSocketServer` class to serve multiple `QWebSocket` clients, so let's define those private attributes in our class, along with a port number where we will run our WebSocket server:

```
private:
    QWebSocketServer    *m_WsServer;
    QList<QWebSocket *>  m_clients;
    quint16             m_port;
```

 You may need to add the appropriate headers that are needed to support the Qt classes we are using by using the **Refactor** menu.

Next, we need to define some private slots for handling connections and a public slot for handling temperature updates:

```
public slots:
    void temperatureUpdate(QDateTime timestamp, float temperature);

private slots:
    void onNewConnection();
    void socketDisconnected();
```

The port to run the WebSocket server on needs to be set when the class is constructed, so we must add it to the constructor:

```
public:
    explicit WSReporter(quint16 port, QObject *parent = nullptr);
    virtual ~WSReporter();
```

That takes care of all of the class definitions. Now, it's time to start implementing the class.

Implementing WSReporter

This is where I got really scared—the implementation, but I found out there was nothing to be scared of.

The constructor and destructor

All of the setup for the WebSocket server is done in the constructor. There are only two main steps:

1. Add the code to create QWebsSocketServer to the class constructor for WSReporter:

    ```
    m_WsServer = new QWebSocketServer(
        "BigProjectReporter",
        QWebSocketServer::SslMode::NonSecureMode,
        this);
    ```

2. Connect the newConnection signal to a handler:

    ```
    if (m_WsServer->listen(QHostAddress::Any, port))
    {
        qDebug() << "WSReport Listening on port" << port;
        connect(m_WsServer, &QWebSocketServer::newConnection,
                this, &WSReporter::onNewConnection);
    }
    ```

We need to specifically craft a destructor for this class so that all of the clients are disconnected and cleaned up:

```
WSReporter::~WSReporter()
{
    m_WsServer->close();
    qDeleteAll(m_clients.begin(), m_clients.end());
}
```

Next, we will look at connection handling.

Handling connects and disconnects

We want to be able to handle multiple clients so that when we get a connection request (see the section on the constructor), we add it to our list of connections and set up a Qt connection between the client disconnect and our own disconnect method:

```
void WSReporter::onNewConnection()
{
    QWebSocket *pSocket = m_WsServer->nextPendingConnection();

    qDebug() << "Client connected:" << pSocket->peerName() << pSocket-
        >origin();

    connect(pSocket, &QWebSocket::disconnected,
            this, &WSReporter::socketDisconnected);

    m_clients << pSocket;    // add a client to our list
}
```

Similarly, we need to gracefully handle disconnects and clean up the clients:

```
void WSReporter::socketDisconnected()
{
    qDebug() << "Client disconnected";
    QWebSocket *pClient = qobject_cast<QWebSocket *>(sender());
    if (pClient)
    {
        m_clients.removeAll(pClient);
        pClient->deleteLater();
    }
}
```

That leaves just one more thing to add—the sending of the updated temperature.

Sending the updated temperature

The updated temperature reading will be sent down the WebSocket in JSON format. JSON stands for JavaScript Object Notation. It is easy for web clients to consume, and it is also very easy to work with in Qt without extra classes.

When `temperatureUpdate(..)` is received, the data is put into a `QJsonObject` class by using simple `insert(..)` methods:

```
QJsonObject jObj;
jObj.insert("timestamp", timestamp.toString());
jObj.insert("temperature", temperature);
```

That `QJsonObject` class is then wrapped in a `QJsonDocument` class, and the text version of the JSON is extracted:

```
QJsonDocument jDoc(jObj);
QString jText = jDoc.toJson(QJsonDocument::Indented);
```

Finally, the JSON text is sent to all of the clients that are connected:

```
for (auto client : m_clients)
{
    client->sendTextMessage(jText);
}
```

The last thing we need to do is instantiate `WSReporter` and connect to its `temperatureUpdate(..)` method.

Wiring in WSReporter

In our `BigProject`, `MainWindow` has become the hub around which everything centers, so it seems like the likely place to connect in `WSReporter`:

1. Add a pointer to an instance of `WSReporter` to `MainWindow.h` and call it `m_wsReporter`.

2. In the constructor, create a new instance of `WSReporter` running on port `8091`:

```
// Create a websockect reporter
m_wsReporter = new WSReporter(8091, this);
```

3. Finally, connect the update from the temperature sensor to the `WSReport` instance:

```
// - websocket reporter
connect(m_tempSensor,
    &TemperatureSensorIF::newTemperature,
    m_wsReporter,
    &WSReporter::temperatureUpdate);
```

Everything is now ready, so try building and running the code. Everything should run as normal, but you still need a WebSocket client to read the output from `WSReporter`.

Monitoring the Host

For monitoring, I decided to keep it really simple and create a simple web page. You will find this web page as `monitor.html` in the HTML directory of this chapter's `BigProject` repository. The web page simply creates a WebSocket connection to the WebSocket server at `ws://localhost:8091`, and then displays the output as alerts. If you want to use your Target, you will need to modify line 10 to point to the correct IP address:

```html
<!DOCTYPE HTML>

<html>
    <head>
        <script type = "text/javascript">
            function WebSocketMonitor() {

                if ("WebSocket" in window) {
                    // Create a Web Socket for messages
                    var ws = new WebSocket("ws://localhost:8091");

                    ws.onopen = function() {
                        // Web Socket is connected, send data using send()
                    };

                    ws.onmessage = function (evt) {
                        var received_msg = evt.data;
                        alert(received_msg);
                    };

                    ws.onclose = function() {
                        // websocket is closed.
                        alert("Connection is closed...");
                    };
                }
```

```
        }
    </script>
</head>
<body>
    <div id = "sse">
        <a href = "javascript:WebSocketMonitor()">Start Monitor</a>
    </div>

</body>
</html>
```

Now that we have a web connected application, we really need to have a short talk about cybersecurity and the role IoT play in it. We don't think about our little connected devices needing security; after all, they don't store credit card details, but that's only one consideration. Read on to get my point of view from dealing with it in medical, intrusion, and fire alarm systems.

Considering IoT security

If you follow information security, or just the latest trends in hacking attacks, you will find that IoT devices are one of the most attacked devices. The security implications of many IoT devices are often not considered because they are so simple. After all, what harm could possibly be done if your internet baby monitor can be hacked? Besides the obvious, which is that it allows someone to see what and where things and people are in your house, it may also be used as a source to compromise other systems. In a connected world, something happening in one place may very well affect something else.

One of my favorite movies is the 1999 version of *The Thomas Crown Affair* starring Pierce Bronson. In the movie, a painting is stolen from an art museum. It was done by compromising the heating and cooling system for the museum. The temperature was raised to a point where the infrared cameras were blind the burglary. No one considered that attack vector, so it was easily exploited. Similarly, connected IoT systems that are incorrectly configured could be compromised to give an attacker access to a house or other premises.

Beyond the interdependence of IoT systems where one IoT device can cause an action on another device, you have to consider an IoT device that can be used as a doorway into an otherwise secure system. A misconfigured IoT device might allow an attacker to tunnel through it into an otherwise secure system from an outside location. The simplest case would be a home router that allows someone to create an SSH tunnel through the router from an outside system into the protected network and to any machine the attacker might wish to try to penetrate.

This brings up the two important parts of IoT or any security—authentication and encryption. From there, we will look at another security concern, anti-playback, and consider what these security issues mean to `BigProject`.

Authentication and encryption

Back when the internet was growing very quickly, a bank created a remote access program that allowed bankers to connect from home and make money transactions. The system was designed to use encrypted communications channels so that no one could see the data going back and forth. Unfortunately, the system didn't do a very good job of authentication. Once the connection between the remote banker and the central banking computer had been made, authentication wasn't used. Anyone with access to that remote banker's machine could access the computer. In their simplest forms, we can define authentication and encryption as follows:

- Authentication is knowing who you are dealing with.
- Encryption is communicating in a way that others can intercept, but they cannot read or change the information being communicated.

Both encryption and authentication are needed for secure communications. Furthermore, authentication shouldn't be a one-time thing. It should be continuous.

Anti-playback

A further protection that can be employed is anti-playback. A playback attack is an attack where a message is repeated. Anti-playback says that no message can be repeated. For instance, the message *Move $100 from Account 1 to Account 2* has no protection against playback. If the system does the action whenever it is sent, we could send the message 100 times and move $10,000. It doesn't matter if the message is encrypted or not if the same data in an encrypted form always causes the same action.

A simple solution is to use something like a sequence number: *Sequence 101: Move $100 from Account 1 to Account 2*. Once a sequence number is used, it cannot be used again. This only really helps if the message is encrypted because spotting the sequence number in an unencrypted message is very simple.

Implications on the BigProject

We haven't looked at any of these security issues in our `BigProject`, but when you are designing your IoT device, I strongly suggest that you consider them and perform a threat analysis to see what security hazards there are and the risk (probability and impact) they have. The CyberMatters blog has a good introductory article at `https://cybermatters.info/2013/12/03/threat-analysis/`.

A few years ago, I worked on a threat analysis of a building system. As I did the analysis, I realized that a relatively mundane system could be compromised in such a way to render a secure building open to anyone walking in. It was dismissed by several people. A few months later, a popular TV crime show came up with the exact same scenario I had. If you can think of it, so can someone else.

Summary

In this chapter, we discovered even more requirements for our `BigProject`, and in the course of implementing them, we learned many new things. We started off by learning how Qt can access SQL databases. Then, we looked at how powerful and simple it is to work with state machines in Qt, especially when we can implement them by just drawing them! Next, we looked at adding a Virtual Keyboard to our project. Finally, we learned about Qt's WebSocket support and discussed cybersecurity in IoT devices.

Along the way, we also touched on other small topics, such as using Qt Style Sheets to control the color (styling) of elements in our GUI.

If you take the time to look at the completed solution in the Git repository, you will discover some other little jewels I have hidden in the code, including how to easily output the active states of a state machine, how to grab screenshots and save them to a file, and even how to rotate the UI display on the target. Take a look and see whether you find some others.

In `Chapter 8`, *Qt in the Embedded World*, we will learn more about where IoT came from, the various roles Qt plays in the IoT space, what options Qt has for embedded development, and how Qt is licensed and what that means to you and your products.

Questions

1. Name two different database backends that Qt supports out of the box on most systems.
2. What advantage does `QSqlTableModel` have over `QSqlQuery` when you want to display data in a table?
3. How could we modify the HVAC state machine so that we don't switch from heating to cooling in less than two minutes?
4. If marketing wanted to store the heat/cooling/fan state changes between runs, how could that be done?
5. What would it take to make the heating/cooling/fan states available through the WebSocket?
6. Even though `BigProject` doesn't store any user data, why should I be concerned with IoT cybersecurity?
7. Do you consider the `WSReporter` implementation of the WebSocket server secure? Why or why not?

Further reading

In this chapter, we have looked into many varied technologies. These books should help you to learn more about some of those technologies:

- *Getting Started with HTML5 WebSocket Programming,* by Vangos Pterneas
- *WebSocket Essentials - Building Apps with HTML5 WebSockets,* by Varun Chopra

3
Section 3: Deep Dive into Embedded Qt

In the previous section, we covered a great deal of material, including different GUIs and a slew of Qt features. Now, we will start learning more directly about using Qt in an embedded way. We begin in Chapter 8, *Qt in the Embedded World*, by taking a look at where Qt fits in the embedded market and the different Qt packages that are available to make it even easier to develop your embedded product. In Chapter 9, *Exploring the IoT with Qt*, we will learn about just a few of the IoT features that Qt offers as BigProject becomes a connected project. Chapter 10, *Using More Qt-Related Technologies*, adds more features to BigProject as we learn how about Qt's support for interprocess communication and develop a web-based GUI.

The following chapters will be covered in this section:

- Chapter 8, *Qt in the Embedded World*
- Chapter 9, *Exploring the IoT with Qt*
- Chapter 10, *Using More Qt-Related Technologies*

Qt in the Embedded World

8

Once upon a time, Qt was very simple to understand. There was essentially only one *flavor* of Qt, and your only real choice was whether you open-sourced the code you wrote so you could use the free, GPL version, or whether you wanted to keep the code to yourself and buy a commercial license. As Qt has grown, the choices and options available have also grown.

In this chapter, we will look at the application spaces that Qt is used in, the difference between the (L)GPL and commercial versions, the various flavors of commercial versions, and some of the extra tools that are available with Qt.

The topics covered in this chapter are as follows:

- Microcontrollers to embedded desktop PCs
- Qt licensing
- Qt's options for embedded development

When you are done reading this chapter, you should be able to do the following:

- Understand the types of embedded system Qt runs on
- Make an informed choice about commercial versus open-source Qt products
- Understand what features and tools Qt can provide for the embedded device space

Technical requirements

This chapter is a *reading* chapter. There is no code to develop or test, although you might want to explore Qt's website (`http://qt.io`) to get more information on the topics presented.

Microcontrollers in embedded super PCs

Depending on who you ask, *embedded software* runs on the following:

- A 4-bit microcontroller surrounded by some custom logic and no OS
- An Atom-based PC-104-sized card buried in the bowels of a machine with a real-time OS
- A network of small, custom boards controlling everything in an automobile, including the brakes, engine, transmission, infotainment system, AC and heating, headlights, wipers, radio, and navigation software
- A 64-bit, multicore AMD Ryzen monster with a GPU that makes a hardcore gamer jealous and costs more than the PC motherboard it is running on

Over the course of my career, I have worked on systems at both ends of the spectrum, and at several places in-between. All of these have qualified as an *embedded system* running *embedded software*.

Some embedded systems have no OS, while others may have full blown OSes, such as Windows or Linux.

The only real commonality is that an embedded system is a controlled system designed for a specific purpose. It is not a multi-use machine that can be used for anything from surfing the web to word processing or gaming.

In this section, we will look at where Qt fits into the wide-ranging embedded world and offer some simple advice about hardware selection.

Qt's place in the embedded world

Embedded Qt systems range from low-end, headless (without display or monitor) systems, to automotive dashboards, to patient-side medical devices, and all the way up to multi-board systems with high-power processors and imaging equipment.

Qt is supported on multiple OSes that have found their way into the embedded space. QNX and Linux are the most common ones seen, but Windows 10 is also a strong player in some embedded designs. Since Qt is cross-platform, porting to a new OS is usually a very straightforward thing to do, especially if you have built a layered architecture.

The cross-platform support also extends to interoperability between OSes. Qt has gone to great pains to make data exchange between different OSes as transparent as possible. I have even developed systems using multiple processing boards running different OSes. Qt was run under Linux or Windows on the *Master* board and talked to multiple QNX-based slave boards running their own headless Qt applications.

 We chose to use Qt for the slave boards even though they did not have any display. The other features that Qt gave us were worth it. Transparently handling data formatting and communications between boards played a big part. Using a common framework allowed developers to create common code and easily move between developing for the master and slave boards.

Last word on hardware choices

Early on in a project, it is very easy to get too caught up in choosing the perfect hardware and OS for your system. Cost and time to market are critical, and sometimes you focus too much on H*ow am I going to get it to run on the hardware?* As you will read in the *Qt's embedded* options section, Qt not only provides support for multiple OSes, but also has pre-made **Board Support Packages** (**BSPs**) for common boards and OSes, and solutions aimed at specific markets. The Qt company and other vendors can even do custom Qt development work if needed.

 A BSP is the software required to provide an OS and software drivers that allow software (in this case, Qt) to run on a given computing board.

Qt licensing and features

Qt is available under two different flavors and licenses—commercial and open-source (**General Public License** (**GPL**) and/or **Lesser General Public License** (**LGPL**)). They differ both in terms of features that are included and legal requirements. It is important to understand the differences.

Legally, the open-source version of Qt brings its own set of limitations. While cost is not an object, complying with open-source preconditions, dealing with product liability, intellectual property, warranties, and source code disclosures, may make it very difficult, if not impossible, to use the open-source version in an embedded product. The commercial license does not have as many restrictions.

> If you have a question about what is appropriate for your project, work with your company's legal, risk management, and intellectual property teams.

Beyond the differences in licensing between the versions, features vary between the different revisions of Qt. Qt is continually being developed. Newer versions of Qt often have features that older versions do not.

> Unlike the days when Qt was part of Nokia, the Qt Company's revenue stream is heavily based on the commercial licensing, training, and consultancy it provides for Qt and its advanced features.

In this next section, you will learn about some of the differences between the open-source and commercial versions.

Open-source version

We have been using the open-source version of Qt in this book. While it is technically marketed at *application development*, we have cross-compiled it for use on an embedded system. This is quite a standard way to build open-source projects for embedded systems.

> In Chapter 1, *Setting Up the Environment*, we looked at how to set up and cross-compile Qt for the Raspberry Pi 3+ running a custom Yocto image. The same basic steps can be applied to any OS and board. You just need the cross-compilation tools and must know how to configure Qt.

The open-source version is made up of GPLv3 and LGPLv3 licensed components. Thanks to the licensing, the open-source version is great for learning Qt (just like this book!) and creating open-source projects. It can even be used for research and internal projects that are not meant for distribution.

You can find out more about the requirements of the (L)GPL version from the Qt Company's (L)GPL obligations page at `https://www1.qt.io/qt-licensing-terms/`.

Some companies have specific requirements associated with using open-source software and tools for development. If you are considering using the open-source version of Qt for within a company you work for, you should understand their requirements and limitations.

Commercial version

The commercial version of Qt's most obvious difference is that it comes with a commercial license. There are also some extra features and tools that are available commercially. The commercial version is targeted at software development professionals making end products based around Qt. In particular, the commercial version is very well suited for developing software for closed IoT and embedded systems that are not user-upgradeable or -modifiable.

There are various flavors of the commercial versions of Qt. The application developer version targets globally applications for desktop and mobile use. The Qt for Device Creation version is geared to embedded devices.

Qt's embedded options

In Chapter 1, *Setting Up the Environment*, we went through the process of building the open-source version of Qt for embedded Linux running on the Raspberry Pi. Now, let's take a look at some commercial Qt embedded options in more detail.

Boot to Qt (B2Qt)

Boot to Qt provides you with a ready-made Qt environment that you can deploy to your target immediately without having to build everything yourself. It allows you to get a quick start on your development.

There are different builds available for a selection of common reference boards and software stacks. Boot to Qt even provides a board emulator that runs within VirtualBox so you do not need to wait for a development board. The emulator couples directly with Qt Creator. The following screenshot illustrates running the BigProject version in `Chapter 7`, *Adding More Features*, in a *tablet*-sized emulator:

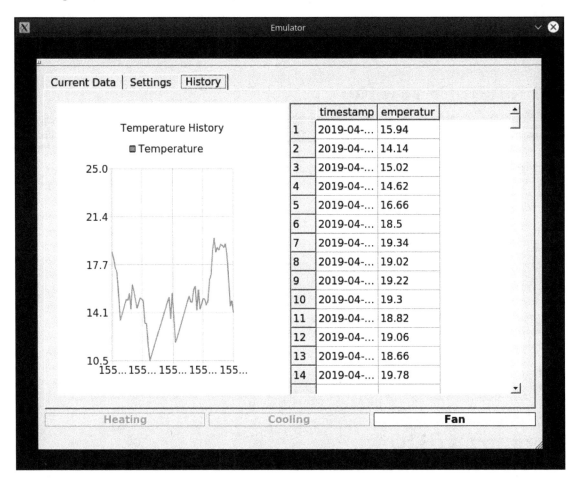

Should you need a customized Boot2qt image, you can either create it yourself, or you can have the Qt Company create it for you. It is one of the services they offer, and a great one if you are not into building custom BSPs.

 For many years, I tried to do everything myself. The embedded landscape of the early 1990s was pretty much the *wild west* of development. If you needed something, you built it. As the industry advanced, I started to realize that it made more sense for me and the companies I worked for to focus on what we did best (for example, fire alarm and security systems, medical devices) and let others provide the pieces they specialized in (OS, GUI framework, database engine).

When developing your product, consider the following points:

- The UI defines the product.
- The **User Experience** (**UX**) defines the success of the product.
- The BSP is the plumbing that makes it happen.

It is recommended that you outsource the plumbing to those who specialize in this and restrict your focus to the UI, the User Experience, and what unique abilities your company brings to the table.

Boot2Qt is one part of Qt for Device Creation, which is explained in more detail in its own subsection.

Qt Configuration Tool

Starting with Qt 5.12, Qt introduced a commercial product called the **Qt Configuration Tool**. This tool simplifies configuring both Qt and Yocto they only build the components you need for your application. For example, if you do not need printer support, you can unselect it and the resultant build will have neither support nor the space requirements for it.

The Qt Configuration Tool is part of Qt for Device Creation, which is explained in its own section.

Once you have installed the Qt source code and created a commercial build of it for your particular target, you can run the **Qt Configuration Tool** to pick and choose what you want.

After launching the tool, you first need to verify that the proper build directory is selected. After that, the tool will automatically load the configuration and present you with a list of categories that you can expand as follows:

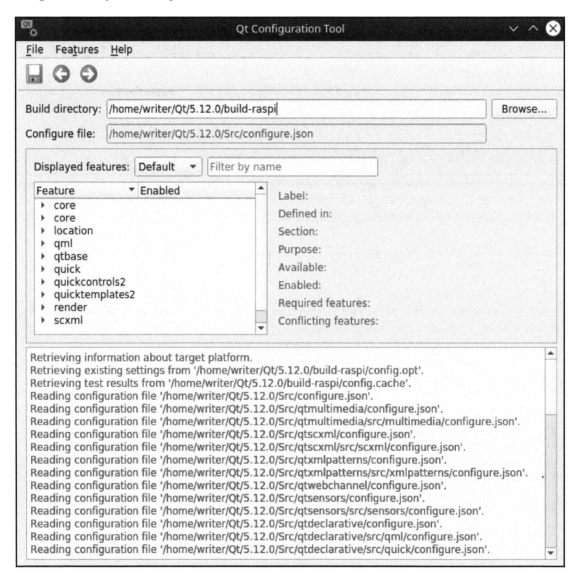

Expanding the categories and clicking on a particular item allows you to enable/disable it from the build (if it is available for your target) and examine a number of details relating to it as follows:

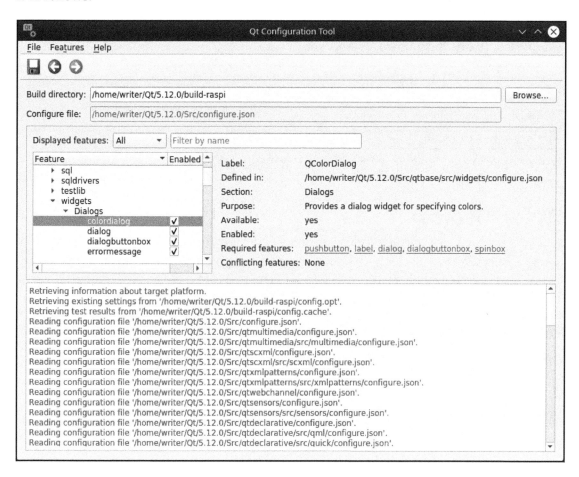

In the previous screenshot, we can see that **colordialog** (**QColorDialog**) is enabled for the build, it **Provides a dialog widget for specifying colors**, and it requires several other features, including **spinbox**, **pushbutton**, and **label**.

You also have the ability to filter for just specific items by using the **Filter by name** field.

Next, let's turn our attention to an important feature of safety-critical systems; making sure that what needs to be displayed to the user is actually shown.

Safety-critical display

Much of the embedded market involves safety-critical systems. In particular, when things go wrong, you need to guarantee that the end user is notified. Qt has developed the **Qt Safe Renderer (QSR)** to meet ISO requirements for safety-critical displays. As of the time of writing, it supports the following standards:

• ISO 26262:2011-6, 2011-8 (ASIL-D)	Vehicle functional safety	Automotive gauges, dashboards, infotainment
• EN 50128:2011 6.7.4 (SIL 4)	Railway software	Electronic systems for railway control and protection
• IEC 61508:2010-3 7.4.4 (SIL 3)	Electrical safety systems	Industrial/manufacturing systems
• IEC 62304:2015 (2006 + A1)	Medical device software	Medical systems

Qt for Medical

When I graduated from college back in 1989, I swore I would never write software for a living. I was trained as an electrical engineer, and I was going to be one—just like my father. That lasted through a job as a sales representative for an electronics company, and even to my first engineering job. There, it soon became obvious that, as good as my electrical engineering skills were and as passionate as I was about not writing software, I was *really* good at writing software, especially for embedded systems.

Over the last couple of decades, I have moved from just control software to safety-critical software—the stuff that can really change (or end) a person's life should something go wrong.

Medical software, which I currently work on, is one of those applications, and government regulatory agencies are very keen on making sure that nothing goes wrong. They do this mainly by requiring hazard analysis, good procedures, testing, and lots of documentation about those areas. (This is where I now spend about 25% of my time—making sure good practices are in place, followed, and well documented.)

This is where Qt for Medical comes in. Qt offers support for the certification processes you will need to go through for medical devices, and even has its own IEC 62304 certifications.

More information on Qt in the medical sector can be found at `https://www.qt.io/qt-in-medical/`.

Qt for Automotive

Qt comes with tools to support automotive system development, from dashboards to infotainment. The open-source version of Qt even comes with an example dashboard as follows:

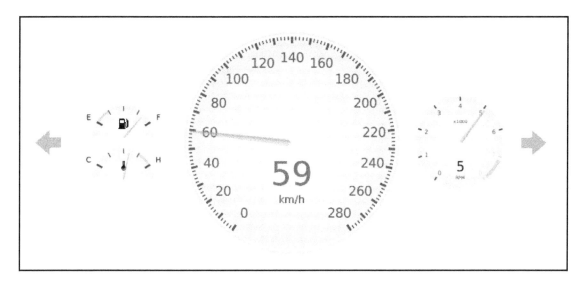

Several automotive companies are already shipping Qt-based solutions in their automobiles, and some have even more interesting ideas planned. More information about Qt for Automotive can be found at https://www.qt.io/qt-in-automotive/.

Qt for Automation

This Qt version includes support for automation. It includes common **machine to machine** (**M2M**) protocols, such as MQTT and KNX. Qt can be used for server, broker, and client sides of the protocols. We will look at Qt's MQTT support in Chapter 9, *Exploring the IoT with Qt*.

Qt has promised to continue to deliver more supported protocols. Even as we finish the final chapter edits, Qt has announced support for yet another IoT protocol, CoAP.

Qt for Device Creation

You have already heard a few things about Qt for Device Creation in this chapter, but I will endeavor to explain a little more about it. After all, it is aimed directly at the embedded development space.

To be totally honest, I didn't really see the need for a specific commercial version of Qt just for embedded work, but then I got a chance to use it. Features such as Boot2Qt, having a virtual embedded machine, and the Qt Configuration Tool, are really nice options to have at your disposal.

More information on Qt for Device Creation can be found at `https://www.qt.io/qt-for-device-creation/`.

Remote objects

An offshoot of the work done in Qt by a major automotive company, **Qt Remote Objects** (**QtRO**), makes it easy to communicate across process and board boundaries. Normally, Qt applications can only communicate using signals and slots within a process. QtRO allows it to work between processes.

Qt UI development tools

As much as I hate to admit it, software developers (like me) are very good at writing software, but very bad at designing UX and UIs. So, most development teams turn to UX designers. The problem is that UX designers are not coders, and going from a pretty design to working code is non-trivial.

Qt has been working hard to solve this problem and now offers tools to make things easier:

- Qt Design Studio is a tool that works by simplifying the process of going from Photoshop drawings to working **user interface** (**UI**) code in QML.
- Qt 3D Studio helps you build 3D user interfaces.

Virtual keyboard

Many embedded systems don't have their own keyboard. Qt provides a virtual keyboard that can be used both in open-source and commercial applications.

The following is how the QWERTY keypad looks as follows:

And the following is how the numeric keypad looks as follows:

The keyboard supports multiple languages and is designed so that other input styles (handwriting, for instance) can be easily added. You can find out more about handwriting support at https://doc.qt.io/qt-5/handwriting.html.

Summary

Choosing the right tool for a job is always important. You have now had a chance to see many of the tools and options available when working with Qt. You understand when and why you might choose a commercial versus an open-source version of Qt. You have also been exposed to some of the advanced tools, technologies, and even certifications Qt can provide.

Using this information, you are now in a good position to determine what options will work best for you own Qt embedded project.

It is important to determine the type of licensing you need for Qt very early in the development of your project. You need to be developing with the license you will ship with. The Qt Company frowns on customers doing all of the development work with the free LGPL version and then, at the very last minute, purchasing a commercial license in the belief that they are complying with the terms.

In Chapter 9, *Exploring the IoT with Qt*, we will be exploring more Qt features that are available under open-source license as we continue to develop our BigProject.

Questions

1. If you have a question about what licensing you need for Qt, who should you consult?
2. Name two OSes found in embedded devices that Qt supports.
3. Can Qt be used to communicate between different OSes?
4. What type of architecture makes porting to a new OS easier?
5. What standard applies to medical devices?
6. What license version is used for the basis of the code we have written in this book?
7. How different is building Qt for QNX from building it for the Raspberry Pi?
8. Is it OK to develop a Qt-based product using the open-source version and then buy a license at the last minute? If so, why?

Exploring the IoT with Qt

9

In this chapter, we will be exploring how **Qt** works with the **Internet of Things** (**IoT**). We will start by to understand what the IoT is comprised of, and then we will look at some examples, using Qt.

The main topics we will cover are the following:

- Examining the IoT and Qt
- Retrieving the weather using a Web API
- Reading the temperature sensor in Qt
- Publishing our status using **Message Queuing Telemetry Transport** (**MQTT**)

As we continue to uncover new requirements for `BigProject`, you will learn the following:

- How IoT came about and what you can use it for
- How Qt can help you with IoT
- How to use Qt to access online data using a web-based API
- How to use the cross-platform Qt Sensor classes to read sensors in Qt
- How to use Qt support for MQTT

Technical requirements

In this chapter, we will be continuing to build `BigProject`, so you will need to refer to your work from `Chapter 7`, *Adding More Features*. You will also need your Target as we will be running code on it.

We also will be using the **Raspberry Pi Sense HAT** as we learn about Qt Sensor support.

Since we will be working with a weather API in this chapter, you will want to obtain a free API ID for `OpenWeatherMap.org`. Follow the instructions at `https://openweathermap.org/appid` to get a free API ID. We will only be using free features.

The source code for `BigProject` and other solutions in this chapter can be found on GitHub at `https://github.com/PacktPublishing/Hands-On-Embedded-Programming-with-Qt/tree/master/Chapter09`.

Examining the IoT and Qt

As we start this chapter, why don't we go back in time and look at how five or six computers talking to one another has now turned into a world where everything is connected? Let's also look at where Qt fits into that world.

The IoT – a brief history

When I graduated from college, shared university computers were networked computers connected together in various ways, and computer addresses always included a path from a well-known machine to the machine you were on. For instance, this was my email signature back in 1988; it contained three different ways to reach me:

```
The Wumpus      UUCP: {cmcl2!decvax}!rochester!ur-tut!aptr
                BITNET: aptrccss@uorvm
                Internet: aptr@tut.cc.rochester.edu
```

UUCP defined one pathway using Unix-to-Unix copy protocols. Each machine was separated by `!`; `cmcl2` and `decvax` were two well-known machines. If you could find a route from your machine to either of these well-known machines, you could make a route to my email.

BITNET was yet another method of specifying an address, and Internet is the address we understand today.

The three different address formats had evolved over a handful of years, but now only the IP (internet) address remains.

Similarly, by the late 1990s and early 2000s, we had devices that were not computers, but rather devices with embedded computers that talked to one another. I personally worked on developing burglar and fire alarm systems that were **internet-enabled**.

Somewhere along the line, in the last decade or so, the idea of *internet-enabled* has been transmogrified into the IoT—a world of devices that all talk over the internet. It's a wonderful and scary world that includes everything from internet-enabled lights and sensors to dedicated control systems for homes and businesses, and web pages serving thermostats. Even `BigProject` is part of the IoT.

So, that begs the question, *Where does Qt fit into all this?*

Where does Qt fit into the IoT?

It does not make sense to use Qt for an IoT-enabled light bulb. The cost and size of the processing power needed to run Qt just wouldn't be worth it. Even a theater-light fixture is probably a poor fit for Qt, for the same reasons.

A room-lighting control system with a touchscreen display starts to make sense though. Even a smart, internet-connected thermostat that takes the weather into account could be a useful application for Qt.

So, Qt works with systems that have a display.

What about systems that control things but do not need to have their own display? Technologies such as **Qt WebGL** allow **Qt Quick** to be streamed to a WebGL-capable browser. This allows the creation of devices (devices without displays) that can be controlled through a Qt Quick GUI displayed in your favorite browser.

It is also possible to use create a GUI-less IoT device that communicates using Qt communication stacks (for example, QWebSockets and `QtMQTT`).

In the next section, we will look at how we can make `BigProject` aware of the weather.

Forecasting the weather using a Web API

Members of the marketing team have come up with another idea. They would like `BigProject` to be able to display the current outside temperature for where we are, so they wrote this:

```
Req. 21: Display the current temperature for a city.
```

This might seem a difficult requirement to fulfill, but Qt comes to the rescue: `QtNetworkAccessManager` makes it incredibly easy to retrieve data from internet sources that support HTTP or HTTPS access, so we will use it.

We will start by finding a weather API we can use, and then we will move on to retrieving weather information using `QtNetworkAccessManager`. Finally, we will test the code and make sure it really does what we want.

Searching for a weather API

The first step is to find a weather API we can access for information. A good source of free information is `openweathermap.org`; it is available at `http://openweathermap.org`. If you have not received your free API ID, now would be a good time to get it.

There are many things that can be done through the API, but we need only focus on fetching the current weather conditions. The particular API calls to do so look like this:

```
http://api.openweathermap.org/data/2.5/weather?q=<location>&appid=<appId>&u
nits=<imperial|metric>
```

Consider the following:

- `<location>` is the name of the location to fetch the weather conditions for (for example, London, UK).
- `<appId>` is the API ID you were given.
- `<imperial/metric>` is your choice of measurement (that is, `imperial`, `metric`, or `kelvin`).

The results are returned as a JSON document, If you want to examine it, you can go to `https://github.com/PacktPublishing/Hands-On-Embedded-Programming-with-Qt/blob/master/Chapter09/SampleWeather.json`.

JSON is something Qt can handle well. We used `QJson` classes when we introduced a web socket to report our temperature readings in `Chapter 7`, *Adding More Features*. In that chapter, that was to create JSON data. This time, we will be using `QJson` to parse the JSON `reply`.

Implementing WeatherFetcher

Like most things we have introduced, we are going to implement `WeatherFetcher` as a new class. Using the techniques you learned in the previous chapters, create a C++ class called `WeatherFetcher` that inherits from `QObject`.

What we need to know

The class should have the following private attributes with getter and setter methods for all but `m_updateTimer`:

```
QTimer *m_updateTimer;    ///< the timer for fetching the weather
int m_updateSecs;         ///< the number of minutes between updates
int m_minUpdateSecs;      ///< minimum time between updates (for
                          /// API)
QDateTime m_lastUpdate;   ///< the date/time of last update
QString m_location;       ///< the location the weather is for
QString m_units;          ///< the temperature units
QString m_key;            ///< the access key for the weather
```

One of the most annoying types of bugs I have had to track down in code is the incorrect or missing initialization of variables or member variables. To prevent that, add member initialization to the `WeatherFetcher` constructor. At the very least, `QObject` (the base class) needs to be initialized to the `parent` parameter, `m_updateSecs` needs to be initialized to 15 minutes (*15 * 60* seconds), and `m_minUpdateSecs` to 60 seconds.

`WeatherFetcher` will need some signals and slots, so add the definitions to the `WeatherFetcher` class definition:

```
signals:
    /// sent when we have updated weather from the API
    void UpdatedWeather(QString forecast, QString conditions,
                        double temperature, double hi,
                        double low);

public slots:
    void start();         ///< (re)start updates
    void start(int secs); ///< start updates after setting update secs
    void stop();          ///< stop getting updates
    bool ForceUpdate();   ///< force an update, ret true if request
                          /// okay
```

Now we need to make sure the `WeatherFetcher` class is constructed correctly.

Constructing WeatherFetcher

In the previous section, we added attribute initializers, but we still have some setup work to do. In the previous chapters, you learned how to do everything that will be needed. Therefore, I will just list most of the setup requirements and let you create the code yourself. You can always check your work by looking at the code for the `WeatherFetcher` class in this chapter's version of `BigProject`:

1. Create a `QTimer` for `m_updateTimer`
2. Make the timer a single-shot timer with an interval of `m_updateSecs`
3. Connect the `timeout` signal to the `doUpdate` slot
4. *Do not* start the timer. This will be done by the `start()` slots

We also need to create a `QNetworkAccessManager` instance so that we can make calls to the Web API. When a `QNetworkRequest` is made through a `QNetworkAccessManager`, the manager's `finished` signal is invoked. In our simple example, we will just connect the `finished` signal to our `handleApiResponse` slot:

```
m_netMan = new QNetworkAccessManager(this);
connect(m_netMan, &QNetworkAccessManager::finished,
        this, &WeatherFetcher::handleApiResponse);
```

With the `finished` constructor, we can start working on the other class methods.

Requesting the current conditions

API requests will be made every `m_updateSecs` seconds, as triggered by `m_updateTimer`; so define a private slot, `doUpdate()`, that takes no arguments.

Access to Network APIs is done asynchronously. A request is sent, and then at some unknown point in the future, a response is received; `doUpdate()` will send the request, and `handleApiResponse(...)` will process the response. Add the following definition as a private slot in the class definition now so we don't have to do it later:

```
void handleApiResponse(QNetworkReply *reply);
```

It is time to start implementing the `doUpdate()` request, so generate the skeleton for the implementation in `WeatherFetcher.cpp` using the *refactor* trick.

We will use `QNetworkRequest(...)` to send the query. In our case, the query is a simple string we build:

```
QString query =
    QStringLiteral("http://api.openweathermap.org/data/2.5/weather?
        q=%1&appid=%2&units=%3")
        .arg(m_location, m_key, m_units);

m_netMan->get(QNetworkRequest(QUrl(query)));
```

Add this definition to `doUpdate()`.

> `QStringLiteral` is an optimizing trick to create a `QString` so that the data is copied into `QString` at compile time instead of at runtime. If we didn't use it, every time we executed `doUpdate()`, we would create a new `QString` and then copy the string into it. This way, that happens before we ever execute the code.

The final things we need to do in `doUpdate()` are to store the last update time and start the timer again:

```
m_lastUpdate = QDateTime::currentDateTime();
m_updateTimer->start(m_updateSecs * 1000);
```

Now that we can send the request, we need to handle the response. Read on to find out how we do that.

Handling the API response

To handle the response, we created the asynchronous response handler slot, `handleApiResponse(QNetworkReply *reply`. Inside that, we need to unpack the response and process it.

For the purpose of `BigProject`, and to keep the book going, we will only code the *golden path*, or the path that the code will follow if everything works correctly.

The response is passed in as a pointer to `QNetworkReply` called `reply`. The response should be JSON, so we will read the whole `reply` and then try to make a JSON document out of it.

We will also use a keyword for which C++11 has changed the meaning. Before C++11, `auto` told the compiler to figure out where to store a variable on its own. Now, `auto` tells the compiler to infer the type of the variable based on what it is set to. The type is not polymorphic like a union; it is a fixed type, and you just let the compiler figure it out. That's a really long explanation to say that we don't want to have to figure out the type ourselves and possibly enter a really long set of characters for it (for example, `QList<QSharedPointer<QImage>>::ForwardIterator`—it's a lot easier to just type `auto`).

Let's start defining the `handleApiResponse(...)` slot:

```
void WeatherFetcher::handleApiResponse(QNetworkReply *reply)
{
    auto data = reply->readAll();
    QJsonDocument    jDoc = QJsonDocument::fromJson(data);
```

Now that the data is in `QJSonDocument`, we need to pull out the parts we need. You may want to refer to the example of the returned JSON that was given at the start of this section as you look at the code to extract it:

1. Find the `main` section in the JSON document, and extract the current temperature, minimum temperature, and maximum temperature:

```
auto            qObj = jDoc.object();
QJsonObject  mainSection = qObj.value("main").toObject();

double temp          = mainSection.value("temp").toDouble();
double lowtemp       = mainSection.value("temp_min").toDouble();
double hightemp      = mainSection.value("temp_max").toDouble();
```

2. Next, gather all of the conditions and form a string:

```
// gather the weather pieces into a string
auto weather   = qObj["weather"].toArray();
QStringList weatherPieces;
for (auto w : weather)
{
    auto element = w.toObject();
    weatherPieces << element["main"].toString();
}
QString weatherDesc = weatherPieces.join(", ");

QString forecast;    // no data, so nothing to set
```

3. Clean up and emit the weather update:

```
reply->deleteLater();

// send out the message
emit UpdatedWeather(forecast, weatherDesc, temp, hightemp,
    lowtemp);
}
```

Did you notice the use of `auto` in the code? What do you think? Does it make the code easier to write? Does it make it easier to understand?

 When I first learned of the `auto` keyword, I dismissed it as too easy to use. *"A real programmer would know what types they were dealing with and not be so lazy as to give the job to the compiler,"* I thought. Then, I used it once, where I had a transient piece of data with a long type name; then I used it again, and yet again in another place. Now, I find it one of the most helpful changes made in C++11. I spend less time worrying about typing the correct type name and more time coding the logic.

There may be times when the user will want to update the weather update. So, we will provide a way to force an update of the weather.

Forcing a weather update

The weather will be updated periodically, but there may be times when we want to update the weather immediately. To allow this, we need one more method—`ForceUpdate()`. We have already added a prototype for it in our class header. Now it's time to add the implementation.

In order to prevent the API server from being overloaded, we want to make sure we don't make requests too quickly. To prevent this, we only allow an update if more than `minUpdateSecs` have passed since the last update. If enough time has passed, we simply call `doUpdate()`.

The code for the method is as follows. Add it to `WeatherFeatcher.cpp`:

```
bool WeatherFetcher::ForceUpdate()
{
    // get the current time
    auto currentSecs = QDateTime::currentSecsSinceEpoch();

    // calculate how long it has been since the last update
    auto timeSince = currentSecs - m_lastUpdate.toSecsSinceEpoch();
```

```
    // figure out if enough time has passed since the last update
    bool requestOk = (timeSince >= minUpdateSecs());
    if (requestOk)
    {
        doUpdate();
    }
    return requestOk;
}
```

Setting the location and weather units

The web API needs to know the location and weather units to use.

For now, we will just use a location string passed in by the user, without doing anything special. This does mean that it is possible that the location name entered will not be valid.

For the weather units, we need to be specific. Unfortunately, C++11 does not offer a *case* statement that works on strings, so we will resort to a series of brute-force `if...then...else if...then...` statements. With only three input values, which will be well-defined by a widget in the **Settings** tab, the code looks quite good:

```
void WeatherFetcher::setUnits(const QString &units)
{
    if (units.contains("Farenheit"))
    {
        m_units = "imperial";
    }
    else if (units.contains("Celcius"))
    {
        m_units = "metric";
    }
    else
    {
        m_units = "xxx";
    }
}
```

Is there an easier way to switch strings?

While it is not possible in C++11 to write a simple `switch` statement that works on `string` values, there are some interesting workarounds that have been proposed, and the capability is under consideration for future C++ versions. If you really have a large number of strings to switch on, lookup-tables and string-tokenizing methods (for example, lex) can be used.

Looking at the code samples so far in the book, you my be wondering "Why do you put the braces on separate lines?"

By now, you have probably noticed that I always use squiggly brackets ({...}) around even single statements in `if` and other clauses, and the braces are by themselves on their own line. Using a set of brackets around even single-line statements in an `if` clause is part of safe programming, and something I instruct all code reviewers to look for and flag for correction if it is not done. Why? Because without the braces, it is too easy to add another indented statement and forget that it will always be executed, not just when the statement above it is. I have actually seen bugs in the field because of this sort of problem. Setting braces off on their own line allows me to easily scan the flow of the code.

Starting and stopping WeatherFetcher

The class header, `WeatherFetcher`, defines two methods for starting the fetching of the weather.

`start()` and `start(int secs)` need to both start the timer and ensure that we make a request immediately. The `doUpdate()` slot will do this for us—it performs the `web` query, and then starts the timer for the next request. The only additional work that `start(int secs)` needs to do is to store `secs` in `m_updateSecs`.

The `stop()` slot simply needs to stop the timer.

With these three things in mind, code up the `start()`, `start(int secs)`, and `stop()` methods. If you want to check your work, look at the finished solution for `BigProject` in the chapter repository.

We have finished creating a class to fetch the current weather for the location, so let's start using it.

Making use of WeatherFetcher

Like most of the other features we have added to `BigProject`, we will patch `WeatherFetcher` into `MainWindow`.

Creating a WeatherFetcher instance

`MainWindow` will need to have a reference to an instance of the `WeatherFetcher` class, and we will need a slot that accepts a weather update from it:

1. Add a reference called `m_weatherFetcher` to the class definition.

2. Create a slot for receiving a weather update called `updatedWeather`. It will be faster to show the definition rather than type out all of the parameters:

```
void updatedWeather(QString forecast, QString conditions,
  double temperature, double hi,
  double low);
```

3. In the class constructor, instantiate `WeatherFetcher` and connect its `UpdatedWeather` signal to the `updatedWeather` slot in `MainWindow`:

```
// Create and start the weather fetcher
m_weatherFetcher = new WeatherFetcher(this);
connect(m_weatherFetcher, &WeatherFetcher::UpdatedWeather,
        this, &MainWindow::updatedWeather);
```

4. Next, we need to set a default value. Use the API ID you received for `<appId>`. You can use any location and units you want (I chose London, UK and Celsius). Set the update interval to 15 minutes and start the update:

```
// ***** PUT YOUR OWN API KEY HERE ***
QString weatherAPI = "<appId>";

ui->locationLineEdit->setText("London, uk");
ui->locationDisplay->setText("London, uk");
ui->unitsComboBox->setCurrentText("Celcius");
m_weatherFetcher->setLocation("London, uk");
m_weatherFetcher->setUnits("Celcius");
m_weatherFetcher->setKey(weatherAPI);

m_weatherFetcher->setUpdateSecs(15 * 60); // 5 minutes
m_weatherFetcher->start();
```

With the weather update coming in, we need to be able to display the data.

Displaying the weather

The current weather will be displayed on the **Current Data** tab of `MainWindow`:

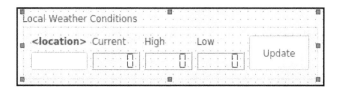

Using what you learned about adding widgets to a UI design, perform the following:

1. Add the previous section to the bottom of the **Current Data** tab of `MainWindow.ui`.

   Here is some information you should know as you add the **Local Weather Conditions** block:

   - The items you see are contained in `QGroupBox` with the name **WeatherGroup**.
   - Items are laid out in a grid.
   - `<location>` is a label named `locationDisplay`.
   - The white box is a read-only `QLineEdit` called **conditions**.
   - `QLCDNumber` items are labeled `currentTemp`, `highTemp`, and `lowTemp`.
   - The **updateWeather** button spans two rows (drag its size handles to expand it).

2. Implement the *clicked* slot from `updateWeather` so that it invokes the `ForceUpdate()` method of `WeatherFetcher`. Since we enforce a minimum delay between updates, we need to check the return value. If it is too soon to make the update, `false` will be returned. In that case, we should notify them with a simple `QMessageBox`:

```
if (!m_weatherFetcher->ForceUpdate())
{
    QMessageBox::information(this, "Weather Update",
                            QString("Please wait %1 seconds
                            between updates.")
                                .arg(m_weatherFetcher-
                                >minUpdateSecs())
                            );
}
```

It's quite probable that you (or the user) will want to know the weather in a location other than London, UK. if the user is in the USA, they will probably want to see the temperature in a unit other than Celsius, so we need to allow them to change that.

Setting the location and temperature inits

WeatherFetcher requires two pieces of information—the location to find the weather for, and the units to use in the weather readings. We will add them to the **Settings** tab:

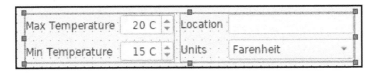

Here are some notes to help you make it compatible with the code:

- **Location** and **Units** are part of a form layout
- The **Line Edit** for **Location** should be labeled locationLineEdit
- The **Units Combo** box should be labeled unitsComboBox
- There should be three selections in the combo box—**Farenheit**, **Celcius**, and **Kelvin**

Right-click and select the **Go to Slot...** method:

1. Implement an editingFinished slot for locationLineEdit. To keep it simple, pass the text() in locationLineEdit to the setLocation(...) method of WeatherFetcher, and also put it in the locationDisplay of MainWindow.

2. Implement a currentIndexChanged(QString) slot for unitsComboBox. As previously, simply pass the new value (passed as arg1) to the setUnits(...) method of WeatherFetcher.

The OpenWeather API provides a couple of different ways to specify the location to use for the weather. We have implemented the simple text search method because it is very simple to use. It is also the most brittle method and can easily result in unexpected results. For instance, the format is <city>, <country>. In the USA, there are several cities that fit Rochester, USA. The one the user wants may not be the one that is retrieved. For a full set of methods to specify the location, refer to https:/ /openweathermap.org/current.

Testing and committing

I have been developing long enough that I take the regular testing and committing of code as a given, but I realize that it may be a new practice for you. So, please do the following:

1. Commit your code.
2. Try running it on the host. Does it work as expected? If it doesn't, try fixing it.
3. When you are happy with how it runs on the host, try it on the target. Does it work as expected? If it doesn't, you know what to do.
4. Commit your code before you start the next section.

 By this point in the book, I have made over 30 commits to 3 branches in my personal `BigProject` library. As soon as I get one section partly working, I commit it. Like I said, it is a habit built from experience, and experience is what you get when things go wrong.

Checking your results

Did the code really work as expected when you first tested it? I doubt it. I left out one small part: updating the display with the new weather conditions.

Were you able to figure out what to do?

Here's how I update the display when the `updateWeather(...)` slot is invoked:

```
void MainWindow::updatedWeather(QString forecast,
                                QString conditions,
                                double temperature,
                                double hi, double low)
{
    Q_UNUSED(forecast);

    ui->conditions->setText(conditions);
    ui->currentTemp->display(temperature);
    ui->highTemp->display(hi);
    ui->lowTemp->display(low);
}
```

Now that we can fetch the current weather, wouldn't it be useful to know the actual temperature and humidity inside? In `Chapter 10`, *Using More Qt-Related Technologies*, we will look at how you can do that with the **Sense HAT** module and QtSensor.

Reading the temperature sensor in Qt

A thermostat is really not a thermostat if it does not know the temperature in the room. Up until now, we have relied on a mock class to provide the temperature, but now it is time to measure the temperature in the room. The Raspberry Pi Sense HAT board has a multitude of sensors, including temperature, pressure, and humidity sensors.

To read the sensors, we will use the QSensor class and a QSensor plugin that reads the sensors on the Sense HAT board.

First, we will need to install the board on our target. Then, we will build the QSensor plugin for the Sense HAT board, along with the required drivers.

Installing the Sense HAT board

Way back in `Chapter 1`, *Setting Up the Environment*, you learned that you would need a Raspberry Pi Sense HAT board, but you were told not to install it yet. The reason I put off installing it until now is that it is slightly more complicated than what we've done before, and I was hoping for a cleaner solution.

The complication comes in that the Sense HAT board connects to the **General Purpose Input/Output** (**GPIO**) connector on the Raspberry Pi, and the LCD touchscreen takes its power from the same GPIO connector. When the Sense HAT board is installed, the power pins from the LCD screen are no longer available.

So, what do you do?

After pondering the problem for a few minutes, I came up with a solution, or, as some would say, a **kludge**.

 The following describes what I did to my Raspberry Pi and Sense HAT board. It is a solution that works, but is by no means optimal. It requires a slight modification of the power wires from the display board. You may choose to make the same modifications, but you assume any risk for doing it incorrectly.

This procedure, which you may perform at your own risk, uses only parts that were provided with the Sense Hat board:

1. Unplug your Raspberry Pi from the network and power, remove any USB devices (such as the miniature keyboard dongle), and remove the Raspberry Pi from the case, if it is in one.
2. Attach two of the provided stand-offs to opposite corners of the bottom (connector side) of the Sense Hat:

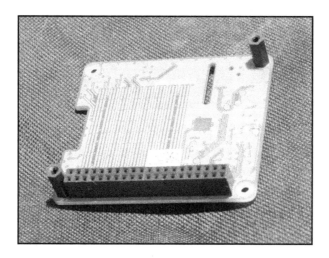

3. Remove the corresponding screws from the Raspberry Pi board. The board will still be connected by two screws, which should be fine for our purposes.
4. Mount the Sense HAT board on top of the Raspberry Pi, making sure the connector is aligned correctly with the GPIO pins:

5. Carefully pry apart the black plastic that covers the pins on the top of the Sense Hat board. This works best if you start from one side and work across. Don't worry if some small metal connectors stay in it:

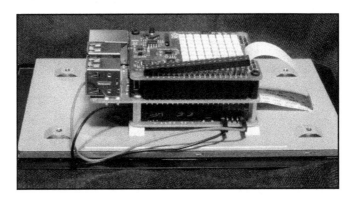

The second and third pins in the row closest to you are the ones we want to use. If there are any metal *caps* still on them, carefully remove them so that they do not get in the way of the connectors:

6. The connectors on the ends of the power wires are designed for longer pins, but we can modify them to fit. Carefully remove the black plastic until the copper can be seen. Then, very carefully, squeeze the connector to make the opening in the copper socket a little smaller so that it fits more tightly on the pins that you exposed (the connector is made for larger pins, hence the adjustments):

5. Carefully pry apart the black plastic that covers the pins on the top of the Sense Hat board. This works best if you start from one side and work across. Don't worry if some small metal connectors stay in it:

The second and third pins in the row closest to you are the ones we want to use. If there are any metal *caps* still on them, carefully remove them so that they do not get in the way of the connectors:

6. The connectors on the ends of the power wires are designed for longer pins, but we can modify them to fit. Carefully remove the black plastic until the copper can be seen. Then, very carefully, squeeze the connector to make the opening in the copper socket a little smaller so that it fits more tightly on the pins that you exposed (the connector is made for larger pins, hence the adjustments):

If you are really daring, it is possible to solder wires on to the main Raspberry Pi board and use them for power, and there are a couple of expansion boards you could add in. Not wanting to purchase yet another piece of hardware, and not wanting you to risk damaging your Raspberry Pi while soldering, I chose not to include them. If you are daring, there is plenty of information you can find online.

With that, I will answer one question you may have about using more than one power supply.

Why didn't you just plug in another USB power supply for the display?

Great question! It has a slightly technical answer.

The USB power supply only guarantees that the + and - have 5 volts between them. There is no guarantee of the relationship between the + and - on two separate supplies. There may be no way the current can flow between them. The signaling between the boards requires that the same + and - are used on all the boards, so we can be sure that the two power supplies will work, or whether something worse (such as shorting the power or providing 10V to a 5V input) might happen. To put it simply—**only use one power supply to supply the target**.

Building the software support

The software is broken up into two parts. The driver level is handled by **RTMULib**, and the Qt is level provided by **QSensor**. In this section, we will build and test RTMULib. Once that is working, we will build a QSensor plugin to interface with the Sense HAT through RTMULib.

RTMULib – the low-level interface

The target image we are using did not come pre-built with the RTMULib needed for the Sense HAT; neither did it come with the ability to simply run an install script. Instead, we will need to do what embedded software developers have been doing for years—we must build it ourselves!

Since we will be building on the host and cross-compiling, we first need to set up the correct build tools. RTMULib is built using **CMake**, so we need to develop a cross-compilation `cmake` file.

Creating a cross-compilation cmake file for the Raspberry Pi

There are a few things CMake needs to know before it can do cross-compilation. These things are stored in a CMake toolchain file. The following file works for our installation of our Raspberry Pi toolchain:

- Create a file called `~/raspi/toolchain-raspi.cmake` and copy the contents into it:

```
# Define our host system
SET(CMAKE_SYSTEM_NAME Linux)
SET(CMAKE_SYSTEM_VERSION 1)

# Define the cross compiler locations
SET(CMAKE_C_COMPILER ~/raspi/tools/arm-bcm2708/gcc-linaro-arm-
linux-gnueabihf-raspbian-x64/bin/arm-linux-gnueabihf-gcc)
SET(CMAKE_CXX_COMPILER ~/raspi/tools/arm-bcm2708/gcc-linaro-arm-
linux-gnueabihf-raspbian-x64/bin/arm-linux-gnueabihf-g++)

# Define the sysroot path for the RaspberryPi distribution in our
tools folder
SET(CMAKE_FIND_ROOT_PATH ~/raspi/sysroot/)

# Use our definitions for compiler tools
SET(CMAKE_FIND_ROOT_PATH_MODE_PROGRAM NEVER)

# Search for libraries and headers in the target directories only
SET(CMAKE_FIND_ROOT_PATH_MODE_LIBRARY ONLY)
SET(CMAKE_FIND_ROOT_PATH_MODE_INCLUDE ONLY)

# Additional compiler directives
add_definitions(-Wall -std=c11 -std=c++11)
```

CMake needs real paths, not ones starting with ~, so replace ~ with the actual path to your home directory.

Now that we have a CMake toolchain file, we can build **RTMULib**!

Building RTMULib

Building RTMULib is a three-step process:

1. Fetch the source code:

   ```
   [On Host]$ cd ~/raspi
   [On Host]$ git clone https://github.com/RPi-Distro/RTIMULib.git
   [On Host]$ cd RTIMULib
   [On Host]$ cd Linux/
   ```

2. Configure the build:

   You have probably noticed by now that Qt Creator builds in a different directory from the source code. Qt calls this a **shadow build**. Building in a different directory from the source is a very good idea, especially if you are re-configuring your build or have multiple build targets. For the `raspi` build of RTMULib, we will be doing the same thing. We start by creating a build directory (`build-raspi`), and then we perform the configuration and build in it:

   ```
   [On Host]$ mkdir build-raspi
   [On Host]$ cd build-raspi

   [On Host]$ cmake -DCMAKE_TOOLCHAIN_FILE=~/raspi/toolchain-
   raspi.cmake .. -DCMAKE_INSTALL_PREFIX=/home/<me>/raspi/sysroot/usr/
   -DBUILD_DEMO=OFF -DBUILD_GL=OFF
   ```

   Did you notice the reference to the CMake toolchain file (see the bold text)?:

   - `..` tells CMake to look for its instructions in the parent directory.
   - `-DCMAKE_INSTALL_PREFIX=/home/<me>/raspi/sysroot/usr/` tells CMake where to install things.
   - The other flags turn off the extra pieces of RTMULib that we won't be using.

   When CMake completes, you should get output that looks similar to the following. In general, you can ignore most warnings, but check that the bold lines look the same:

   ```
   -- The CXX compiler identification is GNU 4.8.3
   -- Check for working CXX compiler: /home/<me>/raspi/tools/arm-
      bcm2708/gcc-linaro-arm-linux-gnueabihf-raspbian-x64/bin/arm-
      linux-gnueabihf-g++

   ....

   -- Using install prefix: /home/<me>/raspi/sysroot/usr/
   ```

```
-- Configuring done
-- Generating done
-- Build files have been written to:
/home/<me>/raspi/RTIMULib/Linux/build-raspi
```

3. Now that CMake has generated what it needs, build and install RTMULib:

```
[On Host]$ make && make install
```

Next, we need to install the drivers on the board, and we should test them to make sure they work.

Installing RTMULib on the target

Now that we have built RTMULib on the host, we need to do some installation and setup with the target:

1. Transfer from the host to the target. The easiest way to do this is to use the `rsync` command, as we did in Chapter 1, *Setting Up the Environment:*

```
[On Host]$ cd ~/raspi/sysroot
[On Host]$ rsync -avz . root@raspberrypi:/
```

2. Next, we need to make sure the proper kernel modules are loaded on boot.

To do this, we will create a file, `/etc/modules`, on the target. Use a `ssh` connection to the target (see Chapter 1, *Setting Up the Environment*, if you've forgotten how) to perform the following:

1. Start `vi` on the target: `vi /etc/modules`.
2. Type `I` (make sure it is a capital *I*) to Insert.
3. Enter the following two lines:
   ```
   i2c-bcm2708
   i2c-dev.
   ```

4. Press *<ESC>:wq<Enter>*.
5. Manually start the required modules so we don't have to reboot and make sure they are installed:

```
[On Target]$ modprobe i2c-bcm2708
[On Target]$ modprobe i2c-dev
[On Target]$ ls /dev/i2c*
/dev/i2c-1
```

The `ls` command should show the italicised line if the modules are started correctly.

Exploring the IoT with Qt

Next, it is time to test RTMULib.

Testing RTMULib on the target

RTMULib comes with a simple Qt program for testing it, so we will use it:

1. Start Qt Creator.
2. Open the `~/raspi/RTIMULib/Linux/RTIMULibDemo/RTIMULibDemo.pro` project.
3. Configure the project for the Raspberry Pi.
4. Build and run it on the target.

If everything is working, you should see a screen full of information. It's a little tight on the 7-inch Raspberry Pi touchscreen, but it should be obvious that things are running as the values change. You might want to try some of the actions to calibrate the accelerometers and the magnetometers.

If you are really daring, `ssh` into the Target, and then try running the program with the following command:

```
[On Target]$ QT_QPA_EGLFS_PHYSICAL_HEIGHT=300
QT_QPA_EGLFS_PHYSICAL_WIDTH=400 /usr/local/bin/RTIMULibDemo
```

It should help you see more of the screen.

More information will be displayed, but it will be really, really small. Changing the values for the height and width will adjust the font size.

 Qt likes to work in point sizes, not pixels. It uses the size of the screen (`QT_QPA_EGLFS_PHYSICAL_HEIGHT/WIDTH`) to do its calculations.

At this point, we have built and tested drivers for the Sense HAT. We may even have calibrated readings. Now we can build the interface from the hardware to Qt, using a **QSensor** plugin.

Building QSensors for the Sense HAT

There are a couple of different packages written in Qt for reading the sensors on the Sense HAT, but the one we are interested in is the one that implements the QSensor interface. The basic QSensor interface is extended by the use of QSensor plugins.

Luckily for us, Lorn Potter wrote one of these and made it available on GitHub at `https://github.com/lpotter/qsensors-Sense HATplugin`.

> If you are like me, you probably fight the do-it-myself syndrome; that is, *"If I can do it myself, I want to do it myself."* This applies to everything from software to simple home repairs. (It is the reason that I still have a leaky faucet, *"Don't call the plumber—I can do it myself!... Sometime!"*) In software, it may mean writing code someone else has already written and tested. **Don't be like me! If someone else wrote something you can use, use it! Don't recreate it!**

The first step is to build the QSensor plugin:

1. Clone the repository:

```
[On Host]$ cd ~/raspi
[On Host]$ git clone https://github.com/lpotter/qsensors-Sense
HATplugin
```

2. Open the `.pro` file in Qt Creator.
3. Configure the build for the Raspberry Pi.
4. Build the project.
5. To install the files, we will need to drop back to the command shell:

```
[On Host]$ cd ~/raspi/build-qsensors-Sense HATplugin-Raspi-Debug
[On Host]$ make install
```

6. Next, we need to fix where the sensors are stored so that they are loaded:

```
[On Host]$ cd ~/raspi/sysroot/usr/plugins
[On Host]$ mv sensors sensors-orig
[On Host]$ ln -s Sense HAT sensors
[On Host]$ rsync -avz . root@raspberrypi:/
```

Wow! That's a lot of little building that probably looked scary as you read through it. It was actually just putting to use a very simple cross-compilation procedure several times:

1. Download
2. Configure/describe the cross-compilation
3. Build
4. Install
5. Test

Oh, *test!* We should test the QSensor plugin!

Testing QSensors for the Sense HAT

Testing is an important part of development, so let's test our QSensor plugin for the Sense HAT. To do this, we are going to use a sample project from the same author as the QSensor plugin, Lorn Potter.

In order to get and build the code, we are going to use a feature of Qt Creator that we have yet to use its ability to create a project from a Git repository, `https://github.com/lpotter/sensors2`:

1. **File | New File or Project...**.
2. Choose **Import Project** from the left-hand projects list.
3. Select **Git Clone** from the middle column.
4. Click **Choose...**.
5. Set the repository field to `https://github.com/lpotter/sensors2`.
6. Click **Recursive**.
7. Click **Next>** to start the repository clone:

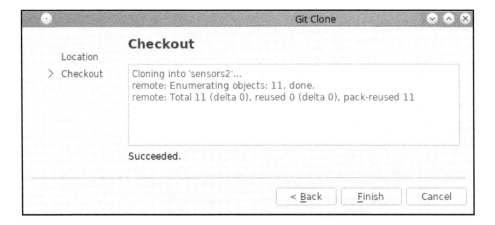

8. Click **Finish**.
9. You will get a message warning about the project configurations. Don't worry; that will be solved in the next step.
10. When the **Configure Project** window opens, select **Raspi**, **Qt 5.12**, and **Configure Project**.

Now that you have configured the project, build and run it on the target:

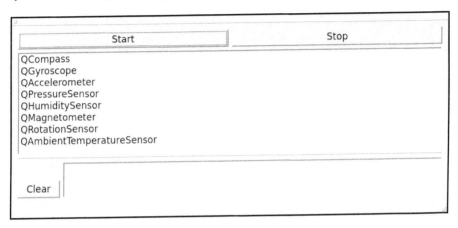

Now that you have it built and running, you can check out the sensors:

1. Select `QAmbientTemperatureSensor`.
2. Click **Start**.
3. The bottom window should fill with temperature readings:

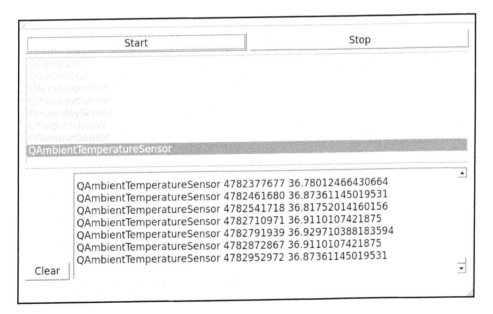

4. Click **Stop**.
5. Select **QHumiditySensor**.
6. Click **Start**.
7. Try breathing on the humidity sensor on the Sense HAT board (it's in the middle of the side away from the LED matrix). If you are in a slightly dry climate, the humidity readings should go up when you breathe on the sensor. When you stop, they should return the following:

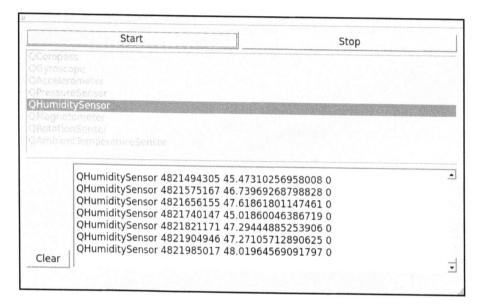

Feel free to try other sensors and see the results you can get and how you get them.

With all of the preliminaries done, we can now read the temperature and display it in our project!

Reading the temperature in BigProject

Now that we have a QSensor plugin for the Sense HAT, we can use it to fetch real temperature readings.

Once again, we start by creating the class for reading the QSensor (`AmbientTempSensor`), and then we wire it into the rest of the code, and finally, we test it on the host.

Creating an ambient temperature sensor class

When we first provided temperature readings for BigProject, we created an interface, TemperatureSensorIF. We then created an instance of the interface called MockTempSensor, which provided mock data. Now we will create a class, AmbientTempSensor, which uses QAmbientTemperatureSensor to retrieve the temperature from the Sense HAT board:

1. In Qt Creator, create a new C++ class called AmbientTempSensor, which inherits from TemperatureSensorIF.

2. In the C++ header file, define the following private member variables. You may need to include some files or insert forward-class declarations:

```
QAmbientTemperatureSensor *m_sensor; ///< The QSensor we will use
bool m_connected; ///< True if we could connect to the sensor
QTimer m_updateTimer; ///< When to update things
```

3. Create a getter method for m_connected. You will also need to define a virtual getter for m_connected in TemperatureSensorIF and implement it in MockTempSensor.

4. Next, define a private slot, which we will use to read the sensor:

```
private slots:
    void readSensor();
```

5. Now modify the constructor so that it takes a QObject * to a parent.

6. Go over to AmbientTempSensor.cpp to start coding the sensor.

7. Modify the skeleton of the constructor to initialize the base class, TemperatureSensorIF, along with m_sensor and m_connected:

```
AmbientTempSensor::AmbientTempSensor(QObject *parent) :
    TemperatureSensorIF(parent),
    m_sensor(nullptr),
    m_connected(false)
```

8. Accessing and starting QAmbientTemperatureSensor is very straightforward, and it takes only three lines of code. Add them to the constructor:

```
// find the sensor and start it
m_sensor = new QAmbientTemperatureSensor(this);
m_connected = m_sensor->connectToBackend();
m_sensor->start();
```

9. Now that we have a sensor, we need to get the readings from it. To keep it similar to our mock implementation, we will read the sensor every second and send an update. To do that, we will use `QTimer` and a slot that reads the sensor. Add the following to the constructor to get it set up:

```
// connect the timer to read the sensor
connect(&m_updateTimer, &QTimer::timeout,
        this, &AmbientTempSensor::readSensor);
m_updateTimer.setInterval(1000);
m_updateTimer.setSingleShot(false);
m_updateTimer.start();
```

10. The final stage of creating `AmbientTempSensor` is to define the slot that reads the sensor and emits the new temperature signal:

```
void AmbientTempSensor::readSensor()
{
  auto reading = m_sensor->reading();
  float temp = reading->temperature();
  auto now = QDateTime::currentDateTime();
  emit newTemperature(now, temp);
}
```

If you guessed that the next step would be wiring our new class into the system, you are correct.

Wiring in the ambient temperature sensor

In order to allow us to test `BigProject` on the host and use the Sense HAT on Raspberry Pi, we need to be slightly creative in how we set up our system in `main.cpp`. First, we try to connect to `QAmbientTemperatureSensor`. If we can connect to it, we use it; if not, we will use the mock temperature sensor:

1. Open `main.cpp`.
2. Change the code that creates `MockTempSensor` to be passed it to the `MainWindow` class to the following code:

```
// create the temperature sensor
TemperatureSensorIF *tempSensor = new AmbientTempSensor();
// -- if we didn't connect to the Sense HAT, create a mock
sensor
if (!tempSensor->connected())
{
    delete tempSensor;
    tempSensor = new MockTempSensor;
```

```
    }
    MainWindow w(tempSensor);
```

The code first creates AmbientTempSensor. If we were not able to connect to the sensor (the backend), we delete the instance of the AmbientTemp Sensor, and then create MockTempSensor. Finally, the remaining temp sensor (either Ambient or Mock) is passed to MainWindow to be used by the rest of the program.

The next step is to test your code.

Testing the temperature reading on the host and the target

Now it is time to test the code:

1. First, commit your code to Git.
2. Next, build the code and try it both on the host and the target.
3. Fix any issues you may find, and when you are happy, commit it to Git. We will be adding to it in the next section.

Since we used the standard QAmbientTemperatureSensor, the code can easily be built for and run on a new board. The only work to do is to create a QSensor plugin for the temperature sensor on the new board and install it.

Publishing our status using MQTT

The following new requirement has come in: **Req 22**: The product must integrate with an IoT protocol such as **MQTT** or **KNX**.

In Chapter 7, *Adding More Features*, we looked at how easily Qt makes working with WebSockets; now we are going to take a look at a couple of more specific IoT protocols—MQTT and KNX. Both of these protocols are supported directly in Qt's commercial product, *Qt for Automation* (see Chapter 8, *Qt in the Embedded World*), and are made available as a source code extension under the (L)GPL license. Since we are using the (L)GPL version of Qt, we will be building them ourselves.

Building IoT extensions

If you can build Qt for the Raspberry Pi, you can build a couple of Qt extensions. In both cases, we will want to build both for the host and the target so you can continue to work with both for development.

The standard build process for a Qt extension is as follows:

1. Fetch the source code
2. Set some environment variables, showing where the Qt version we want to build is (that is, the host or the target)
3. Run qmake from that Qt version
4. Run make
5. Install the built products

That's it! It really is that simple. Now let's look at the specifics for each extension.

Building Qt MQTT

Here are the steps to build the host and the target versions of QtMQTT. The comments explain what is happening in each step:

```
[On Host]$ # fetch the code
[On Host]$ cd ~/raspi
[On Host]$ git clone https://code.qt.io/qt/qtmqtt.git
[On Host]$ cd qtmqtt/

[On Host]$ # create a build directory for the Host
[On Host]$ mkdir build-5.12.0-x64
[On Host]$ cd build-5.12.0-x64/

[On Host]$ # setup the Host build environment
[On Host]$ export QT_INSTALL_DIR=~/Qt/5.12.0
[On Host]$ export QT_MAKE_DIR=$QT_INSTALL_DIR/gcc_64/bin

[On Host]$ # run QMake
[On Host]$ $QT_MAKE_DIR/qmake -r ..

[On Host]$ # build and install
[On Host]$ make -j 4
[On Host]$ make install

[On Host]$ # create a build directory for the Target
[On Host]$ cd ../
```

```
[On Host]$ mkdir build-5.12.0-raspi
[On Host]$ cd build-5.12.0-raspi/

[On Host]$ # setup the Target build environment
[On Host]$ export QT_INSTALL_DIR=~/raspi/qt5pi

[On Host]$ # run QMake, build, and install
[On Host]$ ../../qt5/bin/qmake -r ..
[On Host]$ make -j 4
[On Host]$ make install

[On Host]$ # synchronize changes to target
[On Host]$ cd ~/raspi/sysroot
[On Host]$ rsync -avz . root@raspberrypi:/
```

Building Qt KNX

The build process for Qt KNX is almost identical, except that mqtt is replaced by knx:

```
[On Host]$ # fetch the code
[On Host]$ cd ~/raspi
[On Host]$ git clone https://code.qt.io/qt/qtknx.git
[On Host]$ cd qtknx/
```

Feel free to try downloading and building the code yourself.

Now that you have learned how to build both QtMQTT and Qt KNX, let's make use of one of them. For this book, I have arbitrarily chosen QtMQTT.

Using QtMQTT

Technically, **Message Queueing Telemetry Transport** (**MQTT**) is a lightweight, ISO-standardized, application level, communications protocol designed for devices with limited resources and low-bandwidth connections. Practically, MQTT is a protocol that lives on top of TCP/IP and finds a home in IoT applications.

MQTT uses a publish/subscribe model. Publishers send messages to a broker (server). Clients subscribe to messages. When a publisher sends a message, the broker relays the message to everyone who has a matching subscription.

Each message has a topic that indicates what the message is about, and subscribers can subscribe to topics of interest. Topics may be hierarchical (for example, *light/level* or *light/state*). The publisher and subscriber are responsible for knowing the data format in messages of a given topic. The broker simply passes the message. Messages may be commands or statuses or whatever, as long as the publisher and subscriber agree.

For `BigProject`, we will use a top-level topic of `BigProject-<XXXXX>`, where `<XXXXX>` is a random number generated when the code is run. This was done with the expectation that multiple readers of this book may be using the same MQTT broker at the same time. To make life simple, `BigProject` will only publish `Status` updates (that is, `BigProject-<XXXXX>/Status`) with human-readable data. `BigProject` will not subscribe to anything.

Creating the MqttClient class

The first step will be to add a new `QObject` to our project. This time, the C++ class will be `MqttClient`, and it will inherit from `QObject`:

1. Go ahead and create the skeletons for it using **Add New....**
2. The public signals and slots interface to `MqttClient` will be the following. Add them to the class header:

```
signals:
    /// sent when we are connected to the host
    void HostConnectionUpdate(QString state, const QString &hostname,
                              const quint16 port, const QString& id);

public slots:
    void SendStatus(QString status);    ///< Publish a new status
```

3. We also want to provide a method for consumers of our class to check the connection state. Add this to the class header:

```
QMqttClient::ClientState state() const;
```

4. Internally, we need some private slots and attributes:

```
private slots:
    void messageReceived(const QByteArray &message, const QMqttTopicName &topic);
    void handleStateChange();
    void brokerDisconnected();
```

```
    private:
        QString      m_hostname;      ///< the host to connect to
        quint16      m_port;          ///< the port on the host to
    connect
                                      /// to
        QMqttClient *m_client;        ///< the QMqttClient
        QString      m_deviceName;    ///< A way to uniquely identify us
```

5. Before we move on, we will use the *refactor* trick to create default setters and getters for our private attributes.

When that is done, it will be time to start implementing the remainder of the class methods.

Implementing the MqttClient class

When first learning how to use QtMQTT, I was very afraid of how complex it might be. I was ecstatic to find out how easy it is to work with.

Let's start by implementing our constructor.

Implementing the constructor

The constructor for MqttClient is fairly standard and straightforward:

```
MqttClient::MqttClient(QObject *parent) :
    QObject (parent)
{
    m_client = new QMqttClient(this);

    // Create a Unique Device Name
    m_deviceName = QStringLiteral("%1-%2").arg(qAppName())
                    .arg(QRandomGenerator::system()->generate() %
                    100000);

    // Connect the signals we need to process
    connect(m_client, &QMqttClient::stateChanged,
            this, &MqttClient::handleStateChange);
    connect(m_client, &QMqttClient::disconnected,
            this, &MqttClient::brokerDisconnected);
    connect(m_client, &QMqttClient::messageReceived,
            this, &MqttClient::messageReceived);
```

`BigProject` is becoming an MQTT client. Clients need to talk to brokers. There are a couple of public MQTT brokers that we can use without having to set up our own. They are as follows:

- `broker.hivemq.com`, port 1883
- `test.mosquitto.org`, port 1883

As the author of this book, I have made an arbitrary decision that we will use `broker.hivemq.com` for the purposes of our project. We will hardwire it into the code for now (in Chapter 10, *Using More Qt-Related Technologies*, we learned how to avoid hardwiring and also adding another item to the **Settings** tab):

```
// We need to call these methods so the settings are passed to m_client
setHostname("broker.hivemq.com");
setPort(1883);
}
```

Because the `setHostname(...)` and `setPort(...)` methods pass the information into the `QMqttClient`, we need to use those methods rather than just initializing `m_hostname` and `m_port`.

Implementing our hostname and port setters

The methods to set `m_hostname` and `m_port` need to pass the information on to the `QMqttClient` object, so we need to add that to them:

```
void MqttClient::setHostname(const QString &hostname)
{
    m_hostname = hostname;
    m_client->setHostname(m_hostname);
}

void MqttClient::setPort(quint16 port)
{
    m_port = port;
    m_client->setPort(m_port);
}
```

Once we have methods for setting up the connection, we need to handle the connection to the broker.

Connecting and disconnecting from a broker

Connecting to and disconnecting from an MQTT broker using `QMqttClient` is incredibly easy. You simply call `connectToHost()` or `disconnectFromHost()`, depending on what you are trying to do. Create both the `MqttClient::connectBroker()` and `MqttClient::disconnectBroker()` methods so that they call the appropriate QMqttClient method.

Remember, you can check your code in this chapter's GitHub repository for `BigProject` at `https://github.com/PacktPublishing/Hands-On-Embedded-Programming-with-Qt/tree/master/Chapter09/BigProject`.

Handling connection state changes and incoming messages

In our class constructor, we made the following connections between `QMqttClient` signals and our slots:

```
// Connect the signals we need to process
connect(m_client, &QMqttClient::stateChanged,
        this, &MqttClient::handleStateChange);
connect(m_client, &QMqttClient::disconnected,
        this, &MqttClient::brokerDisconnected);
connect(m_client, &QMqttClient::messageReceived,
        this, &MqttClient::messageReceived);
```

Now we need to actually implement our slots.

When `MqttClient::handleStateChange()` is entered, we are not given what the state change was, but we can get it easily. Unfortunately, the value returned is an enumerated value that does not easily convert to a printable string. Therefore, we need to test the value and set the `stateName` we will emit.

Finally, we emit the `HostConnectionUpdate(...)` signal:

```
void MqttClient::handleStateChange()
{
    auto state = m_client->state();

    // convert enum to text by brute force
    QString stateName;
    if (state == QMqttClient::Connected)
    {
        stateName = "Connected";
```

```
    }
    else if (state == QMqttClient::Connecting)
    {
        stateName = "Connecting";
    }
    else if (state == QMqttClient::Disconnected)
    {
        stateName = "Disconnected";
    }
    // emit the updated state
    emit HostConnectionUpdate(stateName, m_hostname, m_port,
        m_deviceName);
}
```

There are two different ways of telling Qt about enumerated values. One is the old Q_ENUMS macro and the other is the newer Q_ENUM. Although only one letter separates them, Q_ENUM is a bit more powerful. In particular, with Q_ENUM, it is much easier to get the text value (string) that represents the name of the enumeration value; Q_ENUMS has been deprecated, but it was used in the creation of QMqttClient, so we have to do our own comparisons.

For now, we will handle QMqttClient::brokerDisconnected as a specialization of QMqttClient::stateChanged. After all, disconnecting it causes a state change:

```
void MqttClient::brokerDisconnected()
{
    handleStateChange();
}
```

The last slot we need to create is MqttClient::messageReceived(...). We won't use it for anything yet, but it is worth sending what we received out to the debug output:

```
void MqttClient::messageReceived(const QByteArray &message, const
QMqttTopicName &topic)
{
    qDebug() << __FUNCTION__ << topic << ":" << message;
}
```

We still need to implement QMqttClient::ClientState state() const; QMqttClient provides a very simple-to-remember method to return the connection state: state(). You should be able to figure out how to implement our method, so take care of it.

The final implementation piece of MqttClient is the method that publishes our device's status.

Publishing BigProject's status

To keep this example as simple as possible, we will simply publish the status string we have been passed. As with everything else QMqttClient-related, this is a very trivial thing to do, but we only want to do it if we are connected to a broker:

```
void MqttClient::SendStatus(QString status)
{
    if (m_client->state() == QMqttClient::Connected)
    {
        m_client->publish(m_deviceName + "/Status", status.toUtf8());
    }
}
```

With the implementation of MqttClient complete, we'll turn to making use of it. That code goes in MainWindow.

Wiring in and setting up the MqttClient class

Like many of the pieces we have added to BigProject, we first need to modify the MainWindow class header with both a reference to the piece and a slot to receive feedback from it:

1. Add the following private attribute to MainWindow:

```
MqttClient            *m_mqttClient;        ///< the MQTT Client
```

2. Add a public slot to handle connection updates:

```
void    updateMqttConnection(QString state, const QString &hostname,
                              const quint16 port, const QString& id);
```

Now we'll turn to the implementation of MainWindow:

1. In the MainWindow constructor, create a new instance of MqttClient with this as its parent.
2. Connect the HostConnectionUpdate of MqttClient to your updateMqttConnection slot.

3. Implement `updateMqttConnection`:

```
void MainWindow::updateMqttConnection(QString state, const QString
&hostname,
                                       const quint16 port, const
QString &id)
{
    auto statusMsg = QString("%1 %2:%3 (%4)")
            .arg(id)
            .arg(hostname).arg(port)
            .arg(state);
    // show a message box with the information
    QMessageBox::information(this, "MQTT Connection Information",
        statusMsg);
    // Update the bottom statusBar with the status information.
    statusBar()->showMessage(statusMsg);
}
```

4. We will use `updateTempDisplay(...)` to publish our status message. Add the following to that method:

```
// send an udpate
    if (m_mqttClient->state() == QMqttClient::Connected)
    {
        // time: temp activeControlStates
        auto stateString = QString("%1: %2 %3")
                            .arg(timestamp.toString())
                            .arg(temperature)
                            .arg(activeStates.join("|"));
        m_mqttClient->SendStatus(stateString);
    }
```

We are almost there. There is one thing left to do: create a method for connecting to and disconnecting from the MQTT broker.

Starting and stopping the MQTT publication

To start and stop publishing `BigProject/Status`, we will use menu items in `MainWindow`.

Creating menu entries

Creating top-menu items in `QMainWindow` is very easy to do in Qt Creator's design window. Here are the steps to take:

1. In Qt Creator, open `MainWindow.ui`.
2. Click on **Type Here** in the upper-left of the design:

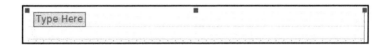

3. Type **My Menu** in the textbox, and hit *Enter*:

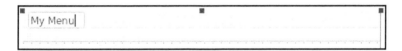

4. Click **My Menu.**
5. Click on **Type Here** under **My Menu**.
6. Enter **Connect to MQTT Broker.**
7. Click on **Type Here** under **My Menu,** and click on **Disconnect from MQTT Broker**:

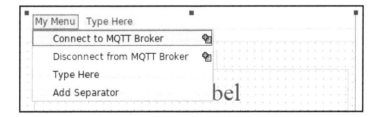

Having created two new menu items, we will not associate actions with them.

Assigning actions to menu items

Every menu item has an action associated with it that is automatically named and created when the menu item is created. They appear at the bottom of the **Design** window:

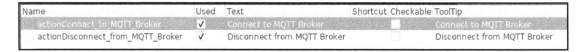

Name	Used	Text	Shortcut	Checkable	ToolTip
actionConnect_to_MQTT_Broker	✓	Connect to MQTT Broker			Connect to MQTT Broker
actionDisconnect_from_MQTT_Broker	✓	Disconnect from MQTT Broker			Disconnect from MQTT Broker

Our job now is to do something with the actions:

1. Right-click on **actionConnect_to_MQTT_Broker**.
2. Select **Go to Slot...** and then select **triggered()**.
3. You should now be in a skeleton method in `MainWindow.cpp`.
4. Complete the code for the method:

```
void MainWindow::on_actionConnect_to_MQTT_Broker_triggered()
{
    m_mqttClient->connectBroker();
}
```

5. Repeat the same steps on `on_actionDisconnect_from_MQTT`, but this time use the code for disconnecting our MQTT client:

```
void MainWindow::on_actionDisconnect_from_MQTT_Broker_triggered()
{
    m_mqttClient->disconnectBroker();
}
```

This is always the scary part for me—testing the code. Are you ready?

Testing the MQTT publication

The simplest way to test that we are publishing correctly is to connect a client to our broker and subscribe to the topics. The `QtMQTT` source code comes with `simpleclient`, which fits the bill well:

1. Navigate to the `examples` directory of the `QtMQTT` source code.
2. Find and open the `simpleclient` example.
3. Build `simpleclient` for the host.

When you are ready to test `BigProject`, do the following:

1. Start `BigProject` (either on the host or the target).
2. Select **My Menu | Connect to MQTT Broker**.
3. Note the broker and the ID (for example, **BigProject-88788**).
4. Open `simpleclient`.
5. In `simpleclient`, do the following:
   1. Connect to the broker shown by `BigProject`.
   2. Subscribe to the `<ID>/Status` topic where `<ID>` is what `BigProject` gave you.

If everything is working, you should see updates in `simpleclient` every time the temperature is updated in `BigProject`:

In the previous screenshot, you can see that we are connected to `broker.hivemq.com`, port `1883`, and that our topics start with **BigProject-48271**. In the following screenshot, you can see the status messages that have been received from our device:

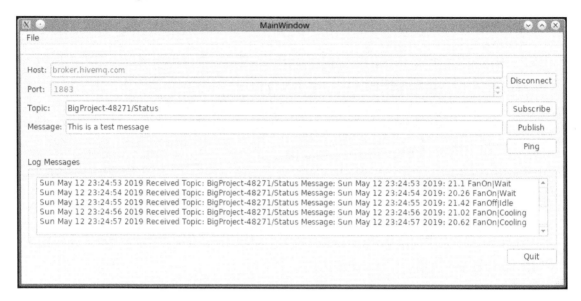

With a temperature one second, `BigProject` generates a fair amount of MQTT traffic. In the real world, we would probably consider not doing an update every second, but in our example, it should be no problem for short runs.

In our testing, we are using a public installation of the **HiveMQ** broker. You may choose to install it on your local Linux, Windows, or macOS X machine, but you will have to change the hostname.

We are almost done with discussing MQTT, but there are still a few final things to say about it. Please read on!

Final words on MQTT

This has only been a very brief introduction to MQTT using `QMqttClient`. Even simple commands such as `publish(...)` have more complex usages that are well worth learning about and considering for your designs.

We also mentioned needing a broker, but we never discussed it in detail. Qt's MQTT support is only client-side, so it made sense not to dive deeper into this in this chapter. Still, you will probably want to learn more about brokers. We used the HiveMQ broker for our testing. You can find out more about HiveMQ's public broker at `https://www.hivemq.com/public-mqtt-broker/`. We also could have used the Eclipse Mosquitto open source MQTT broker. You can learn more about that at `https://mosquitto.org/`.

More details on MQTT can be found at `http://mqtt.org` and the Packt books listed in the *Further Reading* section of this chapter.

Summary

As we have worked through this chapter, we have built out our `BigProject` and learned a few things on the way.

First, we took a quick look at the history of IoT and where Qt fits into that. Then, we started transforming `BigProject` into an IoT device—not a small point device, but an IoT controller. As part of that transformation, we learned how to access web services from within Qt so that we could retrieve weather conditions.

We then learned how to use QSensor to access sensors in our system. In this particular case, it was the temperature sensor on the Sense HAT.

Finally, we took a look at a couple of IoT and automation protocols that are available in Qt and transformed `BigProject` from a simple display-controller to an MQTT client that publishes updates.

In `Chapter 10`, *Using More Qt-Related Technologies*, we will explore a few more Qt-related technologies, including a way to allow the settings of some of the hardcoded values (such as the MQTT broker) without needing to add more to the **Settings** tab. Stay tuned!

Questions

1. Is the IoT a new thing or a new name for something that has been around for almost two decades?
2. Can Qt be used without a GUI?
3. When accessing a web API, is the result returned synchronously or asynchronously?
4. How should asynchronous results be handled?

5. What does `auto` mean in C++11 (and later) versions of C++? Why would you use `auto`?

6. What issues could occur if separate power supplies were to be used for the Raspberry Pi and Touchscreen driver board and panel?

7. Qt is described as cross-platform. How does it handle getting information from sensors on different platforms and operating systems?

8. What IoT protocols have been implemented for Qt?

9. What general steps would you take to add the reporting of humidity and pressure published status from `BigProject`?

10. What would you change in `MainWindow` if you wanted to publish status updates only every 5 minutes instead of every second?

Further reading

As with many topics in this book, we can only touch on a few aspects of several topics in this chapter without creating a volume whose size would rival that of an encyclopedia. Here are some books that should help you learn more about some of the topics we have covered:

- *Hands-On MQTT Programming with Python*, by Gaston C Hillar by Packt Publishing (https://www.packtpub.com/in/application-development/hands-mqtt-programming-python)
- *MQTT Essentials - A Lightweight IoT Protocol*, by Gaston C Hillar by Packt Publishing (https://www.packtpub.com/in/application-development/mqtt-essentials-lightweight-iot-protocol)

10
Using More Qt-Related Technologies

In the previous chapters, we looked at many Qt technologies and solutions. In this chapter, we will continue to develop BigProject and create a couple of other projects along the way. While we do that, you will learn about the following:

- Saving and restoring settings
- Using D-Bus for interprocess communications
- Providing a remote web GUI
- Printing and exporting to PDF

After finishing this chapter, you will have learned about the following:

- How to save and restore settings with QSettings
- How to use D-Bus for interprocess communications
- How to create a WebGL-based GUI that can be used through a web browser
- How to use Qt's printing support to create PDF documents

Technical requirements

In this chapter, we will continue with the development of BigProject. This chapter assumes that you will continue developing in the same code base as you did in previous chapters.

While all of the code that's developed in this chapter may be run on the Host computer, I still strongly suggest that you have your Target so that you can see how the code runs on it.

The code we will develop throughout this chapter is available as complete code in the GitHub repository for this chapter: `https://github.com/PacktPublishing/Hands-On-Embedded-Programming-with-Qt/tree/master/Chapter10`.

Saving settings

Up until now, there have been many hardcoded configuration and user settings. Some of them can be set through the GUI, but others have only been changeable by editing the code and recompiling. Even the ones that can be set through the GUI always start with a hardcoded value and not with the last setting that was made. It's time we changed things so that settings are preserved between runs and so that we can make changes without rebuilding the code.

To do this, we will use the `QSettings` class. `QSettings` provides cross-platform support for saving and restoring program settings.

Searching for settings

Before we can use `QSettings`, it would be useful to figure out what settings we need. The first ones that come to mind are the user accessible settings on the **Settings** tab:

- Maximum temperature for the thermostat
- Minimum temperature for the thermostat
- Location for the weather
- Units for the weather

Digging deeper, we can find some more that are worthy of being adjustable, but aren't presented to the user:

- Seconds between temperature readings
- The weather API key
- Seconds between reading the weather
- The hostname and port for the MQTT broker we connect to

Looking at the list, there are basically three groups of settings:

- Settings related to the thermostat
- Settings related to the weather
- Settings related to the MQTT broker

Since `QSettings` supports hierarchical naming, let's use it to group the settings. The following table shows the setting names we will use, along with what they are for and the default values we had in the code:

Setting name	What it is for	Default value
`thermostat/max`	Maximum temperature for the thermostat	`15`
`thermostat/min`	Minimum temperature for the thermostat	`12`
`thermostat/readingSecs`	Seconds between temperature readings	`30`
`weather/location`	Location for the weather	`London, UK`
`weather/units`	Units for the weather	`Celsius`
`weather/updateSecs`	Seconds between reading the weather	`900`
`weather/apiKey`	The weather API key	`XYZZY`
`mqtt/hostname`	The hostname for the MQTT broker we connect to	`broker.hivemq.com`
`mqtt/port`	The port for the MQTT broker we connect to	`1883`

These values will become important when we start modifying the code so that we can use `QSettings`.

Settings file formats

On Windows machines, `QSettings` typically stores settings in the registry.

On Linux and similar systems, `QSettings` uses a `conf` file to store the settings. The `conf` file is normally stored in `~/.config/<company>/<appname>.conf`. The format of the `conf` file is very similar to that of an INI file from Windows.

The following is the default settings file for `BigProject`. These settings are also in the repository of the `BigProject-default.conf` file:

```
[thermostat]
max=15
min=12
readingSecs=30

[weather]
location="London, UK"
units=Celsius
updateSecs=900
apiKey=XYZZY

[mqtt]
```

```
broker=broker.hivemq.com
port=1883
```

I mentioned that, on Linux and similar machines, the `conf` file is normally stored in `~/.config/<company>/<appname>.conf`. So, where do `<company>` and `<appname>` come from? They come from the values that are given to the `QApplication` object we created in `main.cpp`:

```
QApplication a(argc, argv);

// these identify the application (for QSettings)
a.setOrganizationName("Packt");
a.setApplicationName("BigProject");
```

This means that, for `BigProject`, our configuration file should be in `~/.config/Packt/BigProject`. Since we run as root on the Target, the path on the Target will be `/home/root/.config/Packt/BigProject.conf`.

When you develop your own code, you will probably want to change this to avoid confusion.

> `QApplication`, `QGuiApplication`, and `QCoreApplication` do a lot more than just hold values. Their main purpose is to provide the event loop that powers Qt, but they also provide information about the project (such as application and organization names), along with utilities such as command-line argument parsing. You can find more information in Qt's documentation and the Help System in Qt Creator.

Now that we know what settings we want, we should start using them.

Using QSettings

Using `QSettings` only requires instantiating a `QSettings` object. Once you have a `QSettings` object, there are just a few methods you will need for almost all cases:

- `QSettings::value(<key>)`: This retrieves the value of a setting's `<key>`. If `<key>` is not found, it returns an empty value.
- `QSettings::setValue(<key>, <value>)`: This sets `<key>` to `<value>`.
- `QSettings::sync()`: This synchronizes all settings (saves and reads any changes).

There is also a second form of `QSettings::value(..)`:

- `QSettings::value(<key>, <defaultValue>)`: This retrieves the value of a setting's `<key>`. If `<key>` is not found, it returns `<defaultValue>`.

Early on, we learned the importance of `QVariant` in being a stand-in for any type. Since there may be various types stored by `QSettings`, `QSettings` works with `QVariant`.

To access the settings, start by instantiating a `QSettings` object:

```
// Instantiate a QSettings object to use
QSettings *settings = new QSettings();
```

Once we have the `settings` object, we can retrieve a value by passing its `key` to look up. The value comes back as `QVariant`, so we need to convert it into the type we want:

```
// retrieve a settings value as a QVariant, then convert to an int
QVariant   value = settings->value("key", 0);
int        intVal = value.toInt();
```

Setting a value is the opposite of retrieving it, with one more important step added. We start by creating `QVariant` to hold our value, then we set the value of `key` to `QVariant`. We need to ensure that we don't forget the most important step—syncing the settings. Syncing pushes the data to the appropriate file or registry:

```
// set a value
QVariant   newValue = QVariant("abcdef");
settings->setValue("key", newValue);

// synchronize (save) the settings
settings->sync();
```

Let's consider how `QVariant` is able to store and retrieve so many data types.

Digging deeper into QVariant and meta types

The implementation of `QVariant` shows many basic and Qt-specific types and makes handling them as `QVariant` very easy, but what if you wanted to use your own class?

Qt comes with its own meta type implementation. Meta type information allows Qt to convert classes into `QVariant` and allows you to pass those class values through signals and slots. It take two steps to tell Qt the information it needs for these.

The first step is to tell Qt about the type. You do that with the `Q_DECLARE_METATYPE(..)` macro from the `QMetaType` include file. The macro takes the name of the class you want to declare. It must appear outside the class definition, and the macro tells the toolchain (compilers) about it. I like to put it at the bottom of the header file for the class.

Here are the changes I made to `TemperatureReading` so that it could be used as `QVariant`:

```
#include <QMetaType>

class TemperatureReading
{
    ...
};


Q_DECLARE_METATYPE(TemperatureReading)
```

The second step is to tell the running code about the type by registering it using `qRegisterMetatype<TypeName>()`. `TypeName` is the name of the type. You only need to do it once in the application. For convenience, I like to do it inside the class constructor. That way, I know that, if the class is used, it will be registered.

`TemperatureReading` has two constructors, so I will make sure it is registered in both places:

```
TemperatureReading::TemperatureReading()
    : m_temperatureC(0.0),
      m_timestamp(QDateTime())
{
    qRegisterMetaType<TemperatureReading>();
}

TemperatureReading::TemperatureReading(const QDateTime &timestamp,
    float temperature)
        : m_temperatureC(temperature),
          m_timestamp(timestamp)
{
    qRegisterMetaType<TemperatureReading>();
}
```

Working with `QMetaType` and `QVariant` could take an entire chapter, but I really want you to learn about `QSettings`. I suggest that you refer to the documentation on `QMetaType` and `QVariant` to find out more about their uses. You can read them in Qt Creator or online at `https://doc.qt.io/qt-5/qmetatype.html` and `https://doc.qt.io/qt-5/qvariant.html`.

With the basic background in what we are doing, it is time to start making updates to `BigProject` so that it makes use of `QSettings`.

Changes to MainWindow

As we have developed our `BigProject`, `MainWindow` has become the hub of the project. Since `MainWindow` instantiates most of the classes we want to apply settings to, we will have it access `QSettings`.

In the class definition for `MainWindow`, add a reference (pointer), `m_settings`, to a `QSettings` object as a private attribute. It doesn't need getters or setters. (*Remember*—you can use `Refactor` to make sure `QSettings` is known to the compiler.)

Loading settings

The next major step will be loading and passing out the settings. This needs to be done before we run anything, but after all of the objects we need are created. That suggests it should be done as the last step in the constructor for `MainWindow`:

1. At the end of `MainWindow::MainWindow(..)`, instantiate a reference to a `QSettings` object and assign it to `m_settings`:

   ```
   m_settings = new QSettings();
   ```

2. Using the names and default values from the `Settings Name` table we looked at previously, retrieve the `thermostat` values and distribute them as appropriate. Since `TemperatureSensorIF` doesn't currently have a method to change the time between reads of the temperature sensor, Qt Creator will tell us that the method isn't defined. We will take care of that further down:

   ```
   // - thermostat
      ui->minTemperatureSpinBox->setValue(m_settings-
         >value("thermostat/min", 20).toInt());
      ui->maxTemperatureSpinBox->setValue(m_settings-
         >value("thermostat/max", 15).toInt());
      m_tempSensor->setReadingSecs(m_settings-
         >value("thermostat/readingSecs", 30).toInt());
   ```

3. Repeat the preceding process for the weather fetcher settings. Remember that there are things to update on the **Settings** tab, the **Current Data** tab, and the weather fetcher itself.

4. Repeat it yet again for the MQTT client.

With loading the sensor values done, we need to make sure that, when the user changes something, the values are saved.

Saving settings

The hardest part of saving the settings when the user changes them is to find all of the places we need to update. The good news is that, since we implemented the functionality of the **Settings** tab in `MainWindow.cpp`, all of the locations are in one file!

There are four items we need to look for:

- Changing the minimum temperature
- Changing the maximum temperature
- Changing the location
- Changing the units

The second two are trivial since we already have the perfect places. This is because we already do something when we change values:

1. Update `on_locationLineEdit_editingFinished()` to add saving and syncing `weather/location`:

   ```
   void MainWindow::on_locationLineEdit_editingFinished()
   {
       auto loc = ui->locationLineEdit->text();
       m_weatherFetcher->setLocation(loc);
       m_settings->setValue("weather/location", loc);
       m_settings->sync();
   }
   ```

2. Apply a similar change to `on_unitsComboBox_currentIndexChanged(..)`.

The minimum and maximum temperatures are a bit trickier because changing one can affect the other. The best way to handle this is to create a method, `void saveThermostatSettings()`, that saves both values. The problem we run into is that the value may change many times before the user is done editing it, and we really don't need to be updating the settings until they are done. Therefore, we want to use the `editingFinished()` slot for both maximum and minimum temperatures:

1. Create `saveThermostatSettings()` so that it saves both the minimum and maximum temperature settings.

2. From `MainWindow.ui`, create slots for `editingFinished` for both `maxTemperatureSpinBox` and `minTemperatureSpinBox`. (Remember, you can right-click on **Go to slot...** to do this.)

3. Ensure that the slots invoke `saveThermostatSettings()`.

That concludes the changes to `MainWindow`, but leaves us with having to change a couple of other classes.

Updating TemperatureSensorIF and its children

In order to change the frequency with which the temperature sensor is read, we need to introduce a new method to `TemperatureSensorIF` called `setReadingSecs(..)`. Since it is a base class, we can get away with making as few changes as possible to the children:

1. To the class definition of `TemperatureSensorIF`, add a `protected` attribute, `int m_readingSecs`. We use `protected` so that all of our children can access it.

2. Create getter and setter methods for `m_readingSecs`.

Both `MockTempSensor` and `AmbientTempSensor` need to be adjusted to make use of the new value:

1. In the constructor for `AmbientTempSensor`, do the following:
    1. Locate the call to `setInterval(..)` and change it to `setInterval(m_readingSecs * 1000)`.
    2. Change from a continuous timer to a single shot timer by changing `setSingleShot(false)` to `setSingleShot(true)`.

2. In the code that reads the sensor when the timer expires, `AmbientTempSensor::readSensor()`, add a call to start the timer again, this time passing it the value of `m_readingSecs * 1000`.

3. Apply similar changes to `MockTempSensor`. Remember that we used a lambda method to generate the reading, so you will need to change things there.

These are all of the changes that are needed.

Fire it up and see whether it smokes!

The proof of our work is always in the running and testing.

Commit the code. Then, build, compile, and test the code on the Host.

Be sure to find the `conf` file and verify the contents. Also, try making changes to it and verifying that the new values take effect.

Make any changes you need and, when you are happy, commit the changes and run them on the Target.

I found an issue having to do with how long it took to get the first temperature reading. It was a simple mistake. The temperature sensors send updates based on `QTimer`. `QTimer` is started in the constructor. This implies that the first time a temperature reading is sent, it doesn't happen until the timer expires. There are several ways to solve this. I chose to create a method that forced an immediate update from the sensor by sending it a signal a few milliseconds after the `MainWindow` constructor exited:

```
MainWindow::MainWindow(...)
{
    ...
    // get a temperature reading ASAP after the constructor exits
    QTimer::singleShot(10, [this] () {m_tempSensor->readNow();});

    ...
}
```

The trick to doing so is using a single shot `QTimer` to invoke the `readNow()` method of the temperature sensor.

Feel free to reference the end-of-chapter version of `BigProject` that's stored in the repository at `https://github.com/PacktPublishing/Hands-On-Embedded-Programming-with-Qt/tree/master/Chapter10/BigProject` to see how I solved these problems.

Continuing with QSettings

Unfortunately, we can only explore a little of each topic in this book. `QSettings` is one of those topics you may want to dig deeper into. It is well worth reading the documentation on `QSettings` in Qt Creator's Help System to see all the things that it can do.

Communicating using D-Bus

D-Bus is an interprocess communication system (IPC bus) that allows multiple processes to seamlessly communicate with each other. D-Bus is often used to allow *daemons* (lightweight service providers) and applications wishing to use them to communicate without knowing more than what service they need. In essence, it provides another level of abstraction. A typical setup might be to have a power monitor daemon that can notify when power is failing. Applications and other services that want to do something when power starts failing can find that daemon and use it without knowing how the daemon works. This allows the application to use different hardware as long as a power monitoring daemon is provided for it.

In the typical desktop environment, there are two D-Bus buses defined: the `session` and `system` buses. Since a *bus* is really just an instance of a D-Bus server application, it is possible to spin up more buses as they're needed. For our purposes, we will limit ourselves to using the `system` bus.

Basic D-Bus concepts

Applications that communicate using D-Bus use a *service name* to identify themselves. The service name is typically a dotted hierarchical name starting with the company's domain name in reverse and then the service (for example, `com.packt.bigproject`).

Services provide *objects* on D-Bus. These names are hierarchical and separated by slashes (for example, sensor/temperature).

More details on the full D-Bus specification can be found at `https://www.freedesktop.org/wiki/Software/dbus/`. Qt also has some great documentation that includes an overview of D-Bus. Just search the Qt Creator help section for *Qt D-Bus*.

While it was possible in the past to remotely connect D-Bus buses through TCP, that functionality has been deprecated because of some of the security holes it presented. D-Bus should only be used on single boards.

You are probably wondering: *What does Qt provide in terms of support for D-Bus?* Well, I'm glad you asked, because we will look at that next!

Qt's D-Bus support

Qt has a long history with D-Bus, and it provides both Qt classes and tools for working with D-Bus. Qt's D-Bus supporting classes make interfacing with objects on D-Bus quite easy. The tools make it easy to do everything from monitoring and testing to taking C++ data classes and creating D-Bus interfaces from them.

Read on to learn how this can be done!

Tools

When working with a system, it is always nice to have some tools to make your life as a developer as easy as possible. There are a lot of tools for working with D-Bus included with Qt and in the base support for D-Bus in Linux. We will be using some of them later, but keep them in mind as we add D-Bus support in `BigProject`:

Tool	Source	Purpose
qdbusviewer	Qt	A GUI application that allows the viewing D-Bus services and endpoints
qdbus	Qt	Command-line/text tool for exploring D-Bus
d-feet	Other	A fancy GUI application for working with D-Bus
dbus-monitor	Linux	Command-line/text tool that monitors a bus
qdbuscpp2xml	Qt	Generates an XML representation of a D-Bus interface from a C++ file
qdbusxml2cpp	Qt	Generates a C++ file from an XML representation of a D-Bus interface

Qt classes

It should be of no surprise that Qt's D-Bus support looks very similar to signals and slots. To use it, you need to add the feature to the `QT` line in your `projects` `.pro` file:

```
QT += dbus
```

From here, there are two ways to add D-Bus to your project: the brute-force way and the tool-using way.

Adding D-Bus the brute-force way

The brute-force way is to manually code all of the D-Bus mechanics using Qt's classes. It is really not too hard, but it starts to get painful when you are creating many services.

I have created a simple sample program so that you can see what happens. All of the mechanics of dealing with D-Bus are handled in `MyObject`. Here is what the code is doing:

1. Getting a connection to the `session` bus
2. Creating an interface to the `session` bus
3. Registering as a service with the interface name
4. Seeing who is on the bus
5. Registering to receive a `ping` request
6. Sending a `ping` message
7. Showing the received `ping` message

Everything except the showing of the received ping message is done in a method called `doIt()`. The ping message is handled by `pingReceived(..)`. To keep this chapter from growing too long, I will let you take a look at it in `MyObject.cpp` in the GitHub repository at `https://github.com/PacktPublishing/Hands-On-Embedded-Programming-with-Qt/blob/master/Chapter10/DBusBruteForce/MyObject.cpp`.

 You might be wondering why, in a previous section, I said we would be using the `system` bus, yet this code is using the `session` bus. The reason is that this code will be run on the Target where the `system` bus is rightfully locked down. When we go to the Target, we will open the `system` bus up for our use and use it for our Target applications.

I will let you look up what the different `QDBusMessage`, `QDBusConnection`, and `QDBusInterface` classes and calls do in the Qt help system's very good documentation on using D-Bus.

The complete code for this example is in the `DBusBruteForce` directory of this chapter's repository. You can compile and run this code on the Host. It will not work on the Target.

Let's see what happens when we run `DBusBruteForce` on the Host:

1. Download the code from the repository and open `DBusBruteForce.pro` in Qt Creator.
2. Configure it for the Desktop 5.12.
3. Build and run `DBusBruteForce` on the Host.

When the program runs, you will see that there are a lot of services already on the `session` bus, but if you look for `----- end -----`, you will see that we respond to our ping request.

If you are really brave, you might want to try running dbus-monitor, but be warned: there are a lot of services and applications on your Host that use the session bus, so there may be a lot of extra messages.

That was a fair amount of code to write, so let's learn of a simpler method.

Adding D-Bus the tool-using way

Qt makes it very easy to build complex D-Bus interfaces. Here is an outline of the steps:

1. Write the C++ interface class you want to use with D-Bus.
2. Generate XML from the class definition (the .h file) using qdbuscpp2xml.
3. Make any fixes to the XML.
4. Generate adapter and interface classes from the XML using qdbusxml2cpp.

Rather than going into detail here, we will actually explore these steps in the *Adding D-Bus to our project* section, which can be found later on in this chapter.

Before we do much with it, we need to make sure that our Raspberry Pi Target is ready for us to use D-Bus on it.

Preparing the Target for our D-Bus to enable applications

On the Target, we will be running our application on the system bus. The reason for this is more to do with how sessions are managed than anything else. On the Target, each login (or sshd or program that's started from Qt Creator) is started in its own session. This results in each of them having their own session bus. To deal with this, we will simply use the system bus.

Using the system bus does require us to make a small change to its configuration because it defaults to being locked down. For this book, we will simply allow anything to use the system bus. In real-world code, you should specifically enable users and applications you wrote and/or control, not everything. Let's get started:

1. Make a backup copy of the system bus configuration file:

```
[On Target]$ cp /usr/share/dbus-1/system.conf ~/system.conf.bak
```

2. Edit the `system` bus configuration file:

   [On Target]$ vi /usr/share/dbus-1/system.conf

3. Locate the lines above and below the bold text (in the following block) and insert the bold text between them:

```
<deny send_destination="org.freedesktop.DBus"
send_interface="org.freedesktop.systemd1.Activator"/>
</policy>


<policy context="default">
<!-- Allow everything to be sent -->
<allow send_destination="*" eavesdrop="true"/>
<!-- Allow everything to be received -->
<allow eavesdrop="true"/>
<!-- Allow anyone to own anything -->
<allow own="*"/>
</policy>


<!-- Only systemd, which runs as root, may report activation
failures. -->
```

4. Save the file and exit `vi`.

5. Issue the following command to reload the `system` D-Bus configuration:

   [On Target]$ /etc/init.d/dbus-1 reload

With that set up, we can start adding D-Bus support to our project.

Adding D-Bus to our project

We have been asked to create a lightweight information panel that works with `BigProject` to display the current temperature, HVAC control state, and settings of `BigProject` over a web interface. Before we create that QML application, we need to make some changes to `BigProject`.

The first step is to make sure D-Bus is enabled in the `QMake` `.pro` file of `BigProject`. To do this, add `dbus` to the end of the `QT +=` line in `BigProject.pro`.

By now, that QT line might start looking really long:

```
QT += core gui widgets quick quickwidgets sql scxml websockets
virtualkeyboard sensors mqtt dbus
```

With that done, we will start using D-Bus in `BigProject`.

Writing the C++ interface class you want to use with D-Bus

The first step in using the D-Bus tools is to write the C++ interface class we wish to use:

1. Add a new C++ class to `BigProject`. It should be `QObject` called `ThermostatInfo`.

2. In the header file, provide information about the interface on the line after `Q_OBJECT`:

   ```
   Q_CLASSINFO("D-Bus Interface",
   "com.packt.bigproject.thermostat")These will be used by the tools
   to know what interface to define.
   ```

3. Define the following `Q_PROPERTY` items:

   ```
   Q_PROPERTY(bool fanOn READ fanOn NOTIFY fanOnChanged)
   Q_PROPERTY(bool heatingOn READ heatingOn NOTIFY heatingOnChanged)
   Q_PROPERTY(bool coolingOn READ coolingOn NOTIFY coolingOnChanged)

   Q_PROPERTY(double currentTemp READ currentTemp NOTIFY
   currentTempChanged)
   Q_PROPERTY(double minTemp READ minTemp NOTIFY minTempChanged)
   Q_PROPERTY(double maxTemp READ maxTemp NOTIFY maxTempChanged)
   ```

   These define the values that will be passed, how they are read/written, and what signals are sent when they are modified. We used `double` instead of `float` because the tools recognize `double` natively, and not `float`.

4. Create the signals that are sent:

```
signals:
    void fanOnChanged(bool val);
    void heatingOnChanged(bool val);
    void coolingOnChanged(bool val);
    void currentTempChanged(float val);
    void minTempChanged(float val);
    void maxTempChanged(float val);
```

5. Define private attributes to store the property values:

```
private:
    bool m_fanOn;
    bool m_heatingOn;
    bool m_coolingOn;
    double m_currentTemp;
    double m_minTemp;
    double m_maxTemp;
```

6. Create getters for all of the private attributes.
7. Create public slot setters for m_minTemp and m_maxTemp.
8. Modify the setters for the attributes to emit the appropriate signal when the values are set. The added line is in bold in the following example:

```
void ThermostatInfo::setMinTemp(double minTemp)
{
    m_minTemp = minTemp;
    emit minTempChanged(minTemp);
}
```

This completes the interface definition. Now, we need to generate the XML description of the interface.

Generating XML from the class declaration

The next step is to generate the XML for the interface using qdbuscpp2xml:

1. On the Host, open Command Prompt and navigate to ~/raspi/QtProjects/BigProject (or wherever you have placed the code you are working on).
2. Generate an XML file:

```
[On Host]$ qdbuscpp2xml ThermostatInfo.h -o ThermostatInfo.xml
```

3. Add the new XML file to the project by right-clicking on `BigProject` and selecting **Add Existing Files...**.

4. The output of the XML should look as follows. After examining it, you should see a correlation between the class header and the XML. The properties and signals are clearly identified in the XML:

```xml
<!DOCTYPE node PUBLIC "-//freedesktop//DTD D-BUS Object
Introspection 1.0//EN"
"http://www.freedesktop.org/standards/dbus/1.0/introspect.dtd"><nod
e>
  <interface name="com.packt.bigproject.thermostat">
    <property name="fanOn" type="b" access="read"/>
    <property name="heatingOn" type="b" access="read"/>
    <property name="coolingOn" type="b" access="read"/>
    <property name="currentTemp" type="d" access="read"/>
    <property name="minTemp" type="d" access="read"/>
    <property name="maxTemp" type="d" access="read"/>
    <signal name="fanOnChanged">
      <arg name="val" type="b" direction="out"/>
    </signal>
    <signal name="heatingOnChanged">
      <arg name="val" type="b" direction="out"/>
    </signal>
    <signal name="coolingOnChanged">
      <arg name="val" type="b" direction="out"/>
    </signal>
    <signal name="currentTempChanged">
      <arg name="val" type="d" direction="out"/>
    </signal>
    <signal name="minTempChanged">
      <arg name="val" type="d" direction="out"/>
    </signal>
    <signal name="maxTempChanged">
  <arg name="val" type="d" direction="out"/>
  </signal>
    <method name="setMinTemp">
      <arg name="minTemp" type="d" direction="in"/>
    </method>
    <method name="setMaxTemp">
      <arg name="maxTemp" type="d" direction="in"/>
    </method>
  </interface>
  </node>
```

The next step is to fix the XML if needed.

Making fixes to the XML

qdbuscpp2xml can do a lot of things, but it doesn't know about custom types. If we had used custom data types (for example, ThermometerReading), we would have modified the XML to describe the class using an annotation.

Since we don't use custom types, we will just move to the next step and generate the D-Bus adapter and interface classes.

Generating the Adapter and Interface classes from the XML

Generating the Adapter and Interface classes is done using the other tool, qdbusxml2cpp:

1. Back at Command Prompt, generate an Adapter class using qdbusxml2cpp:

   [On Host]$ qdbusxml2cpp ThermostatInfo.xml -a ThermostatInfoAdapter

2. Now, generate the Interface class:

   [On Host]$ qdbusxml2cpp ThermostatInfo.xml -p ThermostatInfoInterface

3. Add the newly created Adapter and Interface header and implementation files to BigProject and the repository.
4. Look at the added files. Notice that ThermostatAdapter is the class contained in ThermostatInfoAdapter.h.

With all of these things created, we need to actually use them.

Hooking up to D-Bus

Hooking up to D-Bus is fairly simple. We will be using the ThermostatAdaptor class that's defined in ThermostatInfoAdapter.h to do this.

Sending change notifications

We will start by adding code so that we send notifications to the D-Bus when we change things:

1. Add a private `ThermostatAdapter` pointer called `m_thermoAdaptor` to `MainWindow.h`.

2. Before loading the settings in `MainWindow::MainWindow(..)`, instantiate `ThermostatAdapter`:

    ```
    m_thermoAdapter = new ThermostatAdaptor(this);
    ```

3. Now, create the D-Bus connection for it and register `BigProject` as an object and the service we provide:

    ```
    QDBusConnection dbus = QDBusConnection::systemBus();
    dbus.registerObject("/Thermostat", this);
    dbus.registerService("com.packt.bigproject.thermostat");
    ```

4. Next, connect the HVAC states:

    ```
    // connect hvac states
    m_hvacSM.connectToState("Heating", m_thermoAdaptor,
        &ThermostatAdaptor::heatingOnChanged);
    m_hvacSM.connectToState("Cooling", m_thermoAdaptor,
        &ThermostatAdaptor::coolingOnChanged);
    m_hvacSM.connectToState("FanOn",   m_thermoAdaptor,
        &ThermostatAdaptor::fanOnChanged);
    ```

Now that we have wired up the HVAC states, we need to add notifications of changes to the current temperature and minimum/maximum settings. The best places to do this will be in the code that implements them in `MainWindow`:

1. Start with `MainWindow::updateTempDisplay(..)` and send the notification near the end of the method:

    ```
    // notify d-bus adapter
        m_thermoAdaptor->currentTempChanged(temperature);
    ```

2. Since the minimum and maximum temperature settings may change each other, we will place the notification for `min`/`max` settings in the `MainWindow::saveThermostatSettings()` method:

    ```
    // notify dbus changes
        m_thermoAdaptor->minTempChanged(min);
        m_thermoAdaptor->maxTempChanged(max);
    ```

Receiving settings changes

`MainWindow` needs to handle the two D-Bus method calls we handle. Create two public slots that set the appropriate `spinBox` in the GUI:

- `void setMinTemp(double minTemp)`
- `void setMaxTemp(double maxTemp)`

Now that we have made all of the code changes, we really need to build the code, test it, and commit it to the repository.

Testing our D-Bus code

I have gotten into the habit of developing code in small bits and testing it as I go. I would rather catch mistakes early then have to figure them out later. We have done a fair amount of work in adding D-Bus functionality to `BigProject`, and it's time that we test it.

Since the code is now wired to use the `system` bus, we need to test it on the Target:

1. Build and run `BigProject` on the Target.
2. If you have don't have a shell connection open on the Target, start one.
3. Now, issue the following command:

   ```
   [On Target]$ dbus-monitor --system
   ```

4. You should now see output from `BigProject`. Look for our interface name, `com.packt.bigproject.thermostat`.
5. Verify that there are current temperature change messages:

   ```
   signal time=1558578620.486717 sender=org.freedesktop.DBus ->
   destination=:1.1 serial=2 path=/org/freedesktop/DBus;
   interface=org.freedesktop.DBus; member=NameAcquired
     string ":1.1"
   signal time=1558578620.486818 sender=org.freedesktop.DBus ->
   destination=:1.1 serial=4 path=/org/freedesktop/DBus;
   interface=org.freedesktop.DBus; member=NameLost
     string ":1.1"
   signal time=1558578634.156658 sender=:1.0 -> destination=(null
   destination) serial=33 path=/Thermostat;
   interface=com.packt.bigproject.thermostat;
   member=currentTempChanged
     double 36.5184
   ```

6. Now, change the maximum and minimum temperature settings through the GUI on the device and verify that the changes are output on D-Bus:

```
signal time=1558578651.123494 sender=:1.0 -> destination=(null
destination) serial=34 path=/Thermostat;
interface=com.packt.bigproject.thermostat; member=minTempChanged
    double 12
signal time=1558578651.123717 sender=:1.0 -> destination=(null
destination) serial=35 path=/Thermostat;
interface=com.packt.bigproject.thermostat; member=maxTempChanged
    double 17
```

7. Raise and/or lower the minimum and maximum temperature settings until the fan, cooling, or heating lights come on. Verify that messages are shown for these changes. This may take a little time, depending on how often the temperature is read.

8. Test the setting of minimum and maximum temperatures through the bus by using the dbus-send message on the command line. When the commands are issued, the Settings tab of the GUI should change:

```
[On Target]$ dbus-send --system --type=method_call --
dest=com.packt.bigproject.thermostat /Thermostat
com.packt.bigproject.thermostat.setMinTemp double:24.0
[On Target]$ dbus-send --system --type=method_call --
dest=com.packt.bigproject.thermostat /Thermostat
com.packt.bigproject.thermostat.setMaxTemp double:45.0
```

This concludes setting up BigProject to interface to the web-accessible GUI we will be developing.

 Like many of the topics we are touching upon, D-Bus and the tools that work with it are worthy of their own book. The KDE project has a great deal of information on D-Bus. If you are interested in digging deeper, I suggest looking at their tutorials on D-Bus at https://techbase.kde.org/ Development/Tutorials/D-Bus.

Now, we will turn our attention to building a web-accessible GUI.

Remote GUI

We live in an age of web-connected devices, and the marketing department wants to be able to say that `BigProject` can be accessed from the web:

- **Req 24**: The system shall be accessible through a web client.

One of the more interesting features to emerge from Qt in 5.12 is support for remote GUIs using WebGL. Using this, the GUI for an application is accessed through a WebGL-compatible web browser (in other words, Chrome, Edge, or Safari).

QML-based applications can be run through WebGL by simply instructing them to run against the WebGL display platform:

```
[On Target]$ your-qt-application -platform webgl:port=port#
```

Preparing the Target

The distribution of Yocto we are using comes with a firewall already enabled on it. In order to use the WebGL interface, you need to specifically allow our sample application access through the firewall. The other option is to turn it off while testing. The firewall can be stopped and started by using the appropriate command, as shown in the following code:

```
[On Target]$ /etc/init.d/firewall stop      # stop/disable the firewall

[On Target]$ /etc/init.d/firewall start     # start/enable the firewall
```

You may also want to permanently disable the firewall (or any other service) by doing the following:

```
[On Target]$ update-rc.d firewall remove
[On Target]$ rm ./rcS.d/S60firewall
```

A simple GUI

The WebGL interface to Qt must be in written in QML. Since we are interested in WebGL, not QML programming, I have developed a simple interface we can use:

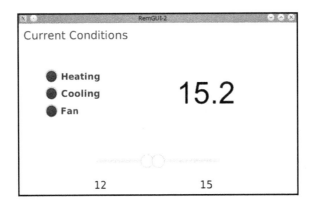

It displays the status of the HVAC system, along with the current temperature. The minimum and maximum temperature settings can be seen and set using the double slider on the bottom.

The code for this project can be found in `RemGUI-2` in this chapter's repository:

1. Download the repository.
2. Build the repository for the Target.
3. Transfer the built code to the Target (remember **Build | Deploy Project** from `Chapter 3`, *Running Your First Application on the Target*):

```
19:46:01: Running steps for project RemGUI-2...
19:46:01: Configuration unchanged, skipping qmake step.
19:46:01: Starting: "/usr/bin/make" -j4
make: Nothing to be done for 'first'.
19:46:01: The process "/usr/bin/make" exited normally.
19:46:01: Connecting to device...
19:46:01: The remote file system has 1133 megabytes of free space,
going ahead.
19:46:01: Deploy step finished.
19:46:01: Trying to kill "/opt/RemGUI-2/bin/RemGUI-2" on remote
device...
19:46:02: Remote application killed.
19:46:02: Deploy step finished.
19:46:02: No deployment action necessary. Skipping.
19:46:02: Deploy step finished.
19:46:02: Elapsed time: 00:01.
```

4. Note where the code was deployed (this is in bold in the preceding *Compile Output* from the Deploy step).

5. Open a Terminal connection (SSH) to the Target.

6. Start `BigProject`, which will be running in the background:

   [On Target]$ /opt/BigProject/bin/BigProject &

7. `BigProject` should now show on the Target display.

8. Run the code so that it starts the WebGL interface on port `8080`:

   [On Target]$ /opt/RemGUI-2/bin/RemGUI-2 –platform webgl:port=8080

9. Open a web browser to and go `http://raspberrypi:8080`. (Depending on the browser chosen and your network setup, you may need to substitute the IP address of your Target or the Target name you used for Raspberry Pi.)

After a few seconds, the GUI should open up in the web browser. It should look like our preceding design, but there is one problem: there is no connection from the web GUI to `BigProject`. We will take care of that now.

Connecting the web GUI to BigProject using D-Bus

To connect the web GUI and `BigProject`, we need some sort of interprocess communications. Interestingly enough, we just learned about something that will do it for us: D-Bus.

D-Bus support is only something that exists in C++, but that is not a problem. Interfacing between C++ and QML is very easy. We start by adding in a D-Bus interface to `BigProject`.

Adding the D-Bus interface code

When we added D-Bus support to `BigProject`, we created two sets of files from the descriptive XML. In `BigProject`, we used the adapter files (`ThermostatInfoAdapter.cpp` and `ThermostatInfoAdapter.h`) so that `BigProject` could be an D-Bus endpoint. In the web GUI we will use the interface files (`ThermostatInfoInterface.cpp` and `ThermostatInfoInterface.h`) instead. To be specific, we will use the exact files we created in `BigProject` so there is not chance of the interface and adapter not matching.

We will add the interface files to the project by using another feature of Qt Creator:

1. Right-click on the **RemGUI-2 project** in the **Projects** list.
2. Select **Add Existing Files...**.
3. Navigate to the source directory for `BigProject`.
4. Select both `ThermostatInfoInterface.cpp` and `ThermostatInfoInterface.h`.
5. Click **Open**.

The files should now show in the **RemGUI-2 project** tree in the directory they are in. Even though the directory looks to be an absolute path, the path is actually stored relatively in `RemGUI-s.pro`. If you like, open that file and take a look.

The next step is wiring in the interface, so follow along.

Wiring in the D-Bus interface

As mentioned previously, the D-Bus interface is a C++ class. The only place we have C++ code in the web GUI is in `main.cpp`. Luckily, we only need to add it to `main.cpp` because `main()` is where we start create our QML environment.

Connecting the D-Bus interface in the C++ program to our QML program is very simple:

1. Instantiate the D-Bus interface.
2. Connect signals and slots between the D-Bus interface and the QML object.

Implementing the changes takes a couple more steps. Here are all of the code changes that need to be made to `main.cpp`:

1. Add `ThermostatInfoInterface.h` as an include file.
2. Change the section of code that creates and starts the QML application so that we can get a pointer to the QML object:

```
QQmlEngine engine;
QQmlComponent component(&engine,
    QUrl(QStringLiteral("qrc:/main.qml")));
auto qmlObj = component.create();

if (!qmlObj) {
    return -1;
}
```

3. After the previous change, we need to connect to the `system` bus, so add the following code:

```
auto bus = QDBusConnection::systemBus();
```

4. Next, we instantiate the interface:

```
ComPacktBigprojectThermostatInterface thermoIF("com.packt.
    bigproject.thermostat", "/Thermostat", bus);
```

5. Finally, we make all of the connections. There are a few of them, one for each data value that we receive and one for each of the settings we send back:

```
    QObject::connect(&thermoIF,
    &ComPacktBigprojectThermostatInterface::coolingOnChanged,
                    [qmlObj] (double value)
{qmlObj->setProperty("coolingOnValue", value);});
    QObject::connect(&thermoIF,
    &ComPacktBigprojectThermostatInterface::currentTempChanged,
                    [qmlObj] (double value)
{qmlObj->setProperty("currentTempValue", value);});
    QObject::connect(&thermoIF,
    &ComPacktBigprojectThermostatInterface::fanOnChanged,
                                    [qmlObj] (bool value)
{qmlObj->setProperty("fanOnValue", value);});
    QObject::connect(&thermoIF,
    &ComPacktBigprojectThermostatInterface::heatingOnChanged,
                    [qmlObj] (bool value)
{qmlObj->setProperty("heatingValue", value);});
    QObject::connect(&thermoIF,
    &ComPacktBigprojectThermostatInterface::maxTempChanged,
                    [qmlObj] (double value)
{qmlObj->setProperty("maxSettingValue", value);});
    QObject::connect(&thermoIF,
    &ComPacktBigprojectThermostatInterface::minTempChanged,
                    [qmlObj] (double value)
{qmlObj->setProperty("minSettingValue", value);});

    QObject::connect(qmlObj, SIGNAL(minSettingSignal(double)),
                    &thermoIF, SLOT(setMinTemp(double)));
    QObject::connect(qmlObj, SIGNAL(maxSettingSignal(double)),
                    &thermoIF, SLOT(setMaxTemp(double)));
```

Let's take a moment and explain a couple of pieces of the code you just entered by breaking down the first line you entered:

- `QObject::connect(&thermoIF,`: Connect to a signal from `thermoIF`.
- `&ComPacktBigprojectThermostatInterface::coolingOnChanged,`: The signal is `CoolingOnChanged`.
- `[qmlObj] (double value) {qmlObj->setProperty("coolingOnValue", value);});`: Connect to a lambda function that uses `qmlObj`, takes a double called `value`, and sets `coolingOnValue` of our QML object, `qmlObj`, to the passed value.

This pattern is repeated for all of the value changes coming from the interface. In the reverse direction, we connect from `maxSettingsSignal` coming from `qmlObj` to the interface's `setMaxTemp` method.

That concludes the changes to the C++ code. Now, let's move onto the changes in the QML code.

QML code changes

The QML code needs to be changed to set up the signals and properties that are exposed by the QML code:

1. Add the following code to the top of the `Window` declaration in `main.qml`. This code declares the signals that the QML object will send:

```
signal minSettingSignal(double value)
signal maxSettingSignal(double value)
```

2. Now, add declarations of the properties we are going to set:

```
property double currentTempValue
property double maxSettingValue
property double minSettingValue

property bool fanOnValue
property bool coolingOnValue
property bool heatingOnValue
```

3. We are almost done with the additions. The next step is to create methods to handle the changes to the properties. The naming of these is dictated for us. For a property named `property`, the method that is invoked is named `onPropertyChanged`:

```
onCurrentTempValueChanged: {currentTemp.text = currentTempValue}
onMaxSettingValueChanged: {rangeSetter.second.value =
    maxSettingValue}
onMinSettingValueChanged: {rangeSetter.first.value =
    minSettingValue}

onFanOnValueChanged: {fanInd.active = fanOnValue}
onCoolingOnValueChanged: {coolingInd.active = coolingOnValue}
onHeatingOnValueChanged: {headingInd.active = heatingOnValue}
```

4. The final step is to generate the signals when the temperature minimum and maximum are changed. In the `RangeSlider` declaration, add the following bolded lines to first and second `onValueChanged` methods:

```
first.onValueChanged: {
minSetting.text = first.value;
mainWindow.minSettingSignal(first.value);
}

second.onValueChanged: {
maxSetting.text = second.value;
mainWindow.maxSettingSignal(second.value);
}
```

That concludes the changes to the QML file. Although there were several of them, they were straightforward in nature.

It is time to try the code out again, but this time we need both `BigProject` and RemGUI-2 running. This time, we will use two SSH connections to the Target:

1. Build RemGUI-2 and deploy it to the Target like we did previously.
2. On the first SSH connection, run `/opt/BigProject/bin/BigProject` to start `BigProject` running.
3. On the second SSH connection, run `/opt/RemGUI-2/bin/RemGUI-2 -platform webgl:port=8080` to start RemGUI-2 running.
4. On the Host, open a web browser to port `8080` of your Target.

As the program is run, you should see both the web and Target displays change as the temperature sensor is warmed or cooled. You may have to blow air on the Sense HAT board to make it cool.

Now that you know how to create a web-enabled GUI, it's a good time to look at one more feature that Qt provides: printing support and PDF file generation.

Printing (PDF)

Would you believe that we have new requirements? They are as follows:

- **Req 25**: `BigProject` shall be able to generate a report of temperature readings for the last 24 hours.
- **Req 26**: The report shall be output in PDF format.

Qt to the rescue!

Qt provides printing capabilities, including the ability to output to a PDF file! We will make use of it here.

The basics

While some Qt GUI objects have special *print* methods that can be invoked to print on `QPrinter`, many don't. This is because of how Qt chose to support printing.

At the base level, Qt *paints* GUI objects onto *paint devices*. When a widget is drawn on the screen, Qt is *painting* it onto the screen. Printing works essentially the same way. Objects are painted (or rendered) on a special paint device, `QPrinter`.

The final piece of the puzzle is that writing a PDF file is part of the built-in operation of Qt's printer support.

Why don't we take a look how this works by adding printing to our `BigProject`.

Adding printing to BigProject

The first step to using Qt's printer support is to let QMake know about it—add `printsupport` to the end of the `QT +=` line in `BigProject.pro`.

To fulfill the printing requirements, we are going to print the History tab from the GUI. As you may remember, the information on the History tab is generated by TemperatureHistoryForm. With this in mind, we will create a DoPrint(..) method in MainWindow:

```
void MainWindow::DoPrint(QPrinter *ap_printer)
{
    ui->historyForm->render(ap_printer);
}
```

Now that the mechanics of printing are done, we only have to provide a method for the user to start printing. Qt provides two different print dialogs. QPrintDialog simply lets you adjust print parameters and then start the printing. I prefer to use QPrintPreviewDialog so that I can see what I am going to print before I print it:

1. Create a new menu option, Export History to PDF, in **My Menu**.
2. Go to the triggered slot for the menu item.
3. In the method, instantiate QPrinter and QPrintPreviewDialog:

   ```
   void MainWindow::on_actionExport_History_to_PDF_triggered()
   {
    QPrinter printer;
    QPrintPreviewDialog preview(&printer);

    preview.connect(&preview, SIGNAL(paintRequested(QPrinter*)),
    this, SLOT(DoPrint(QPrinter*)));
    preview.exec();
   }
   ```

It really is that simple.

Commit your changes to the repository, and then build and run the code on the Target.

Try invoking our new printing option. The print preview dialog doesn't display as well as it could, but you can see enough to navigate it. In the top-right of the dialog, you will see **>>**. Clicking on this will expand the toolbar. Clicking on the newly shown printer icon will bring up the print dialog.

Unfortunately, you will have to use your keyboard to enter the file to save the PDF into.

Once you have clicked on **Print**, the PDF file is generated on the Target. For now, you will need to copy the PDF file off of the device manually, but it is worth doing it using SCP or SFTP and then viewing the output.

With some work, we could improve the **User Experience** (**UX**), but for now, I will leave that for you to do, should you choose to.

Summary

Working through this chapter, you now have hands-on experience with using `QSettings` to save and restore program settings, working with D-Bus to provide interprocess communications, quickly implementing a web-based UI to our `BigProject`, and even creating PDF reports from `BigProject`.

In `Chapter 11`, *Debugging, Logging, and Monitoring Qt Applications*, we will learn more about the debugging, monitoring, and testing of Qt applications. It's going to be fun!

Questions

1. What is the first step in using almost every Qt feature we have worked with?
2. From what you learned in this chapter, why is `QVariant` one of the base Qt concepts?
3. What does IPC stand for?
4. How do you specify that you want to start a Qt application so that its GUI is available to a web browser?
5. What type of Qt GUI can be displayed through a web browser?
6. Why is outputting to PDF so easy in Qt?
7. How do you tell the Qt tools that you want to use printing in your application?

Further reading

While we have briefly touched on many topics, it is good to know that there are other resources out there to help you to learn more about some of the specifics:

- *Qt5 C++ GUI Programming Cookbook* by Lee Zhi Eng
- *Application Development with Qt Creator - Second Edition* by Ray Rischpater

Section 4: Advanced Techniques and Best Practices

So far, we have set up our development environment and target device, learned how to use Qt Creator, looked at modern software development, and learned many things about Qt while transforming our BigProject from a simple digital clock into a connected thermostat. In this section, we will look at a number of more advanced Qt topics.

We begin in Chapter 11, *Debugging, Logging, and Monitoring Qt Applications*, by looking at ways to debug, log, and otherwise monitor Qt applications. In Chapter 12, *Responsive Application Programming – Threads*, we talk about the different ways Qt supports threads and how they can be used to generate more responsive programs. In Chapter 13, *Qt Best Practices*, our concluding chapter, we look at a number of best practices for Qt development that will help you in your projects.

The following chapters will be covered in this section:

- Chapter 11, *Debugging, Logging, and Monitoring Qt Applications*
- Chapter 12, *Responsive Application Programming – Threads*
- Chapter 13, *Qt Best Practices*

11
Debugging, Logging, and Monitoring Qt Applications

Probably the most important part of developing software is the one most people think the least about—ensuring that the software performs as expected. In medical and safety-critical applications, we refer to this as **verification** and **validation**. Verification confirms that the written requirements are met. Validation confirms that the system meets the users' needs.

Although it sounds complex, it really breaks down to testing, monitoring, and debugging. In this chapter, we will take a look at ways this can be done in embedded Qt applications as we work through the following topics:

- Testing Qt applications
- Debugging Qt applications
- Monitoring Qt applications

When you are finished with this chapter, you should be able to do the following:

- Use either Google Test or Qt Test to test your application
- Use the code inspection tools that come with Qt to look for silly programmer mistakes (SPMs)
- Monitor the functionality of a Qt application
- Debug issues found in a Qt application

Technical requirements

All of the work in this chapter is Host-based and can be done without a Target.

While we will not be adding code to `BigProject`, we will be testing, debugging, and monitoring it. Therefore, you will need your copy of `BigProject`.

While not required, you may want to install Google Test from `https://github.com/google/googletest/tree/master/googletest` so that you can try the Google Test example in the repository.

The source code for this chapter can be found in this book's GitHub repository at `https://github.com/PacktPublishing/Hands-On-Embedded-Programming-with-Qt/tree/master/Chapter11`.

Testing Qt applications

There are two basic ways of verifying that code is functioning:

- Inspection: Looking at the code to find errors
- Testing: Running the code with multiple inputs and verifying the correct functionality

In this chapter, we will learn about both the strategies and the tools Qt brings to the table to help with them. We will also talk a little about the importance of code coverage for any verification or testing effort.

 Some may break this into two parts for each category I listed—*Inspection and Analysis* and *Testing and Demonstration*. Personally, I feel that just confuses things. You can either inspect the code, including analyzing the logic/calculations, or you can test the code, which is really just a demonstration that it works.

We will start with code analysis because Qt makes it so easy to do some of the work.

Code analysis

As I was writing this book, I have submitted sentences that looked perfectly fine when I wrote them, but made no sense when someone else (usually my editor) read them. There is something about reading what you wrote yourself that lets you miss obvious mistakes. You know what you meant to say and don't catch the mistakes.

The same applies to writing code. Complete nonsense is caught by the compiler, but things that are syntactically correct are not; for example, *The ball dug a refrigerator* is syntactically correct (subject, verb, object), yet it still makes no sense.

In this section, we will look at code inspection tools that help find these sensical mistakes, along with SPMs, which are the common things programmers do that they should catch themselves, but don't. In C++, a typical SPM is using $a = b$ to check for equivalence, instead of $a == b$.

Clang analysis

Qt Creator comes with several Clang-derived static analysis tools. The advantage of these tools is that they are actually run while you are editing your code. Instead of waiting to complete your code, you can see the necessary corrections as you type.

The disadvantage is that because they are run while you are typing, they may be a couple of lines behind, flag things you are yet to get to, or they just slow down the system a little.

You can choose the tool(s) and strength from the **Analyzer** section of the **Options** menu:

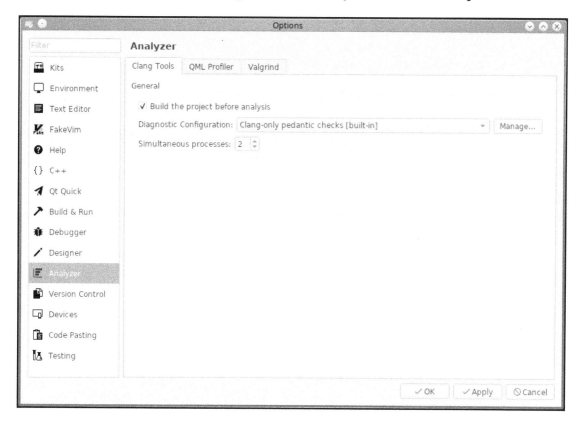

The pull-down menu allows you to choose one of several different analysis tools and levels:

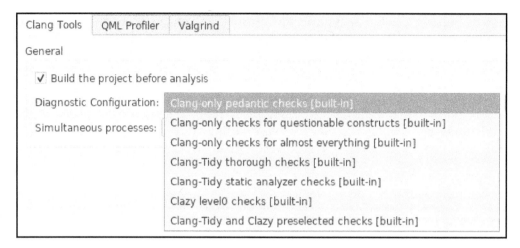

The list of options looks daunting, so let me provide some explanations:

- **Clang-only** is the Clang Static Analyzer. It is good at picking up syntax errors and some SPMs.
- **Clang-Tidy** is designed to help you use modern (C++11) coding techniques. It will also catch easy code optimizations. One of the ones I trigger the most is passing by value when a const reference would be better (as it saves memory and processing power).
- **Clazy** is a Qt-specific plugin. It understands Qt semantics and can make recommendations on how to improve your Qt code.

The feedback is shown as warnings in your code.

Manually running Clang analysis

The **Analyze** menu allows you to manually run several different analysis. The C++ analysis option you chose in the **Options** menu is the top selection:

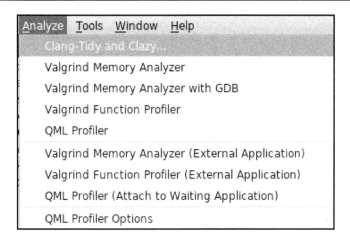

As you can see in the following screenshot, I like **Clang-Tidy and Clazy** at the same time. For me, it gives me the best feedback. After you manually run the analysis, the results are shown in their own pane:

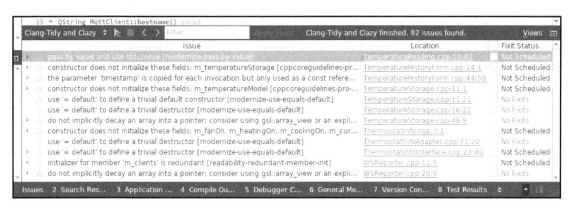

At the risk of scaring you, I will bring up one of the oldest methods for analyzing code, but with a new twist.

Code reviews

I said *code reviews*, and I am sure I just lost everyone reading this book. No one will read this section because everyone remembers those late Friday night meetings where someone hands out 200 pages of code listing, and then everyone pretends to read through them line by line, looking for mistakes, even though they are just thinking, *When can we get out of here? I want to start my weekend. Why did they schedule it now? Isn't there a better way?*

The good news is that there are much better ways.

Nothing, including automated code analysis, can replace the power of having three or four sets of eyes read through the code looking for logic blunders or even poorly commented code. They are still as important as ever, but how we do code reviews has evolved past the entire team sitting in one room being bored. Modern code review tools such as Atlassian's Crucible allow for distributed code reviews over the web. Reviewers are free to review code at their own pace and time. They can make comments about the code (or other comments) and read feedback.

Distributed code review tools take the drudgery out of reading through code, and can turn it into a learning experience.

 Both the literature and my personal experience have shown that distributed code reviews that are done by two or three reviewers as the code is checked in are actually better at finding and ensuring that issues are solved than doing giant code reviews at the end of a project.

Now that we have dealt thoroughly with code analysis, we will move on to actively testing the functionality of the code.

Active testing

Active testing is what we have been doing since the beginning of this book. This is running the code and making sure it behaves both as specified and as expected.

In this section, we will look at both hand and automated testing. We will apply automated testing to part of `BigProject` using two powerful test frameworks, Qt Test and Google Test.

Writing good tests

It is very easy to write a few tests, run them, and assume that the code is correct because all of the tests passed. This assumes that all of the tests are written in such a way to ensure things are correct.

Consider the following method, which will add two numbers together:

```
int plus(int a, int b) {
    return (a - b);
}
```

Now, let's feed a set of values into it to make sure it works:

- $a = 1, b = 0, result = 1$ -- Passes
- $a = 2, b = 0, result = 2$ -- Passes

If all my tests use a value of 0 for b, then they will all pass, but the method is wrong. We can see that from visually inspecting the code. The problem is our test set doesn't have good coverage. By *good coverage*, I mean two things. The first is that we check every line is tested. What we are missing is the second item, where data covers every reasonable type of case. The data we used only covers cases where $b == 0$. We need to test with other cases where b $!= 0$. We don't have to test every number, just the ones that make sense to the method we are testing.

While this is a simple example to analyze and would be easily caught, when complex methods are tested, it can be very easy to write `always passes` tests. This also demonstrates why testing and static analysis cannot fully replace code reviews.

Hand testing

At the end of `Chapter 1`, *Setting Up the Environment*, what did we do when we finished setting up our Target? We tested the Target with a piece of code and verified that it displayed a photograph.

This trend has continued with us throughout virtually everything we have done—building, running, and testing the code!

It's just good practice to make sure what you are doing works and hasn't broken something else.

Hand testing takes time, and it can be very hard to test exactly the same each time. Automated testing is a solution to that. There are a couple of test frameworks that are supported in Qt Creator, and we will look at two of them—Qt Test and Google Test. First, let's look at Qt Test.

Automated testing

Automated testing allows us to repeatedly apply multiple tests to code without having to do very much work. It is part of a good continuous integration environment.

For our example, we will test a piece of code that I didn't know was broken until I started working on the D-Bus integration: the code that determines when to turn on heating and cooling! (in *Debugging Qt applications* section, we will look at ways to debug the problem.)

Preparing for testing

Back in the 1990s, there was an oft-used phrase: *design for manufacturing*. The idea was to create your mechanical designs so that they could be easily made.

I often say *design for testing*. Design and write your code for testing. One of the key ways of doing this is making sure that you can test small portions (units) without having to use and deploy the entire code base. It also requires exposing test points where you can inject data and check the results.

In developing my `BigProject` code, I... well... I forgot about it. The logic that figures out which transition to send to the HVAC state machine was embedded in `MainWindow::updateTempDisplay()` and required the presence of the state machine. To make the code testable, I first extracted the method (using the **Refactor** | **Extract** function) and dropped it in `HVACController`, where it seemed to make better sense. I then changed the interface so that it didn't need the state machine and returned the name of the state transition.

I made the algorithm testable.

With that done, I set about writing test code using Qt Test.

 You can see the changes that were made in the version of `BigProject` in the GitHub repository for this chapter.

Qt testing

Qt testing consists of a set of classes and macros that make writing unit tests rather easy.

We will start by learning about a few of the basic macros that are used by Qt testing. We will then look at making sure we have good test input coverage (are we testing all the possibilities?), after which we will run the tests and learn how to view the results.

Basic tests

Here is a very simple test that demonstrates the basic test macros:

```
private slots:
    void sampleTests() {
        QWARN("This is a simple warning message.");
        QVERIFY((3 - 2) == 1);
        QCOMPARE(3 - 2, 1);
    }
```

Let's take a look at what the bold macros do:

- `QWARN(..)` simply prints a warning message in the test log.
- `QVERIFY(..)` is used to check Boolean conditions (for example, $x == y$, $x < y$, `x.contains(y)`, ...). Should the test fail, then the rest of the test method isn't executed.
- `QCOMPARE(..)` checks if the two passed parameters are equal. Should they not be equal, the test fails, and the rest of the code in the test method isn't executed.

Test methods are private slots in a QObject. The slots are executed in the order they are defined in the class header file.

There are a few specially named slots you may override by defining them in your code:

- `initTestCase()`: This is run before any tests are run
- `cleanUpTestCase()`: This is run after all of the tests in the test case have been run

Covering the possibilities

There are nine conditions that need to be tested to cover the possible cases in `HVACController::updateSMfromTemperature(..)` to ensure we have good input coverage. We could code each one as a test, but that violates the **DRY (Don't Repeat Yourself)** principle. A better solution would be to write one test method that is run nine times, once for each case. Qt Test support allows us to do this using test data.

Test data for a test method is provided by a `_data` method. For a test named `xyzzy`, test data is provided by `xyzzy_data()`.

To test `updateSMfromTemperature(..)`, we need to have the following data:

- A `QStringList` class of active states in the state machine
- Float values for the minimum, maximum, and current temperature
- The expected transition as `QString`

These are defined as columns using `QTest::addColumn<T>("name")`, where `T` is the type of data. Consider the following code:

```
/// The data for the test
void updateSMfromTemperatureTest_data()
{
    QTest::addColumn<QStringList>("states");
    QTest::addColumn<float>("min");
    QTest::addColumn<float>("max");
    QTest::addColumn<float>("current");
    QTest::addColumn<QString>("transition");
```

Once the fields are defined, we can start defining rows (cases) of test data using `QTest::newRow("dataset name")`. For each column, we add it to the row using `<<`:

```
QTest::newRow("Idle-Between")
    << QStringList({"FanOff", "Idle"})
    << 10.0f << 15.0f << 12.5f
    << QString("none");
QTest::newRow("Idle-High")
    << QStringList({"FanOff", "Idle"})
    << 10.0f << 15.0f << 20.0f
    << QString("TooHot");
```

Did you notice how the numeric values are defined? The f character at the end tells the compiler we are defining *float* values instead of *double* values. Qt Test will complain if the value type of the data doesn't match the defined type.

The associated test will be executed once for each row that is defined.

In the test, we need to retrieve the fields in the row so that we can use them. The QFETCH(T, name) macro does that for us. The name must match the field and becomes the variable name that contains the value:

```
/// The Test
void updateSMfromTemperatureTest()
{
    QFETCH(QStringList, states);
    QFETCH(float, min);
    QFETCH(float, max);
    QFETCH(float, current);
    QFETCH(QString, transition);
```

With the values retrieved, we can use QCOMPARE(..) to verify the results of the method call:

```
    QCOMPARE(HVACController::updateSMfromTemperature(min, max, current,
states),
            transition);
}
```

The complete code for these tests is in the BigProjectQTester directory, which is in the GitHub repository for this chapter.

Running the tests and viewing the results

While the tests can be run by using the **Build and Run** button in the left column of the Qt Creator window, a better way to launch tests is from the **Main** menu under **Tools** | **Tests**. If you use the second way, the **Test Results** pane will open as soon as the test run is completed:

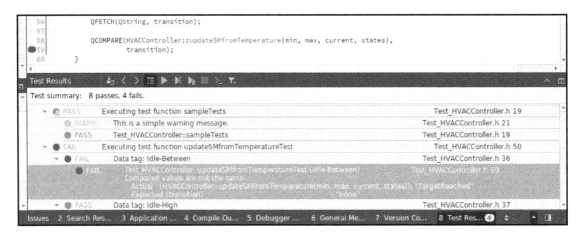

You can see from the **Test summary** on the **Test Results** pane that out of 12 tests, we had four that failed. By clicking on the failures and expanding them, we can see the results of one of the failures.

Also note that in the code listing above the test results, the line where the test failures were recorded is marked.

On the top of the **Test Results** pane, there are a set of buttons:

- The green play button will run all of the tests in the currently active project.
- Pressing the green play button with check marks will run only the selected tests.
- The **Filter** button will allow you to filter the results you see.

You can see and select the tests in a project by selecting **Tests** from the left **Projects and Open Documents** panes.

Qt Test is not the only testing program supported by Qt Creator. The ever popular Google Test is also supported.

Google Test

Google is known for Google Chrome, browsers, Gmail, and a whole host of consumer software. What most people don't realize is that they spend a lot of money developing tools to help them create all of that software.

Google Test, which is supported by Qt Creator's testing support, is one of these tools. It is designed to do testing on generic C++ code and supports many compilers and platforms. It supports more types of test checks and data inputs. It can also run multiple unit tests both sequentially and in parallel on some platforms.

Google has also added support for defining and substituting mocks during tests.

There is one drawback to using Google Test with Qt: it doesn't have direct support for Qt constructs. Even so, I prefer it to Qt Test because of the extra features it offers over Qt Tests and that there are many articles and references on the web for it. There are even articles about how to use Google Test with signals/slots and the Qt event loop.

Unfortunately, size limitations don't allow us to take a deeper look, but the `BigProjectGTester` directory contains the same tests as we saw in `BigProjectQTester`, only implemented in Google Test instead of Qt Test.

If you want to run the tests, you must first install Google Test from `https://github.com/google/googletest/tree/master/googletest`.

Good testing requires not only good tests, but also good test coverage.

Checking code coverage

To have truly safe software, you must verify that every possible path of code execution is covered. Consider the following pseudocode snippet for running a water heater:

```
TurnOnPropane();
IgnitePropane();
if (everything_is_ok == true) {
    when (temperature >= desired) {
        TurnOffPropane();
    }
} else {
    // handle the error
}
```

Testing needs to ensure that when `everything_is_ok`, the right thing is done, and also that we *handle* the error correctly. If handling the error doesn't include turning off the propane, there is going to be a *big* problem. If that branch is never tested, they won't know if it is correct or not.

This is why checking for code coverage is very important.

The traditional way

The traditional Linux and Unix way for finding code coverage is to use `gcov` to generate the coverage map and `lcov` to make the output pretty. A good write-up of how this can be done can be found at `https://codeflu.blog/2014/12/26/using-gcov-and-lcov-to-generate-beautiful-c-code-coverage-statistics/`.

Testing doesn't have to be hard!

Do you remember this diagram from `Chapter 5`, *Managing the Overall Workflow*?

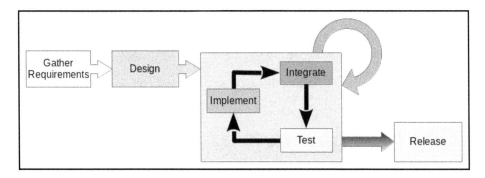

Here, we briefly talked about continuous integration (the gray box). It is such a key process in producing safe, reliable software that it bears mentioning again. By continually testing your code and making sure it works with the code for the rest of the system, we catch mistakes early and fix them sooner. The job of testing is broken up into small portions instead of one big effort at the end of the project when you have forgotten everything you did.

Testing and static analysis can easily be added to continuous integration systems, such as Jenkins and Hudson. I strongly urge you to try it if you can.

Now is a good time to debug the failures we found during testing.

Debugging Qt applications

Debugging is part of code development, so let's explore some ways we can debug our applications.

Old school is a term that seems to follow me. It started in some online video games where new players would say, "He's cool. He plays old school." Now, it even adorns the 1988 car I bought as a project. The previous owner put it on, but I sort of like it.

I say that because we will be looking at old-school debugging methods that are still applicable today; then, we will look at how to use the modern debugging interface that is integrated in Qt Creator.

Old-school debugging

I wrote my first program in 1983. It was an MS-BASIC program running under CPM to help me manage a newspaper delivery route I worked for a friend. That became the first program where I had to do real debugging, but there weren't any debuggers.

So, how did I do it? I used PRINT statements. When I was tracing the code execution, I would put PRINT statements in, telling me what was happening in the code.

Fast-forward 30 years, and PRINT statements are still useful, but in Qt we call them the qDebug() statements.

One of the advantages of the qDebug() statements is that they allow us not only to see where we are but also to see values that may not be visible in a debugger because of how the compiler decided to optimize the code it generated.

You have already seen qDebug() in use in several places, but let me show you an optimization I use in most of my code:

```
#define DEBUG_OUT          (qDebug() << __FUNCTION__ << ":")
#define DEBUG_OUT_EXPR(x) DEBUG_OUT << #x << "=" << x;
```

DEBUG_OUT simply makes typing easier. __FUNCTION__ (one underline character on each side of FUNCTION) is a macro that outputs the current function name so that I know where the message came from.

The second DEBUG_OUT_EXPR(x) expression is one I use quite often to output the value of some expression or variable. #x tells the C++ preprocessor to use the text of x as a string. For example, DEBUG_OUT_EXPR(4 + 2) produces DEBUG_OUT << "4 + 2" << "=" << 4+2;.

One of the most useful places for PRINT statements is in multi-threaded programs. These can be tricky to debug, especially if the code is paused and continued like it is with a debugger.

Now, let's look briefly at the Qt Creator debugger.

Working with the Qt Creator debugger

In Chapter 2, *Writing Your First Qt Application*, we learned how to use Qt's debugger to find a problem with our application. Instead of repeating that material, let's look at a couple of advanced uses of the debugger.

Examining threads

We will start by looking at the **Threads** menu:

1. Start debugging BigProject on the host.
2. Click the **Pause** button in the debugger pane.
3. Now, click on the **Threads** dropdown in the top bar of the debugger pane:

From here, we can choose a thread, and the debugger will update the screen to show you where you are on that thread.

Try it!

Debugging and the target firewall

The Yocto build we are using comes with a fairly aggressive firewall. Before using the Qt debugger running on the Host against a program running on the Target, you need to verify that the firewall on the Target has been disabled. Refer to the *Preparing the Target* section in Chapter 10, *Using More Qt-Related Technologies*, to learn how to disable the firewall on the Target.

Monitoring Qt applications

In addition to debugging code, it is also useful to monitor the code to look for opportunities to improve performance or cases where memory usage can be reduced.

We will start by looking at Qt's logging capabilities.

Logging the Qt way

We have already met and discussed qDebug(), but there are other methods available for logging:

- qDebug(): To log a debug message
- qWarning(): To log a warning
- qInfo(): To log an informational message
- qCritical(): To log a critical message
- qFatal(): To log a fatal message and exit

Controlling the logging format

At one point, my DEBUG_OUT macro grew fairly large. I wanted to be able to output a timestamp for the message, along with other information. That was before I learned about the QT_MESSAGE_PATTERN environmental variable and the qSetMessagePattern(..) method. These two tools allow you to control the format of the logging messages.

In the end, I found a very useful message pattern in the Qt documentation. See if you can figure out what it is doing from looking at the help information, then look at the following sample output (it really is just one line):

```
"%{time yyyy-MM-dd hh:mm:ss.zzz} | [%{if-debug}D%{endif}%{if-
info}I%{endif}%{if-warning}W%{endif}%{if-critical}C%{endif}%{if-
fatal}F%{endif}] | %{function} [%{file}(%{line})] | %{message}"
```

A full description of what can be done can be found in the help information for qSetMessagePattern(..).

Here is the output from using the message pattern I gave previously to output the different message type:

```
02:04:30: Starting ~/raspi/QtProjects/build-LoggingExamples-
Desktop_Qt_5_12_0_GCC_64bit3-Debug/LoggingExamples...
2019-05-27 02:04:30.712 | [D] | main [../LoggingExamples/main.cpp(14)] |
This is a debug message
2019-05-27 02:04:30.712 | [W] | main [../LoggingExamples/main.cpp(15)] |
This is a warning message
2019-05-27 02:04:30.712 | [I] | main [../LoggingExamples/main.cpp(16)] |
This is an informational message
2019-05-27 02:04:30.712 | [C] | main [../LoggingExamples/main.cpp(17)] |
This is a critical message
2019-05-27 02:04:30.712 | [F] | main [../LoggingExamples/main.cpp(19)] |
This is a fatal message. Good Bye!
02:04:33: The program has unexpectedly finished.
02:04:33: The process was ended forcefully.
```

The sample code that generated this is in the LoggingExample directory in the repository of this chapter on GitHub.

But what if I want to change where messages are logged to? How can I do that? Read on to find out.

Controlling the logging destination

One of the more powerful features of Qt's logging/message system is that you can control where a message goes by creating your own `QtMessageHandler` and installing it using `qInstallMessageHandler(..)`.

If you are interested in finding out more regarding how to do this, refer to the Qt help system. The documentation on `qInstallMessageHandler(..)` even includes an example of how to use these methods.

The last monitoring method we will look at is Valgrind.

Using Valgrind

Valgrind is one of the more interesting programs out there. It can be used both for analyzing memory usage for leaks and for profiling functions. We will start by using Valgrind to do some function profiling, and then look at how it can be used to look for memory leaks.

Function profiling

Valgrind can be used to profile your code down to the method/function level. To start it on the current active project, use **Analyze | Valgrind Function Profiler** from the **Main** menu.

The `AnalyzeMe` program, which can be found in the GitHub repository for this chapter, is a very short program that's designed to use up processing power.

Try running the Valgrind function profiling on `AnalyzeMe`!

You should get something that looks like this:

```
< >  ⌂  ≣    AnalyzeMe/main.cpp              ↕ X  ◆ notFib(int) -> int

          1    #include <QDebug>
          2
          3  ▼ int notFib(int x)
  81.4%   4    {
          5        int result = x;
          6  ▼     if (x < 1000) {
          7            result = (notFib(x + notFib(x + 1)));
          8        }
          9        return result;
         10    }
         11
         12
         13
         14  ▼ int main(int argc, char *argv[])
  98.7%  15    {
         16  ▼     for (int i = 0; i < 1000; ++ i) {
         17            QList<int>   nums{1, 4, 7, 8, 12, 17, 31};
         18
         19  ▼         for (auto n : nums) {
         20                qDebug() << n << " --> " << notFib(n);
         21            }
         22        }
         23    }
         24
```

From this result, we can see that 98.7% of the time is taken up in main(), and 81.4% is taken up in notFib(..). While those numbers might look wrong, they are actually correct. When the code is in notFib(..), we are also in main() because notFib(..) is called from main().

You will also have noticed three other sections that opened beneath the code. These allow you to dive deep into the call stack.

Analyzing for memory issues

One of the most tricky things about embedded systems is that they need to run forever without restarting or crashing. One of the most common failure modes in embedded systems is a slow memory leak.

Another common issue, especially if you don't use smart pointers, is incorrect pointer usage that leads to trying to use the wrong pointer location. These types of issues are what Valgrind was designed to find.

In the Qt Creator environment, you can run the Valgrind memory analyzer on a piece of code simply by selecting **Analyze | Valgrind Memory Analyzer** from the **Main** menu.

Try running the Valgrind memory analyzer on `BigProject` overnight!

Summary

I love learning new things, and I hope you found some new things in this chapter. We started off in the *Testing Qt applications* section and learned multiple ways to test applications. In the *Debugging Qt applications* section, we looked at methods of debugging applications the old-school way and by using the Qt Creator debugging screens. Finally, we looked at monitoring Qt applications.

None of these were exhaustive looks. They were more of a survey to let you know what is out there. I encourage you to continue looking into these topics as you find the need for them.

In the next chapter, we will talk about responsive application programming using the Qt thread support libraries.

Questions

1. What is an SPM and how are they made?
2. Can static analysis replace code reviews? Why or why not?
3. How much of the code should be tested?
4. What is a classic Linux code coverage tool?
5. Are `PRINT` statements still valid for debugging?
6. If I want to provide a warning message in a log file, which Qt method do I use?
7. What does function profiling tell me?
8. Does function profiling provide code coverage?
9. What is a mock?

12
Responsive Application Programming - Threads

We have covered a lot of material up to this point. Way back in `Chapter 4`, *Important Qt Concepts*, we talked about threads in relation to signals and slots. In this chapter, we will take a deeper dive into Qt's multifaceted thread support.

I have broken down our discussion of Qt's thread support into three sections:

- Examining Qt's different threading models
- Solving problems with threads
- Overcoming cross-thread communication and synchronization

When you have finished with this chapter, you should have learned the following subjects through hands-on examples:

- Which threading models Qt supports and where they can be used
- How to use threads to make a responsive UI
- How to look at problems in terms of threads
- How to synchronize threads
- The different methods of sharing data between threads
- What Qt does to support communicating between threads

Technical requirements

This chapter assumes that you have a working Qt system on a Host computer. While the Target is not specifically used, as with most Qt programs, you should be able to build and run the examples on the target. (That's the power of Qt!)

As in previous chapters, I assume you have been working and following along with the material in the book and are familiar with C++11 and basic Linux commands.

Source code for this chapter can be found in the GitHub repository at `https://github.com/PacktPublishing/Hands-On-Embedded-Programming-with-Qt/tree/master/Chapter12`. In it you will find several small projects to help you explore threading with Qt.

Examining Qt's different threading models

Before we start exploring how we can use Qt's thread support, we should understand the support Qt has for threads. Most of Qt's thread support is on the C++ side, but there is also support in QML.

In this section, we will learn about the following Qt thread models:

- Simple Threads
- Thread pools
- Qt Concurrent (`run`, `map`, `filter`, and `reduce`)
- QML WorkerScript

We will start with simple threading using QThreads.

Simple threads

As Qt has evolved over almost 30 years, its thread support has also evolved. One of the earliest and most simplistic support methods for threading is `QThread`. `QThread` encapsulates the idea of a thread and it provides its own event loop. The event loop allows it to process events, slots, and signals.

Each instance of `QThread` has a priority that can be used to tell the operating system how to schedule it. The special `QThread::InheritPriority` priority is the default priority of a newly created `QThread` class. It tells the new thread to inherit the priority of the thread that created it.

Once you have created `QThread`, you need to actually start it for it to do any work. If you don't start it, nothing will happen.

 Calling `QThread::start()` seems like a simple thing to remember to do, but, in my experience, it is one of the more frequent causes of threads not running.

We will discuss how threads communicate in the *Communicating between threads* section at the end of this chapter.

Using QThread

There are two different ways that `QThread` can be used, and it is one of the most contentious issues in Qt. Experts on both sides of the debate claim theirs is the only way. The more enlightened realize that both are valid and have their place.

The first method is to subclass the `QThread` class, and make a custom version that does the work in the subclass.

The second method is to do the thread work in `QObject` and `move(..)` the `QObject` class to a new thread in which it will run.

I have done both, but have come to realize that in 90% of the cases I encounter, running `QObject` in its own thread is the easiest and best method. So, this is the approach we will learn about. That doesn't say subclassing is bad; it is just not the approach we will learn about in this book.

Running a QObject in its own QThread

In order to run a `QObject` in its own thread, it must be moved to that thread. Qt makes this very easy:

```
auto thread = new QThread();
auto myObject = new QObject();

myObject->moveToThread(thread);
```

Once you have done that, you can wire up signals and slots. Also remember to start the thread or `QObject` will not send signals or receive slots!

The GuiThread project in the chapter repository contains an example of creating an object (CalcObject) that has a long-running calculation and running that on the thread. It was designed to allow you to experience the difference threading makes to a GUI application.

The code has only two classes, MainWindow and CalcObject. Pressing **Run** and **Run Threaded** will ask CalcObject to make the number of calculations shown in the center spin box. The difference is that **Run** uses a direct call, and thus the calculations run on the same thread as MainWindow. **Run Threaded** creates a thread, moves CalcObject to it, and then starts the calculations:

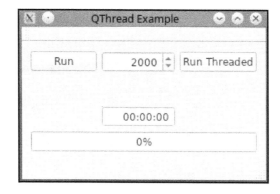

Open the project, build it for the Host (or Target, if you are brave), and experiment so that you get some idea about the difference running calculations on a separate thread makes.

Some things to look at as you experiment are as follows:

- When does the message box appear?
- When are the timer and progress bar updated?
- What was the difference in overall time?
- What was the difference in how the GUI behaved?

Feel free to examine the code and try making changes to it.

Now that you have some experience and understanding of QThread, why don't we move on to QThreadPool?

Thread pools

Creating threads is expensive in both time and resources. If you only have one or two threads that will last the length of the programs run, it isn't really that much of an issue. If your application needs a large number of threads or the program will be creating and destroying threads often, then the time and resource overhead will add a large burden to your program.

The solution is thread pooling. A thread pool is a collection of premade threads that can be quickly assigned and reassigned things to run. In the Qt world, QThreadPool is the thread pool, and QRunnable is the thing that can be run.

The requirements around your QRunnable are pretty basic—it must terminate in a reasonable time so that other QRunnables may have a chance to be run. QRunnables are designed to be things with a fixed, relatively short lifespan, not processes things that are started and run the entire length of the program.

There are a couple of interesting things about QRunnables. The first is that they are not QObjects. If you wish to use signals and slots with them, you must inherit both from QRunnable and QObject. The other interesting thing to note is that you can mix and match QRunnable things. As long as the item in question inherits from QRunnable, it can be added to a thread pool.

When a QRunnable is started, QRunnable::run() is invoked. When run() terminates, QRunnable is removed from the pool to make room for a new QRunnable class.

The basic sequence of using QThreadPool with the QRunnable objects is as follows:

```
// create the thread pool
auto pool = new QThreadPool();

// create a bunch of Runnables
for (int i = 0; i < NUM_RUNNABLES; ++i) {
    auto runThing = new QRunnable();    // create a runnable
    pool->start(runThing);              // start
}
```

GuiThreadPool in the chapter repository contains a revised version of GuiThread that has been modified to use QThreadPool and QRunnable:

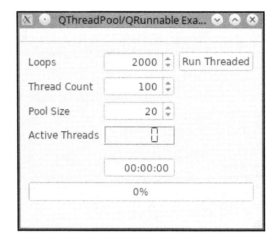

Like the previous program, the number of loops is controlled by the top spin box. This time, there is only a **Run Threaded** button. When that is pressed, QThreadPool with **Pool Size** spots is created, then the CalcObjects **Thread Count** is started.

You should now be asking a question about the illustration: if you only have 20 spots in the pool, how can you start 100 threads? That's a good question. The answer is that QThreadPool will queue up the other 80 threads and as soon as a spot opens up, it will fill it.

Why don't you build, run, and experiment with this project? Here are some questions to think about as you do:

- When does the message box appear?
- When are the timer and progress bar updated?
- What was the difference in overall time for the same number of loops between the two programs?
- What happens if you increase/decrease the number of threads?
- What happens if you increase/decrease the number of spaces in the pool?

The difference you see will also be closely related to the threading ability of your computer. On my Quad Core AMD A6 laptop there is about a 10:1 difference. Running the test on the Raspberry Pi 3B+ Target also yielded about a 10:1 difference. On an octa core machine I am developing image processing routines on, the difference is more like 100:1!

Examine the code and feel free to change it and see what happens.

> For me, experimentation is the greatest way to learn. I am not sure about you, but I am guessing since you chose a hands-on book, it might be the same.

We have now looked at ways of doing threading in Qt in C++. There is one more to consider, Qt Concurrent.

Qt Concurrent

Qt Concurrent is the newest and highest-level API for working with threads in Qt. This high-level API takes care of many of the more difficult tasks of thread synchronization. It automatically manages the thread count to adapt to the system it is running on.

Qt Concurrent methods are built around executing functions. Functions may be executed by themselves using `QtConcurrent::run()`, or applied to sets of data using the Map, Map-Reduce, Filter, and Filter-Reduce methods.

The concept of applying functions hints at a definite push to enable Qt to handle some aspects of functional programming in addition to the procedural programming C++ and Qt are known for.

> **Procedural** (or **imperative**) **programming** is the way C++ is usually used. You have procedures or steps that are run in order. **Functional** (or **declarative**) **programming** is a different paradigm. In functional programming, you have functions that are applied to data. HASKELL is purely functional, while LISP can be used functionally.

One could probably write a small book or class on how to effectively use the different forms of Qt Concurrent, but we are limited to part of a chapter. Nevertheless, let's take a brief look at a couple of concepts.

Running concurrent functions

The simplest application of Qt Concurrent is the running of functions in separate threads. Consider this simple example that sums all the numbers from 1 to *n*. I know there is a very simple one-step calculation that will do this, but I needed something for an example:

```
int sumToN(int n) {
    int sum = 0;
```

```
        for (i = 1; i < n+1; ++i) {
            sum += i;
        }
    }
```

Now, we will apply the function to three different values for *n* such that all three will be calculated separately in their own threads:

```
// run with 3 different values of n
QFuture<int> f1 = QtConcurrent::run(sumToN, 1000);
QFuture<int> f2 = QtConcurrent::run(sumToN, 6421);
QFuture<int> f3 = QtConcurrent::run(sumToN, 9999);
```

If we want to block execution on our thread until all three have completed, we can use `QFutureWatcher` with `QFutureSynchronizer`:

```
QFutureWatcher<int> fw1(this);
QFutureWatcher<int> fw2(this);
QFutureWatcher<int> fw3(this);
fw1.setFuture(f1);
fw2.setFuture(f2);
fw3.setFuture(f3);

QFutureSynchronizer<int>    sync;
sync.addFuture(f1);
sync.addFuture(f2);
sync.addFuture(f3);

sync.waitForFinished();    // wait/block until all finished
```

By extrapolation, we can see that we can run the function in parallel on as many values as we wish. The only issue is that each time we add another value, we have to create almost identical code again for that value. Wouldn't it be nice if we could just pass in a container (for example, `QList`) of values and use a couple of commands to apply our function to all of the values? That is what `QtConcurrent::map(..)`, `QtConcurrent::mapped(..)`, and `QtConcurrent::mappedReduce(..)` were designed to do.

Mapping, filtering, and reducing data

Qt Concurrent support for threading work on dataset splits into two types: mapping and filtering. The mapping support maps a function onto data. The filtering support is used to filter (remove) data from dataset.

Both the mapping and filtering support can be used with a reducing method. The reducing method can be used to post-process the results from mapping and filtering.

Mapping a function onto data example

In the previous section, we demonstrated how to use `QtConcurrent::run(..)` to run the same function on three different pieces of data. It was a fair amount of almost, but not quite, identical code. Mapping solves this problem by allowing us to create a Qt container class (`QList`, `QVector`, and so on) and in one line apply the function to all the members in that container.

In the following code, we create a container with three different values (1). We then apply the `sumRandom` function to each of them using just one statement (2). Finally, we wait for the function to finish on each of the `values` we applied it to (3):

```
void MainWindow::MappedExample()
{
    // (1) Define the values to work on
    QList<int> values({1000, 6421, 9999});

    // (2) apply sumRandom to all
    QFuture<int> f = QtConcurrent::mapped(values, sumRandom);

    // (3) Wait for the results
    auto sync = new QFutureSynchronizer<int>();
    sync->addFuture(f);
    sync->waitForFinished();

    QMessageBox::information(this, "All Threads Done", "All threads
        done.");
}
```

Next we look at filtering and reducing data.

Filtering and reducing data

We have a dataset with the height of a city's population. We would like to find the average height of the children aged 12-13 years. This is how we would use the Qt filtering and reducing methods:

- Filter the dataset so that only the children aged 12-13 years are present.
- Reduce the dataset to create a total height for the remaining population.
- Divide the total by the number of people in the remaining population.

Here is an example based on the other `QtConcurrent` examples. This time we want to produce the average of the sums. We start out defining the values like we did before (`1`), then we apply `sumRandom` to each of the `values` (`2a`). The difference is that as each calculation is completed, we feed the result to `workingAvg`, which calculates the average of the `values` (**2b**):

```
// calculate the average when given an item at a time;
void workingAvg(int &avg, int v) {
    static int count = 0;
    static int sum = 0;
    sum += v;
    ++count;
    avg = sum/count;
}

void MainWindow::MapReduceExample()
{
    // (1) Define the values to work on
    QList<int> values({1000, 6421, 522});

    // (2) Apply sumRandom to all values and apply workingAvg to
    // results
    QFuture<int> f = QtConcurrent::mappedReduced(values,
                                        sumRandom,      // (2a)
                                        workingAvg      // (2b)
                                        );

    // (3) this will wait until f is finished!
    auto result = f.result();
}
```

Let's close out Qt Concurrent with an example program.

Concurrent examples

The `GuiConcurrent` directory in the chapter repository contains an example program that exhibits how to apply `run(..)`, `map(..)`, `mapped(..)`, and `mappedReduce(..)` to the same problem:

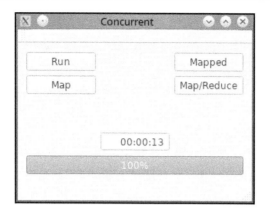

Feel free to look at the code to see how things are implemented. Note the heavy use of lambda functions:

- The **Run** button uses `QtConcurrent::run(..)`.
- The **Map** button uses `QtConcurrent::map(..)`.
- The **Mapped** button uses `QtConcurrent::mapped(..)`.
- The **Map/Reduce** button uses `QtConcurrent::mappedReduced(..)`.

In this section, we learned about the highlights of `QtConcurrent`. There are a few things I left out. I encourage you to look at the Qt Creator help system and the online Qt tutorials and blogs if you wish to dig deeper into `QtConcurrent`.

QML WorkerScript

The support for multithreaded operations in QML is done through the `WorkerScript` QML type.

Using `WorkerScript` is very straightforward:

```
Rectangle {
    anchors.fill: parent
    // define the worker
    WorkerScript {
        id: worker
        source: "scriptfile.mjs"

        onResult: {... do something ...}
    }

    MouseArea {
```

```
            anchors.fill: parent

            // start the worker when the rectangle is clicked
            onClicked: worker.sendStartMsg({'data1': data1,
                                            'data2': data2,
                                            ...})
    '   }
    }
```

Now, we need to define the contents of `scriptfile.mjs`:

```
    WorkerScript.onStartMsg = function({'data1': data1,
                                        'data2': data2,
                                        ...})
    {
        // do something
        Workerscript.sendResult(...)
    }
```

Having examined the different thread support methods in Qt, we will move on to seeing the types of problems we can solve with the threads.

Solving problems with threads

There are many problems that lend themselves to using threads. Why don't we learn more about them? Here is a short list:

- Responsive GUIs
- Image processing
- Real-time control versus GUI

Responsive GUIs

My first software engineering job was writing control software for Xerox machines. Usually, people are told that Xerox is a trademark name and to use *photocopiers* rather than *Xerox machines*, but seeing as I was working for Xerox and the software was going into their machines, I think it is appropriate. As part of the work, I learned about customer expectations. One of the biggest expectations is that when the user does something, such as pressing a button, he or she immediately expects some sort of feedback. Even if the user presses the **make copy** button while the machine is finishing powering on and warming up, you need to display something that tells the user the button press did something. In the start up case (or anytime we were busy), we replied with *Adjusting Copy Quality*.

If we break our system into a GUI thread and logic/worker threads, we can easily achieve this. The GUI thread continues to process user events while the worker threads do their work. We saw an example of this in our `GuiThread` and `GuiThreadPool` examples.

Image processing

Image processing is a field that is well suited to the application of threads. A typical image processing routine applies a simple function to every pixel in an image. It sure sounds like a massively parallel problem—a perfect application for map, map-reduce, filter, and their related Qt Concurrent methods.

 The power of **Graphic Processing Units** (**GPUs**) comes from the number of core graphics processors they contain. Instead of one processor handling the transformation of all of the pixels in an image, hundreds of processors each handle the transformation of a few pixels. All of these run in parallel. It is basically a multithreaded/parallel application.

Near real-time control

Another useful application of threads is handling near real-time control applications. In this case, we can run a high-priority thread (or threads) to handle the real-time control tasks, and use lower- priority threads to handle communication and GUI type issues.

Overcoming cross-thread communication and synchronization

There is an old saying, with great power comes great responsibility. Using multiple threads gives you great power to solve problems, but it also brings great responsibility to not introduce cross-thread problems.

The first thing we will learn about is synchronization between threads using Qt's support for mutexes and semaphores. That rolls directly into a more specialized type of synchronization, protecting data from corruption as it is accessed from multiple threads. We will then learn about using Qt signals and slots to communicate between threads, and then finally we finish off discussing Qt GUI objects and their limitations in regards to threads.

Synchronization

In procedural programming, we tend to think of things happening sequentially. We then tend to write our code with an assumption that once we start executing a method nothing will interrupt it until it completes. We also assume that only the code we are currently writing can change the data. Put another way, let's look at some code:

```
int val = 100;

void myMethod() {
    int oldVal = val;
    val = val + 10;
    // do some more stuff, but don't change val

    ASSERT(oldVal + 10 == val);
}
```

If we don't consider threads, we assume that ASSERT will always pass. Furthermore, myMethod() only changes val in one place, and we take that into account in ASSERT.

But what happens if there are two threads running myMethod()? Since threads are executed independently, it is possible that we enter myMethod() in one thread, execute the addition, and just then we enter myThread() in another thread and execute after the addition. Then the first thread starts running again. In this case, the first thread will find that val has been incremented by 20 (10 in the first thread and 10 in the second). Now ASSERT will fail for the first thread!

Note that oldVal is thread safe as it is created on the stack, and val is shared between all threads since it is stored in the heap (common memory).

Solving this issue comes down to *synchronizing* the interaction of threads. Qt provides several different ways of handling synchronization.

Mutexes and semaphores

The lowest level of synchronization can be done using QMutex , which is just a wrapper around a standard mutex. To get the mutex, you use the lock() method. To release it, use the unlock() method:

```
int val = 100;
QMutex      mutex;

void myMethod() {
    mutex.lock();
    int oldVal = val;
    val = val + 10;
    mutex.unlock();
}
```

There is a danger here, which is evidenced by the removal of ASSERT. If the method is left before unlock() is invoked, the mutex will remain locked.

The solution to the unlock problem is QMutexLocker(..) , which ensures that the mutex is appropriately released when it goes out of scope. Consider the following code:

```
int val = 100;
QMutex      mutex;

void myMethod() {
    QMutexLocker      lock(&mutex);
    int oldVal = val;
    val = val + 10;

    ASSERT (oldVal + 10 == val);
}
```

If myMethod() leaves through ASSERT or by finishing, the mutex will be automatically unlocked.

You can think of a QSemaphore class as a QMutex class that counts. QSemaphore is used to control access to a limited resources.

Pretend we are renting cricket bats. We have 10 bats to rent, and a customer may request as many bats as they want:

```
QSemaphore      bats(10);

bats.acquire(1);      // 10 available, so customer gets bat
bats.tryAcquire(10); //  9 available, none given
bats.tryAcquire(5);  //  9 available, 5 given
```

```
bats.release(4);      //  4 were available, now 8 available
bats.acquire(10);     //  8 available, wait for 10 available,
                      //    then give 10
```

The customer will either get the number of bats requested or none at all.

Waiting with mutexes

QWaitCondition is a class that makes it easy for threads to wait for conditions to be met. Finding examples to demonstrate code can be hard. This example took a while, but it actually works very well to demonstrate QWaitCondition. The example is taken from one of my favorite past times, motorsports.

The code excerpts below are from two different classes. The Track class imitates a race track that starts cars. The Car class simulates a race car running on the track. The simulation is very simple, the track can start 1 or all cars, and when the cars run, they print out when they start and when they finish. Each of the objects run in their own thread.

The Track::run() method is shown below.

```
void Track::run()
{
    QTextStream qcout(stdout);

    qcout << "Track is running." << endl;
    forever {
        qcout << "Press 1 to start 1 car, a to start all cars" << endl;
        auto c = getchar();
        if (c == '1') {
            qcout << "Starting 1 car" << endl;
            m_condition->wakeOne();
        } else if (c == 'A' || c == 'a') {
            qcout << "Starting ALL cars" << endl;
            m_condition->wakeAll();
        }
    }
}
```

Track::run() starts by printing out a message, then falls into a forever loop. The loop is fairly straight forward. It first asks you to press '1' to start one car or 'a' to start all cars. To start one car, QWaitCondition::wakeOne() is called. To start all cars, QWaitCondition::wakeAll() is used.

`Car::run()` is shown below.

```
void Car::run()
{
    QTextStream qcout(stdout);
    qcout << "Car is running.";
    forever {
        m_trackMutex->lock();
        m_condition->wait(m_trackMutex);
        m_trackMutex->unlock();
        qcout << "-> Starting Car #" << m_carNumber << endl;
        QThread::sleep((qrand() % 5) + 2);
        qcout << "-< Car #" << m_carNumber << " finished." << endl;
    }
}
```

`Car::run()` is similar to `Track::run()`. It prints out a message, then falls into a forever loop. This time the code tries to grab the mutex and then falls into `QWaitConditon::wait(..)`. When the car is woken, the mutex is releases so other cars may run, and then the car waits for a random time to finish.

Here is what happens when 4 Cars are used on the Track. First 1 car is released, then all cars are woken, and finally, just one car is run.

```
Track is running.
Press 1 to start 1 car, a to start all cars
1
Starting 1 car
Press 1 to start 1 car, a to start all cars
Press 1 to start 1 car, a to start all cars
Car is running.-> Starting Car #1
-< Car #1 finished.
a
Starting ALL cars
Press 1 to start 1 car, a to start all cars
Press 1 to start 1 car, a to start all cars
-> Starting Car #1
Car is running.-> Starting Car #36
Car is running.-> Starting Car #24
Car is running.-> Starting Car #902
Car is running.-> Starting Car #201
-< Car #201 finished.
-< Car #902 finished.
-< Car #24 finished.
-< Car #36 finished.
-< Car #1 finished.
1
```

```
Starting 1 car          ·
Press 1 to start 1 car, a to start all cars
Press 1 to start 1 car, a to start all cars
-> Starting Car #201
-< Car #201 finished.
```

The sample code for this example can be found in the GitHub repository, `https://github.com/PacktPublishing/Hands-On-Embedded-Programming-with-Qt/tree/master/Chapter12/CarStarter2`.

Having seen how to synchronize execution between threads, we will next learn how to protect data in an multithreaded environment using some specialized synchronization that Qt provides.

Protecting data

There are many cases where more than one thread may want read or write access to the same data (or file). In the generalized case, there is no problem if several consumers read the same piece of data at the same time, but there are problems if writing occurs while it is being read or if more than one producer tries to write the same data as before.

To handle this, Qt provides `QReadWriteLock`.

Read access is given as long as no write access has been granted. Multiple threads can lock for read at the same time.

To gain read access, the `lockForRead()` and `tryLockForRead(..)` methods are used. The first blocks until it is possible to obtain read access. The second version will try to get the lock and return `true` if the read lock was granted, otherwise, it returns `false`.

Write access is only given if no read or write access is currently granted. The methods are `lockForWrite()` and `tryLockForWrite(..)`.

Communicating between threads

While communication between threads can be done with variables (protected by `QReadWriteLock`), the proper Qt way is to use signals and slots. Signals and slots are the truly basic building blocks of Qt.

When discussing signals and slots in Chapter 4, *Important Qt Concepts*, you learned that the way you connect them determines which thread the slot is executed in:

- Slots that are invoked as function calls will always execute in the same thread as the caller.
- If a signal is connected to a slot through a direct connection, then the slot will be executed in the same thread as that which sent the signal. A direct connection works like a function call.
- If a signal is connected to a slot through a queued connection, the slot will be executed in the same thread as that of QObject containing the slot.

> The connection(..) method is smart. If you use Qt::AutoConnection when setting up the connection, Qt will check to see which thread the sender and receiver are in. If they are in the same thread, a direct connection will be established. If they are in different threads, a queued connection is established. This does require that QObjects are assigned to their proper threads before making the connection.

Being careful mixing threads and Qt GUI

As you can see, the Qt thread support is fairly comprehensive. There is one caveat to be aware of: Qt's GUI objects can only be run on the main GUI thread. That is easy to say, but may not be clear.

Let me explain by example.

In an application, I have a button that launches a long calculation. The calculation is done in a separate thread. The last statement in the calculation function is supposed to display a message box to say the calculation is done. Since that statement is in the calculation function, it will be run on the calculation thread. But, since the message box is not being launched from the GUI thread, it will not be displayed!

Summary

Threading is a big topic. As we worked our way through the chapter we learned that Qt comes with a great deal of support for handling threads.

We started by learning about the different threading models Qt provides. We then moved onto looking at the different classes of problems Qt works well for, including how we can use threads to provide a responsive UI. We then discussed the Qt support for thread synchronization and inter-thread communication.

This is the second-to-last chapter of the book. In the final chapter, we will look at some best practices for developing Qt applications, and talk a little more about how Qt became what it is today.

Questions

1. What is used for threading in QML?
2. Why is a thread pool helpful?
3. What will happen if more runnable objects are assigned to a thread pool than there are slots in the pool?
4. What is the highest-level API for threading in Qt?
5. How do I use Qt to apply a function to all elements in a list at the same time?
6. What is functional programming, and why is it different?
7. What is the Qt way of communicating between threads?
8. How does `Qt::AutoConnection` work?
9. What is an easy way to allow multiple threads to safely read and write data?
10. What happens if I try to open a second `MainWindow` class for a thread launched by the original `MainWindow` class?

Further reading

In the section on thread synchronization, I briefly described how a GPU does its work. The programming of GPUs for graphic usage is often done in OpenGL. Programming GPUs for more general math problems is done in CUDA. If you want to learn more about how to program to do this, refer to these books:

- *OpenGL 4 Shading Language Cookbook – Third Edition*, David Wolff, by Packt publishing
- *Hands-On GPU-Accelerated Computer Vision with OpenCV and CUDA*, Bhaumik Vaidya, by Packt publishing
- *Hands-On GPU Programming with Python and CUDA*, Dr. Brian Tuomanen, by Packt publishing

13
Qt Best Practices

We have reached the last chapter of this book!

As we have worked our way through the chapters in this book, we have fulfilled 23 requirements for an imaginary product. In the process, we had a chance to learn the *Qt Way* by implementing, testing, and debugging code.

In the last two chapters, we left the project behind, but I hope that, as you learned about more Qt capabilities, you have thought of ways you could not only apply them to the project, but also to future projects you might have a chance to work on. The nice part is that you have a premade Target system that you can use. As I completed this book, I already thought of the next thing I want to build with my Raspberry Pi, Sense HAT, and Qt—an in-car performance monitor that can show and record how hard the car is turning, accelerating, and braking when I am competing in motorsports. I know there are plenty of other devices that can do this, including my phone, but I think it would be fun if I built it myself. Another project I thought about was a Wi-Fi controller for my DSLR camera.

For this final chapter, I wanted to take one step back and look at the some of the best practices for Qt development. By doing so, we will cover the following topics:

- Understanding the *Why?* of Qt
- Choosing between C++ features and the Qt Way
- Increasing efficiency in Qt

By finishing this chapter, you will understand why Qt has its own constructs for modern C++ language features, know how to avoid the hidden traps that cause slow Qt code, and be able to make good choices between Qt and C++ language features.

Technical requirements

Like all of the chapters in this book, it is expected that you have worked through the previous chapters.

This chapter will be primarily about information sharing, but where there are code snippets, you should feel free to try them both on your Host and Target. For me, I don't really learn about something until I have tried it myself.

Understanding the Why? of Qt

Several decades ago, as a young teenager, I had a chance to watch a very interesting video series called *You Are What You Were When*. The series was made to teach managers how to understand how the people on their teams thought and behaved. Beyond watching the teacher work his way around a room filling every white board that surrounded it with notes and drawing, I found the idea incredibly powerful—everyone (and everything) is shaped by where they came from.

With that in mind, let's look at where Qt came from so that we can understand the Qt we can see today.

The time was 1991. Personal computers were just starting to be something you might see in a regular office. Development of graphical interfaces was incredibly fragmented. There were competing display technologies, all with their own programming methods.

The C++ language was fragmented beyond belief. It was new, but there were only a few standard ways of doing things. Support for the simple idea of what a string was differed depending on whose compiler you were using and what options there were for compilers for the operating system you were running.

Out of that chaos came Qt. It was aimed at graphical workstations running Unix. The problem was that even those didn't always run the same tools or use the same display technologies.

Therefore, the developers of Qt went about creating the tools they needed so that they could have a standard platform. They wrote their own string class (`QString`), they created their own container classes (`QList`, `QQueue`, `QMap`, and so on), and they created an ordered environment for development.

As Qt continued to be developed, some APIs changed as the major versions (1, 2, 3, 4, and 5) were introduced, but they always tried to maintain as much compatibility with the past version as reasonable while introducing new features. As C++ continued to evolve, some of the biggest Qt changes were actually in how things were implemented.

Often, Qt introduced concepts before others standardized them. For instance, the ranged-for loop, `for (i : container)`, which makes it easy to iterate over a standard container, wasn't part of the C++ standard until C++11, but Qt had `foreach(i, container)` before C++11 was a standard. If you dig more into Qt, you will find that there are many examples of this, including `QSharedPointer`, `QFile`, `QFileInfo`, `QDir`, and more that I don't have room to enumerate.

Does that mean it is better to user the Qt version? I'll leave that question for the next section.

Choosing between C++ features and the Qt Way

Throughout this book, I have pretty much stuck to teaching you the *Qt Way* of doing things. Does that mean it is right for all cases? Well, that depends.

> *If you are finding it hard to do something that should be simple in Qt, then (a) you aren't doing it the right (Qt) way or (b) you really shouldn't be doing it at all.*

We saw this in the last chapter when we learned about Qt Concurrent. I learned about threading in Qt before Qt Concurrent was developed. As I learned about Qt Concurrent, I discovered that it was easier to do certain tasks using Qt Concurrent rather than QThreads. Still, I tend to resort to `QThread` and `QThreadPool` out of habit.

Should I use the `pthread` *library or* `QThread`?

It's a valid question that I have seen more than once, so let's look at it and see whether we can get some guidance that we can use for other areas:

- `pthread` is written for C:
    - It doesn't have an object-oriented interface
    - Interfacing to objects would be tricky
    - `pthread` is well understood and available outside Qt
- `QThread` has a C++, object-oriented interface:
    - I can easily create `QObject` to do work and assign it to `QThread`
    - `QThread` requires `QtCore`

Which should I use—foreach (i: container) or for (i : container)?

- Qt's foreach is available with any compiler that can build Qt
- for (i: container) is only available in C++11 or later compilers
- To the untrained eye, foreach is more obvious than this *new* C++11 feature
- Qt's foreach can easily create a copy of the container if you don't use it correctly. (Here are two good articles about this: https://blog.qt.io/blog/2009/01/23/iterating-efficiently/, and https://doc.qt.io/qt-5/containers.html#the-foreach-keyword.)

By looking at these questions, we can come up with simple guidelines to consider:

- If we aren't already using Qt, is it worth introducing Qt for one feature?
- If we introduced Qt, would it make our development more efficient?
- Which is easier to interface with if we are using Qt?
- What side effects are introduced in either instance?
- Is there a better/newer way we should be using?

When I looked at these guidelines, I came up with the following results:

- For threading in a Qt application, use QThread, QThreadPool, or even QtConcurrent
- For iterating over containers, use for (i : container)

Now that we have some guidelines on how to decide when to do things the Qt way, let's learn about how we can make our Qt code more efficient.

Increasing efficiency in Qt

Originally, I was going to call this section *Writing faster Qt code*, but as I was developing the outline, I realized that what I was really talking about is writing efficient Qt code. Let me explain.

When I was young, unmarried, and living with my parents, I had money to play with so that I could build faster cars. One time, I decided to make the motor of my car more powerful without having to increase its displacement. When I was finished, the car had 50% more horsepower, and when I used the horsepower, it went through fuel 50% faster.

However, I also got something else out of this. I took the car on a long (several hour) expressway trip. What I found was that the fuel economy of the car (when driven like a sane person) went up by 50%. Why? Because in order to get more power out of the engine, I have to increase the efficiency of the engine. I used all sorts of trick to eliminate wasted energy. This gave me more power when I demanded it, but also saved the fuel that would have just gone to generate wasted energy.

In order to speed up my car, I made it more efficient. Writing faster code often results in more efficient code. That's why I chose *Increasing efficiency in Qt*.

The Qt developers have already put a great amount of effort into making Qt as efficient as possible, but it is still possible to do things that make it work hard. (Just like driving overly fast takes more fuel, no matter how efficient your car is.) In this section, we will look at areas that tend to give the most payback for the effort they take.

Let's start with what I call the *low-hanging fruit*. These are the simple things that are easy to do and can really cut waste.

Don't make extra copies

Every time we copy something in our code, we use more memory, which makes the computer spend more time duplicating the data.

Passing parameters

This is not as much a *Qt thing*, but rather a general C++ programming thing. Consider these two method signatures:

```
void methodA(MyClass m);
void methodB(const Myclass &m);
```

If neither methodA nor methodB are modifying MyClass, the second is faster. Why?

- In methodA, we are *passing by value*. A copy is made of MyClass and then the copy is passed to methodA

- In methodB, we are *passing by reference*. Instead of making a copy of MyClass, we simply tell methodB where it can find an instance of Myclass to reference. No copying is done

This is probably the most common optimization that's found, and one of the ones with the biggest return for the effort it takes.

A lot of work has been put into writing many of the Qt classes to make them as efficient in speed and memory as possible. One of the techniques they use is **implicit sharing**. Simply put, when you make a copy of the class, you aren't copying the data—you are just generating a new reference to the data. Only if you change the data is a copy made (copy on write). The Qt Help for implicit sharing has a very good explanation on how this works and what classes use it and provides a long list of commonly used classes.

Hidden copies

This is one that I was subtly aware of, but didn't fully appreciate until it was explained to me.

In many cases, class implementations and compiler rules may make a hidden copy of items. Modern compilers (which includes basically every C++11 capable one) have become much better at detecting compiler generated copies. That leaves class implementation issues.

QString is a very powerful class, but if it isn't used correctly, you can quickly introduce hidden copies. Many QString methods will do this, but the most dangerous ones are probably the replace(..) methods.

If you think about it, it really does make sense that copying or moving data is going to be an issue when you're replacing parts of a string. If the replacement string is a different size than the string it is replacing, then something is going to have to be moved or copied. Hence, doing the following could cause four different copy/move operations:

```
QString b = a.replace("1", "one")
            .replace("2", "two")
            .replace("3", "three")
            .replace("4", "four");
```

While there is no easy way around the problem should 1, 2, 3, and 4 exist in the string, depending on the size of the string, it might be conditionally doing the replacements after checking whether it needs to be made with contains(..).

Keep it DRY

I have explained that **Do not Repeat Yourself** (**DRY**) for several times, but it is one of the fundamental principles of coding. In previous discussions, we talked about copying and pasting code in several places and the problem of maintenance. Now, we will look at how DRY applies to code efficiency.

Avoiding pointless initializations

One of the more common issues is the unnecessary initialization of variables. This is one of those things that you want to look for once you are happy that the code works as it should since it tends to violate the safe programming philosophy of always ensuring that variables are initialized:

```
int sum() {
    int sum = 0;
    int i = 0;
    QString resultString("");

    for (i = 1; i <= 10; ++i) {
        sum += i;
    }

    resultString = QString("The result is %1").arg(sum);
    return sum;
}
```

I found two occurrences where values are initialized but never used—i and resultString. The best solution to this is not to remove the initialization, but to move it to the point of use. Here's a revised version:

```
int sum() {
    int sum = 0;

    for (int i = 1; i <= 10; ++i) {
        sum += i;
    }

    QString resultString = QString("The result is %1").arg(sum);
    return sum;
}
```

The initializer for `i` has been moved into the `for(..)` statement. We don't use it anywhere else, so we don't need it outside the scope of the `for(..)` statement. Likewise, we don't even declare `resultString` until we set its value. If this wasn't a contrived example, I would question why we are bothering with creating `resultString`. It isn't used anywhere, which brings us to another way of increasing efficiency.

Avoiding useless work

I have always developed my software by solving little problems one by one and combining the solutions into bigger solutions until I have delivered what I need to provide to the project. In this process, I have often discovered that I wanted to change something before I combined it. That's good, except that I would sometime leave things that are no longer needed in the code—things like `resultString` from the previous example. If it were a part of a bigger project, then I may have put it in there so that I could use `qDebug()` to output a message that made sense, and when I went through the code to remove the `qDebug()` statements, I missed removing `resultString`.

As you are developing—especially toward the end of development, but before testing – take some time to go through your code and find places you are doing useless work and resolve them.

On the topic of useless work, consider whether you really need to create something that has already been created.

Using the best solution

We only tend to apply DRY to the code we write, but the application is much bigger. One common mistake is *reinventing the wheel*. Don't develop a solution for something that has been solved before.

The preceding code example shows this very well. Instead of looping through numbers and adding them, we could use a simple formula:

```
// sum of 1..n
sum = (n * (n+1)) / 2;
```

If we used what's shown in the preceding example, we could have significantly cut down the amount of code the CPU has to execute:

- In the original, we need to (1) add a value, (2) increment a counter, (3) test a condition, and 9 out of 10 times (4) jump back to the top of the loop. Three of the steps are executed 10 times, and one is executed nine times. That is 39 steps in total.
- By using the formula, we only need to (1) increment a number, (2) multiply, and (3) divide.

Which one is going to take less time to process?

This may seem like a trivial example. What about rewriting methods that have already been optimally written, tested, debugged, and even made safe for threads? `QString` already provides several methods that are fairly straightforward to quickly hack together (`toUpper`, `toLower`, `split`, and so on). We shouldn't be writing these ourselves. We should be concentrating on writing code for the unique problems of our project.

Speaking of `QString`, one of the frequent traps is not using `QString::empty()`, and instead using `QString::size() > 0` or even `QString::operator==("")`. Implementation-wise, the first is much faster as it doesn't have to figure out how big the string is. The last one is by far the worst. I will actually create a new, empty `QString` instance and then test it to see whether the two instances are equal!

Stay in one place

By *stay in one place*, I refer to the temptation of mixing solutions. If you have committed to using Qt, stick with using Qt. Don't go back and forth between Qt and something else unless there is a real need to.

For example, when you're reading data to be used by a method that takes `QStringList`, don't use `stdlib` methods to read the file into `std::list<string>` and then convert it into `QStringList`. Instead, use the Qt file methods (`QFile` and `QTextStream`) to read the data directly into the `QStringList`. You save yourself the trouble and time of converting.

Letting Qt Creator help

In Chapter 11, *Debugging, Logging, and Monitoring Qt Applications*, we talked about some built-in Qt Creator tools for static code analysis. In particular, we talked about clang-tidy and clazy. Like code reviews, these tools are great at helping you to find areas to improve your coding.

Try opening up your BigProject code and analyzing your project using the combined clang-tidy and clazy analyzer.

When I run the analysis on the final version I created for Chapter 10, *Using More Qt-Related Technologies*, I found a fair number related to copying data—*the xyzzy parameter is copied for each invocation, but is only used as a const reference.* The analysis also found a few places where I was redundantly initializing member variables.

> *Like code reviews? Isn't that like having your tooth pulled?*

> Actually, no. I have learned more by having other people with different experiences read my code and suggest better ways than almost any other way. Consider that if you code like you always do and it works, why would you bother seeing if there is a better way? However, whether someone suggests a better way, you learn something that can help you to grow as a developer. A good code review can create just that type of learning environment.

Summary

In this final chapter, we started by trying to understand why Qt has its own ways for doing some things that are now considered standard parts of modern C++11 or other libraries. That led us to trying to come up with some guidelines on when we should use Qt or other libraries. From there, we discussed how to increase the efficiency of our Qt code and found that some methods have applications outside of just Qt programming.

While this is the end of the teaching section of this book, I sincerely hope that this is not the end of your learning when it comes to how to develop embedded applications using Qt. We have only hit the high level of some of the topics that could be discussed. There are many things I wish I could have added to the discussion and discussed more in depth since the technology is continuing to grow. At the time of writing, Qt 6 is actively being developed, C++17 compiler support is finally emerging, and C++20 is just around the corner.

Go out, find something to learn about, and learn it!

Questions

1. In a Qt application, is it better to use `std::string` or `QString`?
2. Why does Qt have its own `QSharedPointer` class?
3. Efficiency-wise, is it better to pass by reference or value?
4. If you were to pass by reference, but are not going to modify what was referenced, what decorations should you use in the function prototype?
5. Why can `QString::replace()` negatively affect the performance of an application?
6. Why do I like code reviews, and why should you like them too?
7. What aid can Qt Creator offer in helping you to create more efficient code?
8. Now that you have finished the learning section of this book, what should you do?

Further reading

What is it you want to learn next?

Packt has a variety of books on many subjects. In fact, while writing this book, I purchased one on CUDA programming for an image processing project I was working on. Here are some books that caught my attention as a learner/teacher of C++ and Qt:

- *C++17 By Example,* by Stefan Björnander
- *Hands-On Embedded Programming with C++17,* by Maya Posch
- *Computer Vision with OpenCV 3 and Qt5,* by Amin Ahmadi Tazehkandi
- *Raspberry Pi 3 Home Automation Projects,* by Ruben Oliva Ramos and Shantanu Bhadoria

Find a book about something you are interested, get it, and learn something!

Appendix A: BigProject Requirements

Throughout this book, we have been given requirements for `BigProject` and implemented them. Let's take a look at all of them here:

- **Req. 1**: The device will display the current date and time.
- **Req. 2**: The device will be run on simple hardware.
- **Req. 3**: We must develop using Qt.
- **Req. 4**: The device must display the current ambient temperature.
- **Req. 5**: The user will be able to see a historical table of temperature readings.
- **Req. 6**: The user will be able to see a scrolling, real-time graph of temperature readings.
- **Req. 7**: The system will maintain a history of readings across power cycles.
- **Req. 8**: Deleted
- **Req. 9**: The user will be able to set a minimum acceptable temperature.
- **Req. 10**: The user will be able to set a maximum acceptable temperature.
- **Req. 11**: If the temperature falls below the minimum acceptable temperature, the heater must be turned on.
- **Req. 12**: If the temperature is above the minimum acceptable temperature, the heater must be turned off.
- **Req. 13**: If the temperature rises above the maximum acceptable temperature, the cooler must be turned on.
- **Req. 14**: If the temperature falls below the maximum acceptable temperature, the cooler must be turned off.
- **Req. 15**: The minimum and maximum temperatures must be separated by 3 degrees.
- **Req. 16**: The minimum temperature must be lower than the maximum temperature.
- **Req. 17**: The HVAC unit needs to wait 30 seconds between activations of either the heating or cooling sections.

- **Req. 18**: When heating or cooling, the fan must be on.
- **Req. 19**: The system will have a virtual keyboard for entering text onscreen.
- **Req. 20**: It will be possible to remotely monitor the temperature reading.
- **Req. 21**: Display the current temperature for a city.
- **Req. 22**: The product must integrate with an IoT protocol such as MQTT or KNX.
- **Req. 24**: The system shall be accessible through a web client.
- **Req. 25**: `BigProject` shall be able to generate a report of temperature readings for the last 24 hours.
- **Req. 26**: The output report will be in the PDF format.

Appendix B: Bonus Code - Simplifying Q_PROPERTY

I love using Q_PROPERTY in my code, but I really don't like all of the manual work that is needed to make it work. Thus, I have written a couple of macros to make things a little simpler.

The code is part of the PropertyClassTemplates.h file in the GitHub repository at https://github.com/PacktPublishing/Hands-On-Embedded-Programming-with-Qt.

Simplifying defining Q_PROPERTY()

This is the simplest of the macros, PROPERTY. It takes a data Type and the Name of the property, then takes care of not only generating the Q_PROPERTY statement, but also the required getter and setter methods:

```
/**
 * @def PROPERTY(Type, Name)
 *
 * @brief   A macro to define a class "Property" (Q_PROPERTY).
 * @param   Type    - the type of the property
 * @param   Name    - the name of the property
 *
 * This macro defines a Q_PROPERTY, its storage, and the required getter
and
 * setter methods.  This allows the property to be accessed by through the
 * QObject or Q_GADGET system.  It also makes importing and exporting the
class
 * to XML Streams very easy as the property system does most of the work
for you.
 *
 * @note    This can only be used with a class that inherits from QObject
or Q_GADGET
 */
#define PROPERTY(Type, Name)   \
    private:
\
        Type m_##Name;
\
        Q_PROPERTY(Type Name READ Name WRITE set##Name)   \
```

```
    public:
\
        void set##Name(const Type &value) { m_##Name = value; }
\
        /*void set##Name(const QVariant &value) {
set##Name(value.value<Type>()); } */ \
        Type Name() const { return m_##Name; }
```

Using the macro is straightforward, as follows:

```
class MyObject : public QObject
{
    Q_OBJECT

    PROPERTY(QString, bookName)
    PROPERTY(QString, author)
    PROPERTY(QDate,   publishDate)
...
}
```

 This macro does not support data types of `QVariant` or pointers. It does not support notification from `Q_PROPERTY` either.

The `NOTIFYING_PROPERTY(..)` macro allows us to create a property that also provides a `NOTIFY` element, but you need to define the notifying signal separately:

```
/**
 * @def NOTIFYING_PROPERTY(Type, Name)
 *
 * @brief   A macro to define a class "Property" (Q_PROPERTY).
 * @param   Type    - the type of the property
 * @param   Name    - the name of the property
 *
 * This macro defines a Q_PROPERTY, its storage, and the required getter
and
 * setter methods.  This allows the property to be accessed by through the
 * QObject or Q_GADGET system.  It also makes importing and exporting the
class
 * to XML Streams very easy as the property system does most of the work
for you.
 *
 * @note    This can only be used with a class that inherits from QObject
or Q_GADGET
 * @note    You must define the signal void _Name_Changed() manually.
 */
#define NOTIFYING_PROPERTY(Type, Name)    \
```

```
    private:
\
        Type m_##Name;
\
        Q_PROPERTY(Type Name READ Name WRITE set##Name NOTIFY Name ##
Changed)  \
    public:
\
        void set##Name(const Type value) { m_##Name = value; emit Name ##
Changed();}                    \
        void set##Name(const QVariant value) {
set##Name(value.value<Type>()); } \
        Type Name() const { return m_##Name; }
```

Simplifying working with Q_PROPERTY items

Once it is easy to define Q_PROPERTIES, you'll soon want to make using it easy, so I have developed some template functions to do the work. Here is a list of them:

```
/// A generic template for stream the properties of a Q_GADGET or QObject
template <class OT> QString DumpProperties (const OT &obj);

/// Stream the properties of a class to a QDataStream
template <class OT> QDataStream &operator<<(QDataStream &stream, const OT
&obj);

/// Retrieve the properties from a QDataStream.
template <class OT> QDataStream &operator>>(QDataStream &stream, OT &obj);

/// Check that all of the properties of two objects of the same type match.
template <class T> bool ArePropertiesMatched(const T &left, const T
&right);

/// Copy all of the properties from one instance to another.
template <class T> void CopyProperties(T &left, const T &right);
```

With a little imagination, you can see that it would be reasonably easy to expand these functions and macros to handle reading and writing XML and JSON.

Assessments

Section 1: Getting Started with Embedded Qt

Chapter 1 – Setting Up the Environment

1. **Qt is available under what types of licenses? How are they different?**
   Commercial and open source (L/GPL). The open source (L/GPL) version requires that you abide by the applicable GPL and LGPL licenses, while the commercial version does not.

2. **What project allows you to custom build a Linux distribution for embedded use?**
   Yocto.

3. **How do you prepare to build Qt from its source code?**
   You run the correct `configure` command for the device you are building for.

4. **What command can be used to synchronize directories across remote machines?**
   `rsync`.

5. **What are two methods for sharing filesystems between remote machines?**
   Cloning the filesystem from the Target to the Host, and by remote mounting the Target filesystem.

6. **Is it okay to use the Qt version that's installed via Ubuntu? Why or why not?**
   No. This is because we don't control the version of Qt installed by Ubuntu and this book has been written for a specific version (5.12) of Qt.

7. **What are the major steps that are needed to prepare Qt for working on a new device?**
   1. Obtain the source code.
   2. Configure the build.
   3. Build the code.
   4. Install the code on the device.

8. **How can you identify the device that's assigned to an SD card?**
By using `dmesg` to see what device the card was assigned to. If you run `dmesg` before inserting the device, insert the device, then run `dmesg` immediately, you should see what device it was assigned to. This works for almost any device you connect.

Chapter 2 – Writing Your First Qt Application

1. **Can Qt Creator interface to Version Control Systems? If so, which ones?**
Yes. Mercurial (Hg) and Git.
2. **Give two ways in which you can create a new project in Qt Creator.**
   1. Clicking the button in the **Projects** screen of the **Welcome** page.
   2. Selecting **New File** or **Project...** from the **File** menu.
3. **How do you add a C++ class to a Qt Project?**
Use the New File or Project Wizard, which can be launched from the File Menu.
4. **Do Qt and Qt Creator only support GUI development?**
No.
5. **What resources does Qt Creator provide for learning more about a Qt topic?**
The built-in Help pages that can be accessed from the Help button in the left-hand menu, or by pressing *F1* on a Qt variable, class, or method name in the editor.
6. **What is the basic process for adding elements to a design?**
Click and drag the element from the left-hand column of the Design page to the form you are working on.
7. **Describe ways in which can you compile and run your application.**
   1. Select **Build** and then **Run** from the menu bar on the Qt Creator Window.
   2. Press *Ctrl+R*.
   3. Click on the **Run** (▶) icon in the left icon bar.
8. **How can you start debugging an application being developed in Qt Creator?**
   1. Press *F5*.
   2. Click on the debug icon (▤) from the left icon bar.
   3. Select **Debug** | **Start Debugging** | Start debugging project_name.
9. **How do you set a break point in the debugger?**
In the **Code Editing** screen, left-click on the left-hand side of the line number where you want to set your break point.

Chapter 3 – Running Your First Application on Your Target

1. **What is a Qt Creator kit?**
   A collection of Device, Compiler, Debug, Qt Build, and optional Qt `mkspec`, which is used by Qt creator to know how to build and run your code.

2. **Where are kits configured?**
   In the **Kits** tab of the Kits selection in the Options dialog.

3. **How do you add a new device to Qt Creator?**
   Open the **Options** dialog, select **Devices** from the left-hand menu of the dialog, and then define the device.

4. **How can you tell where the application is deployed to on the Target?**
   By looking at the Compile Output from the deploy step. The line that shows *Trying to kill* shows where the code is deployed to.

5. **What is a layout?**
   A flexible way of arranging items on the screen in which their relative locations are consistent, regardless of the dimensions of the screen.

6. **If you are designing a form, what kind of layout would you use?**
   A Form Layout.

7. **How can you space things out in a layout?**
   You can use horizontal or vertical spacers.

8. **How can you switch layout types for the main window?**
   Right-click in the **Form**, select **Layout**, and then select a **new Layout**.

9. **How do you switch between different configurations for a project?**

   Click on the Configuration icon () from the left icon bar and then select the appropriate kit and build type.

10. **In Qt Creator, how do you start debugging an application on the Target?**
    Click on the Debug Icon

11. **How would you configure Qt's Analog Clock Window Example to run a build for and then run on the Target?**
    1. Open the example.
    2. Select the **Raspi** configuration.

Section 2: Working with Embedded Qt

Chapter 4 – Important Qt Concepts

1. **If a signal is emitted, when is a slot that's connected by a direct connection executed?**
   Immediately, and in the same thread.
2. **Can console-only (non-GUI) applications be written in Qt?**
   Yes.
3. **Can a signal with two parameters (`int` and `QString`) be connected to a slot that accepts one parameter (`QString`)?**
   No. The parameter count and types must match.
4. **What must be defined for `Q_PROPERTY` when creating a property?**
   1. All the methods named by `READ`, `WRITE`, `NOTIFY`, or other keywords.
   2. Storage for the property.
5. **Can properties be added to QObject at runtime instead of when the class is defined?**
   Yes, dynamic properties can be added at runtime.
6. **What is `QVariant`?**
   A generic container for any type that the Qt meta-object system knows about.
7. **Which Qt class would you use to find out if a file is read-only?**
   `QFileInfo`.
8. **What is one advantage of the model/view architecture?**
   1. It separates the data (model) from the display (view) of the data, allowing the view to change without affecting the model.
   2. You can easily add filters between the model and the data without changing the model or the view.
   3. You can create custom renderers to control how the data is shown without changing the model or view.
9. **Is it possible to link more than one proxy model?**
   Yes.

Chapter 5 – Managing the Overall Workflow

1. **The process where software is continuously integrated, built, and tested is called what?**
   Continuous Integration.

2. **Why should code be integrated often and as soon as possible?**
   Bugs, misunderstandings, and other code issues are found out much sooner, making it easier to fix them.

3. **What kind of software architecture can be used to separate the display of data from the code that provides the data?**
   Model/View Architecture.

4. **Why do all the code examples use `m_` as the prefix to class member variables?**
   It is a convention that helps readers know that the variable is a member of the class, and it is well supported by Qt Creator.

5. **How do you run code on the target instead of the host?**
   By changing the build and run configuration. (See `Chapter 3`, *Running Your First Application on the Target*.)

6. **What is Dependency Injection?**
   Dependency Injection is a technique where you give (inject) dependencies to a class that will use them instead of defining them in the class.

7. **What is Mocking?**
   Mocking is replacing a class with one that pretends to be the same class. It is used for testing and developing.

8. **Why is testing and debugging at an early stage important?**
   The earlier bugs are found, the easier they are to fix. (See the section on *Continuous Integration* in `Chapter 5`, *Managing the Overall Workflow*.)

9. **Do the author's source listing always execute as expected?**
   No.

10. **How well does the implemented code fit into the Presentation—Data—Hardware Layer model?**
    It is reasonably close. Data presentation is handled by `MainWindow`, and the sensor is handled by `TemperatureSensorIF`. The data model, however, is not really to be seen.

Chapter 6 – Exploring GUI Technologies

1. **What is the difference between QML and Qt Quick?**
   QML is the Qt Modeling Language. Qt Quick is a toolkit for developing UI applications in QML.
2. **Why were QML and Qt Quick originally developed?**
   To provide a simpler way to define user interfaces than using Widgets and C++.
3. **Are Qt Widgets a dead-end technology?**
   No.
4. **What types of application are best suited for Qt Widgets?**
      1. Desktop applications, such as Spreadsheet/Word Processor applications.
      2. Applications that need to interface heavily with C++ or C libraries.
5. **What types of applications are best suited for Qt Quick and QML?**
      1. Games.
      2. Dashboards.
      3. Infotainment systems.
      4. Display/GUI heavy applications.
6. **How did we expose data stored in a C++ QObject to QML code?**
   By using `Q_PROPERTY` and a signal.
7. **What keystroke can be used to go from a C++ method declaration in a class to its implementation?**
   F2.
8. **What language or data format is QML based on?**
   JSON.

Chapter 7 – Adding More Features

1. **Name two different database backends that Qt supports out of the box on most systems.**
      1. MySQL & MariaDB.
      2. SQLite.
      3. Generic ODBC.
      4. PostgreSQL.

2. **What advantage does** QSqlTableModel **have over** QSqlQuery **when you want to display data in a table?**
   QSqlTableModel provides QAbstractItemTable that can be directly used by a QAbstractItemView class.

3. **How could we modify the HVAC state machine so that we do not switch from heating to cooling in less than two minutes?**
   Change the *delay* on the onentry event for the Wait state.

4. **If Marketing wanted to store the heat/cooling/fan state changes between runs, how could that be done?**
   Add it to the data sent to TemperatureStorage, most likely by modifying TemperatureData, and update the database schema to include it.

5. **What would it take to make the heating/cooling/fan states available through the websocket?**
   Add them to the data that's being sent to WSReporter::temperatureUpdate(..) and the JSON data that is being sent out by the method.

6. **Even though BigProject does not store any user data, why should I be concerned with IoT cybersecurity?**
   Because of the potential of an indirect attack using BigProject, as either a platform for the attack or as a way to create a secondary issue that compromises security (for example, set off a temperature alarm that causes doors to be unlocked).

7. **Do you consider the WSReporter implementation of the websocket server secure? Why, or why not?**
   No. There is neither encryption nor authentication.

Section 3: Deep Dive into Embedded Qt

Chapter 8 – Qt in the Embedded World

1. **If you have a question about what licensing you need for Qt, who should you consult?**
   The Qt Company.

2. **Name two OSes found in embedded devices that Qt supports.**
   1. QNX.
   2. Linux.

3. **Can Qt be used to communicate between different OSes?**
   Yes.
4. **What type of architecture makes porting to a new OS easier?**
   A layered architecture.
5. **What standard applies to medical devices?**
   ISO 62304 applies to software for medical devices.
6. **What license version is used as the basis for the code we have written in this book?**
   The open source (L/GPL) license.
7. **How different is building Qt for QNX from building it for the Raspberry Pi?**
   The toolchain that's used to build and the configuration command line.
8. **Is it OK to develop a Qt-based product using the open source version and then buy a license at the last minute? If so, why?**
   No. The Qt company explicitly prohibits this. Code developed using the open source version of Qt must be released under the applicable open source rules.

Chapter 9 – Exploring the IoT with Qt

1. **Is IoT something new, or a new name for something that has been around for almost two decades?**
   It is an old thing that has been renamed.
2. **Can Qt be used without a GUI?**
   Yes.
3. **When accessing a web API, is the result returned synchronously or asynchronously?**
   Asynchronously.
4. **How should asynchronous results be handled?**
   They should be processed by a slot.
5. **What does auto mean in C++11 (and later) versions of C++? Why would you use auto?**
   Since C++11, `auto` tells the compiler to figure out the data type for you. Using it simplifies the code, especially when it comes to long, complex data types.
6. **What issues could occur if separate power supplies were to be used for the Raspberry Pi and Touchscreen driver board and panel?**
   - The power supplies may fight one another.
   - The voltage levels supplied to the two boards may not be compatible and cause malfunctions or even damage to the boards.

7. **Qt is described as cross-platform. How does it handle getting information from sensors on different platforms and operating systems?**
It provides a generic QSensor class that supports plugins for different systems and boards.

8. **What IoT protocols have been implemented for Qt?**
At the time of writing, the list includes the following:
   - MQTT
   - KNX
   - OPC UA

9. **What general steps would you undertake to add the reporting of humidity and pressure published status from Big Project?**
   1. Read those sensors.
   2. Provide `Mock` data for the sensors for host testing.
   3. Update the `QString` data that's sent to `MqttClient`.
      Note: There is no need to update `MqttClient` since the message is composed by the class that calls `MqttClient::SendStatus(..)`.

10. **What would you change in** `MainWindow` **if you only wanted to publish status updates every 5 minutes instead of every second?**
   - **Option 1**: Decouple the handling of the temperature update from the sending of the MQTT data and use a different timer for the sending of the MQTT data.
   - **Option 2**: Lengthen the time between temperature readings to 5 minutes.

Chapter 10 – Using More Qt-Related Technologies

1. **What is the first step in using almost every Qt feature we have worked with?**
Adding the name of the feature to the `QT +=` line in the .pro file.

2. **From what you have learned in this chapter, why is** `QVariant` **one of the base Qt concepts?**
They can hold almost any data type, including those you define yourself, and they are used almost everywhere.

3. **What does IPC stand for?**
Interprocess communication.

4. **How do you specify that you want to start a Qt application so that its GUI is available to a web browser?**
   Add `-platform webgl:port=XXXX` to the command line for the application.

5. **What type of Qt GUI can be displayed through a web browser?**
   A QML/QtQuick GUI.

6. **Why is outputting to PDF so easy in Qt?**
   PDF printing is handled just like any other printer.

7. **How do you tell the Qt tools that you want to use printing in your application?**
   Add `printsupport` to the `QT +=` line in the `.pro` file.

Section 4: Advanced Techniques and Best Practices

Chapter 11 – Debugging, Logging, and Monitoring Qt Applications

1. **What is an SPM and how are they made?**
   SPM stands for Silly Programmer Mistakes. These are common mistakes C++ programmers make that can be hard to find. They include things such as `a = b` instead of `a == b` in an `if` statement.

2. **Can static analysis replace code reviews? Why or why not?**
   No. Static analysis is good at catching syntactical errors, while code reviews are good at catching logical errors.

3. **How much of the code should be tested?**
   All of it.

4. **What is a classic Linux code coverage tool?**
   gcov.

5. **Are PRINT statements still valid for debugging?**
   Yes. They still have their place, especially in systems where stopping code during debugging is not possible.

6. **If I want to provide a warning message in a log file, which Qt method do I use?**
   `qWarning()`.

7. **What does function profiling tell me?**
   How much of the execution time is taken in a given function (method) in the code.

8. **Does function profiling provide code coverage?**
No. It only goes down to the function level. It does not show individual lines of code.

9. **What is a Mock?**
A `Mock` is a class that mocks (pretends) to be another class. It is used for testing and development.

Chapter 12 – Responsive Application Programming – Threads

1. **What is used for threading in QML?**
`WorkerScript`.

2. **Why is a thread pool helpful?**
It saves the time that's needed to create and destroy threads by providing a pool of pre-made threads that can be assigned and reassigned to different objects.

3. **What will happen if more runnable objects are assigned to a thread pool than there are slots in the pool?**
The thread pool will fill all of the available slots, and then queue up the remainder of the runnable objects. When a runnable object finishes, its thread will be assigned to one of the items in the queue.

4. **What is the highest level API for threading in Qt?**
Qt concurrent.

5. **How do I use Qt to apply a function to all of the elements in a list at the same time?**
`mapped(..)`.

6. **What is functional programming, and why is it different?**
In functional (or declarative) programming, you have functions that are applied to data, often in parallel. In procedural (or imperative) programming, you have procedures or steps that are run in order.

7. **What is the Qt Way of communicating between threads?**
Signals and slots.

8. **How does** `Qt::AutoConnection` **work?**
If the objects are assigned to the same thread, it creates a direct connection. If the objects are assigned to different threads, it creates a queue connection.

9. **What is an easy way to allow multiple threads to safely read and write data?**
Use the `QReadWriteLock` class.

10. **What happens if I try to open a second `MainWindow` class for a thread launched by the original `MainWindow` class?**
Since the second `MainWindow` is not in the same thread, it will not work. Qt supports GUI work in only one thread.

Chapter 13 – Qt Best Practices

1. **In a Qt application, is it better to use `std::string` or `QString`?**
`QString`, because you are already working in the Qt Framework and the framework methods take `QString`, not `std::string`.

2. **Why does Qt have its own `QSharedPointer` class?**
It was developed before shared pointers became part of the standard libraries for C++.

3. **Efficiency-wise, is it better to pass by reference or value?**
Pass by constant reference.

4. **If you were to pass by reference, but are not going to modify what was referenced, what decoration should you use in the function prototype?**
A const class.

5. **Why can `QString::replace()` negatively affect the performance of an application?**
It can cause multiple memory copies and moves.

6. **Why do I like code reviews, and why should you like them too?**
Because I (and you) learn new and better ways of coding from them.

7. **What aid can Qt Creator offer in helping you to create more efficient code?**
The build in static analysis tools, such as CLang analysis, CTidy, and CLazy.

8. **Now that you have finished the learning section of this book, what should you do?**
Go off and learn something else!

Other Books You May Enjoy

If you enjoyed this book, you may be interested in these other books by Packt:

Hands-On Mobile and Embedded Development with Qt 5
Lorn Potter

ISBN: 9781788994019

- Explore the latest features of Qt, such as preview for Qt for Python and Qt for WebAssembly
- Create fluid UIs with a dynamic layout for different sized screens
- Deploy embedded applications on Linux systems using Yocto
- Design Qt APIs for building applications for embedded and mobile devices
- Utilize connectivity for networked and machine automated applications
- Discover effective techniques to apply graphical effects using Qt Quick apps

Qt5 C++ GUI Programming Cookbook - Second Edition
Lee Zhi Eng

ISBN: 9781789803822

- Animate GUI elements using Qt5's built-in animation system
- Draw shapes and 2D images using Qt5's powerful rendering system
- Implement an industry-standard OpenGL library in your project
- Build a mobile app that supports touch events and exports it onto devices
- Parse and extract data from an XML file and present it on your GUI
- Interact with web content by calling JavaScript functions from C++
- Access MySQL and SQLite databases to retrieve data and display it on your GUI

Leave a review - let other readers know what you think

Please share your thoughts on this book with others by leaving a review on the site that you bought it from. If you purchased the book from Amazon, please leave us an honest review on this book's Amazon page. This is vital so that other potential readers can see and use your unbiased opinion to make purchasing decisions, we can understand what our customers think about our products, and our authors can see your feedback on the title that they have worked with Packt to create. It will only take a few minutes of your time, but is valuable to other potential customers, our authors, and Packt. Thank you!

Index

www.ingramcontent.com/pod-product-compliance
Lightning Source LLC
LaVergne TN
LVHW081511050326
832903LV00025B/1450